Conflict and Integration in Indo-Pakistan Relations

Sarbjit Johal

Monograph No. 30
Monograph Series
Centers for South and Southeast Asia Studies
University of California at Berkeley

I dedicate this book to my
mother and my father.

Distributed by:
Centers for South and Southeast Asia Studies
260 Stephens Hall
University of California at Berkeley
Berkeley, CA 94720

Library of Congress Catalog Number 89-83322

Printed in the United States of America.

Acknowledgments

First of all I want to express my appreciation for the guidance that I received from the members of my dissertation committee, Professor Michael Gordon, Professor Wolfram Hanrieder, and Professor Peter Merkl. Also, I sincerely thank Rasul Bux Rais for reading and commenting on an earlier draft of this book. The final version has been improved by Yvon Johnson's competent editing for which I am grateful. In producing the typeset copy I am indebted to the advice and assistance of Barbara Gaerlan, Betty Wong, and Tanya Smith of the Centers for South and Southeast Asia Studies. Finally, I want to thank my wife, Satu, for the support she has given me from the beginning of this project to its conclusion.

Table of Contents

CHAPTER ONE

REGIONAL POWERS AND INTEGRATION

Despite attempts at regional integration, many less-developed countries (LDCs) are in conflict with each other. Some large LDCs, such as Brazil and Argentina, are regional rivals; other much smaller countries have territorial, ethnic, and resource disputes with their neighbors. Leaders of small states are apprehensive about local dominance by regional or middle powers such as Brazil, Iran, India and Indonesia. From the viewpoint of these small states, regional integration under the leadership of a middle power may be a guise for a new regional imperialism.[1]

This study examines such relationships between national power and regional integration in the case of one pair of states in South Asia--India, the regional power, and Pakistan, the countercore of this region.[2] It will examine their regional foreign policy goals, their capabilities of either promoting or resisting regional integration, and, finally, their record of integration and conflict.

Most of this record has been one of conflict. Pakistan has challenged India's claim to be the regional power in South Asia. Its governments have argued that accepting Indian leadership would lead to a loss of national sovereignty, particularly since Pakistan has an outstanding territorial dispute with India in Kashmir.

South Asia is an important region for analyzing the relationship between national power and integration. First, it is a clearly-defined geographical region with a definite hierarchy of national power. Second, scholars often classify South Asia as a *conflict region* because of the history of Indo-Pakistani conflict.[3] It is a suitable case-study for examining the reasons why conflict has predominated over integration. Finally, the benefits of regional integration are potentially very large. While South Asia has one of the largest concentrations of absolute poverty in the world, it also has much untapped economic potential. Successful integration there would promote world-order concerns of economic equity, the nonproliferation of nuclear weapons, and improvement in living standards.

The wide differences in economic, political, and military capabilities between India and Pakistan may be reasons why regional integration has been slow in developing in South Asia. Yet size of regional units by itself does not allow one to predict the success or failure of regional integration. There are several instances of regional integration where the process was guided by a larger state and supported by smaller states. One example is Saudi Arabia's leadership in 1981 in forming the Gulf Cooperation Council with the United Arab Emirates, Bahrain, Kuwait, Oman, and Qatar.

The question is: Under what conditions will small states accept or reject the leadership of regional or middle powers? At stake here is the nature of community formation. What are the conditions for being a core area? How does a core area use its economic, political, military, and cultural assets to influence its regional environment? How does it extract concessions from the smaller states for achieving its regional goals? These are pivotal questions. Any satisfactory answer needs to be guided by theory.

THEORETICAL APPROACH: POWER AND INTEGRATION

A substantial literature has developed that looks at the factors determining successful regional integration among developed and developing countries. Its consensus is that success will depend on the external economic and political environment (for example, the material and military support from an external power such as the United States) and on the costs and benefits of integration as seen by national policymakers.[4]

One approach sees integration as a process of creating *security communities*, which are defined as groups of people which have attained within a territory "a sense of community and of institutions and practices widespread enough to assure for a long time, dependable expectations of peaceful change among its population."[5] Integration may result in either an *amalgamated security community,* where there is a formal merger of the units, or a *pluralistic security-community,* where the units retain their legal independence.[6] This approach has been called the pluralist pretheory of integration. In this study, *integration* refers to the process of creating peaceful relations among nations.

Deutsch's emphasis on several possible institutional outcomes of regional integration is a major reason why the pluralist approach is applicable to developing countries. For some developing countries the issue is not whether to create new political units but how to safeguard their international identity, maintain peace with their neighbors, and establish norms of peaceful change.[7] The key is a *core area.* Deutsch argues that it is a political unit that acts as the nucleus of an integration process among several units. Core areas are distinguished from the smaller units by two sets of capabilities--*power* and *responsiveness.*[8] Power refers to a core area's greater political, administrative, and economic capabilities; responsiveness refers to the core area's ability "to control its own behavior and redirect its own attention" to other political units, thereby taking into account their wishes and needs.[9]

Despite a large number of historical case studies of integration, and despite their many theoretical advances, Deutsch and his colleagues gave few empirical indicators of core areas. One attempt at operationalization is by Barrera, who identifies core and countercore areas according to positional indicators, such as population, economic strength, and prestige, and behavioral indicators, such as leadership roles, during the integration process.[10]

Another work relevant to core areas and integration is Etzioni's *Political Unification.* Etzioni is concerned with power, communications, and responsiveness. He applies a theory of power to case studies of what pluralists would term amalgamated security-communities.[11] I suggest that Etzioni's framework may be used to look at the formation of pluralistic security-communities.

Etzioni defines power as a "unit's capacity to induce or influence another unit to carry out directives or any other norms it (the first unit) supports."[12] He distinguishes between *power* and *assets;* the former is a relational property between the units while the latter "are possessions that a unit or system has, regardless of those others may have."[13] For Etzioni, three types of assets are available to an *elite*, or leading, unit to achieve its goals of integration: *utilitarian, coercive, and identitive.*

Utilitarian assets include a country's "economic possessions, technical and administrative capabilities, manpower, etc."[14] Coercive assets are "the weapons, installations, and manpower that the military, the police, or similar agencies command."[15] Identitive assets are "usually values and symbols, built up by educational and religious institutions, national rituals, and other mechanisms. The larger the potential appeals of these values and symbols to other units, the larger the identitive assets of the unit under examination."[16]

Etzioni's concept of identitive assets is especially useful in analyzing the integrating power of core areas because it captures the *ideal* elements of integration not found under the categories of utilitarian and coercive assets. Such values and symbols may be racial, religious, ideological, or they may be derived from the historical experiences of the units (for example, the common experience of colonialism may give rise to anti-colonial and anti-imperialist symbols and values). Etzioni's framework also draws attention to some of the potential obstacles to integration among nation-states. Identitive factors have been a major source of dispute between India and Pakistan, as shown in the opposition between Pakistan's *two-nation* theory and India's secularism.

I adopt Etzioni's framework in this study, though with some modifications. First, the term *material assets* is preferred to utilitarian, to make his terminology more consistent with other theories of power.[17] Second, the term *military assets* is preferred to coercive assets because material assets may also be used for coercion. Thirdly, Etzioni's definition of power incorporates the concepts of *coercion* and *influence*. In this study, I use the term power in the sense of punitive and coercive actions in order to distinguish it from influence, which implies voluntary actions rather than compulsion. Finally, I have modified the application of Etzioni's framework by considering only a few key indicators of the three types of assets. What follows is an elaboration of each type of asset and its corresponding use for power and influence.

Material

Three key material assets are economic, scientific, and political capabilities.

Economic capabilities are measured by gross national product (GNP). This is a particularly useful indicator of economic assets because it subsumes and measures many of the economic assets of a country, such as the size and quality of its population and its income from abroad. This study will examine whether the changes in the GNP of the core increase the surplus available to it for punishing, coercing, or rewarding other units. It will also examine whether changes in the GNP of the periphery allow it to resist the core.

By themselves, high GNP growth rates give an inaccurate picture of the assets of a country. The periphery may have larger growth rates than the core but from a smaller initial economic base and in economic sectors that contribute little to the material or military assets, power, and influence of the periphery. So, besides looking at proportional GNP growth rates, it is also necessary to look at the absolute increases, the changes in per capita GNP (in order to control for population differences between units), and changes in the structure of GNP. The latter two more accurately indicate a country's economic assets. A high per capita GNP tends to be associated with high levels of economic productivity. The structure of GNP (that is, the values added to the economy by its primary, secondary, and tertiary sectors) shows the level of development reached by the economy. A modernizing economy is one in which the share of GNP added by the secondary and tertiary sectors is increasing relative to the primary sector.

The second material asset is scientific capability. In contemporary international relations this determines a country's economic growth, military capabilities, and international status.[18] This study will examine the growth of Indian and Pakistani capabilities in nuclear science and technology for two reasons: first, these advanced fields allow us to compare India and Pakistan with the more developed countries; and, secondly, these fields affect Indian and Pakistani military power and influence.

The final material asset is political capabilities. The political elites of developing countries face several problems in political development. They have to establish a strong central authority, weld several diverse ethnic, religious, and other social groups into one nation, and, finally, they have to mobilize domestic and foreign resources for social and economic development. Under political capabilities, then, I examine the skills of each unit's political leadership in legitimizing the political system, in politically integrating the country, and in extracting resources for development. This component of material assets is crucial because responsiveness clearly depends on a core area's ability to control its own behavior.

A core area may use its material assets to punish, coerce, or to reward other units. To punish or coerce, it may deny access to its markets, impose trade embargoes, and suspend aid and technical assistance. It may also disrupt the political integration of the periphery by supporting autonomy or secessionist movements in the periphery. To reward other units, the core area may give economic and technical aid, share scientific knowledge, give access to its markets, ease the transit of goods to a third country, or underwrite the political security of elites facing domestic challenges in the periphery.

Military

The military assets of a country are made up of: the quality and quantity of its weapons and installations; the size and quality of its armed forces; the skills, morale, organization, and leadership of the armed forces; and its military reputation.[19]

A core area may use these assets to punish, coerce, or reward the periphery. It might, for example, threaten to use force to coerce the periphery to resolve ethnic disputes between. Or a core area might be interested in using its military assets to reward the periphery. It may provide other units with military support in case of military pressure or intervention from a third country. This could take the form of sharing of military information, military training or joint exercises with the periphery. It may deploy its military assets or conclude a diplomatic agreement in such a way as to signal to the periphery that it has no aggressive intentions. For instance, Brazil promoted the Amazon Pact of July 1978 with Bolivia, Colombia,

Ecuador, Guyana, Peru, Surinam, and Venezuela in order "to assure its uneasy neighbors that projects like the Trans-Amazon Highway were not intended to lay the groundwork for military expansion."[20] Finally, a core area might use its military assets to bolster the domestic political positions of elites in the periphery. The Shah of Iran, for example, provided troops and other military aid to Oman in 1973 to enable the Sultan of Oman to quell the Marxist-led Dhofar rebellion.

Identitive

The third type of asset available to a core area is identitive. As noted earlier, this may include racial, religious, and ideological values and symbols. Etzioni writes that these "assets are transformed into power when a member unit or the system (through its representatives) succeeds in showing that a particular course of action it seeks other units or all member-units to follow is consistent with, or an expression of, these values and symbols that other units have come to be committed to."[21] Here Etzioni is referring to the identitive influence of core areas, which may be manifested in shared cultural, religious, and ideological values. But a core area might also use its identitive assets to punish and coerce. It might label a peripheral unit a heretic in some ideological value (for example, the USSR and Yugoslavia's alleged deviation from Marxist-Leninism in the late 1940s). The core area might also attempt to prevent the peripheral unit from developing values and symbols that it opposes. Indian governments, for example, have tried to use India's composite Hindu-Muslim culture to deny Pakistani claims that religion is a sufficient basis for nationality in South Asia.

The pluralist approach contains a number of hypotheses about the relationship between core areas, capabilities, and integration.

Deutsch and his colleagues found that integration is more likely to be successful if the capabilities of the core area (and perhaps other regional units) are increasing. Rising capabilities allow the core area to meet some of the loads or burdens of integration, including "military or financial burdens, drains on manpower or wealth; the burden of risk from political or military commitments; costs of social and economic readjustments," and burdens "upon the attention-giving, information-processing, and decision-making capabilities of administrators, political elites, legislatures, or electoral majorities."[22]

But Deutsch and Etzioni agree that integration does not necessarily follow from increased power. The rising military capabilities of a regional power may make the periphery more insecure. Nor does responsiveness automatically follow from power, although it is a precondition of it. A regional power may have greater capabilities than other units and yet be unresponsive to them. In this case, such a large unit is only potentially a core area. Whether the periphery becomes insecure or the regional power responsive will depend upon other factors, such as extraregional military threats, the existence of identitive assets, or the national goals and traditions of the regional power, for instance, regional integration, conquest or indifference.

In developing countries, a regional power's major goal might be to increase its own internal development. It might be too preoccupied with domestic problems to devote much attention to its regional neighbors, let alone promote integration. This may be termed the *attention hypothesis* of responsiveness. But Etzioni argues that this "argument assumes a necessary contradiction between the development of a country and regional unification.[23] It also emphasizes the domestic interests of the regional power and neglects its regional and international concerns, such as regional security.

Another hypothesis of power and responsiveness is that a regional power's goals of either internal development, integration, and conquest will depend upon the material, military, and identitive opportunity costs associated with each. By opportunity costs are meant here the costs incurred by an actor in foregoing the highest-valued alternative to a particular course of action.[24] Like the first hypothesis, this one derives from the fact that regional powers in the developing areas have some of the same low standards of living as the periphery. If the regional power attempts to promote regional integration by offering rewards to the periphery, this might be at the cost to its own development. But unlike the first hypothesis, this one views a particular type of regional goal as a conscious, calculating policy of the regional power. The regional power might accept the costs to its internal development of rewarding the periphery, if it achieves other higher-valued benefits, such as regional security. Or, it might find that the benefits of regional integration are too small in relation to the costs of persuading the periphery to cooperate. This may be termed the *opportunity cost hypothesis* of responsiveness.

These hypotheses assume that policymakers are rational. But are they irrelevant in cases where emotional factors play a part in interstate relations? This objection seems particularly true of the religious and cultural conflicts of Indo-Pakistan relations, and may be framed in terms of a null hypothesis. Thus formally stated, the hypotheses of this study are:

1. Where emotional factors predominate, national policymakers do not weigh the costs and benefits of integrating with other countries. [the null hypothesis]

2. Regional powers in developing areas may be too preoccupied with their domestic development to devote attention to regional integration [the attention hypothesis]

3. A regional power will concentrate on its internal development when it calculates the costs of internal development to be smaller than the costs of regional integration. [The opportunity cost hypothesis.]

4. Regional integration is more likely to be successful where the regional power can convince the periphery that it can match or surpass any material, military, or identitive support to the periphery from extraregional powers. [This is an elaboration of the opportunity cost hypothesis of responsiveness.]

INDIA AND PAKISTAN

According to Brecher, an ideal analysis of the South Asian subordinate system would be made up of:

> a three stage construct: the subordinate system of South Asia, its structural and textural features in 1948, and the changes that occurred in these salient characteristics at certain nodal points in time; a parallel analysis of the dominant system of global politics, focused on inter-bloc relations since 1948; and, most important, the linkages between the two systems.[25]

As Brecher admits, such a study would be both "challenging and novel," but, unless it covered several volumes, it would have to sacrifice depth of analysis for depth. This study concentrates on the first stage of this construct, and is thus intended to be an introduction to the larger construct outlined above by Brecher. The role of the dominant system and external powers will be considered only in so far as they have affected the power relationships between India and Pakistan. Indeed, some of the nodal points of time have resulted from external power intervention in the subsystem; for example, May 1954, when the United States began a strategic relationship with Pakistan; October 1962, when communist China launched a military attack along India's Himalayan borders; and December 1979, when the Soviet invasion of Afghanistan brought Soviet power to the doorstep of the regional subsystem. The other nodal points have taken place when India and Pakistan have fought large-scale wars. Thus the phases of Indo-Pakistan relations may be divided into:

1. August 1947 to May 1954
2. May 1954 to October 1962
3. November 1962 to September 1965
4. September 1965 to December 1971
5. December 1971 to December 1979
6. January 1980 to the present

The South Asia region includes Bangladesh, Bhutan, India, the Maldives, Nepal, Pakistan, and Sri Lanka.[26] In this study I concentrate on Indo-Pakistan relations. Both states have been the strongest economic and military states in the region. Though the 1971 War reduced their combined share of the population of South Asia, they are still the strongest economic and military states

Moreover, Indo-Pakistan relations historically have determined whether South Asia has been a peaceful or a conflictual region. Some of the smaller states now appear to be the most enthusiastic proponents of a formal regional integration scheme. Nevertheless, only India and Pakistan have the potential to either disrupt the region or to make relations more cooperative.

In this study, I use the term *balance of power* to refer to the existing distribution of power between India and Pakistan.[27] It could be argued that such an examination is unnecessary because India has always been the strongest state in South Asia since 1947. This argument fails to take into account the following factors: First, I examine the balance of power in order to explain their conflict or integration. Over the last forty years, Pakistan's potential and actualized power have fluctuated markedly relative to India. Its power increased when it signed the Mutual Defense Assistance Program with the United States in April 1954 and when the Pakistan military took over power in 1958, thereby ending the political instability in Pakistan. Pakistan's power decreased when India built up its military following the Sino-Indian War of 1962, when western countries imposed an arms embargo after the 1965 Indo-Pakistan War, and, most important, when India defeated Pakistan in 1971.

Secondly, India's absolute level of assets is less impressive if both countries are compared on a per capita basis. When India's larger population is taken into account, the gap between India and Pakistan in indices of potential power, such as per capita income, gross manufacturing output, and food and energy consumption, either narrows or disappears. History is replete with examples of small countries that have overcome their disadvantages in territory, natural resources, and population by greater industrial and agricultural productivity, technical and administrative capabilities, and by greater mobilizational efforts. This study examines whether Pakistan has offset its quantitative disadvantages by emphasizing the qualitiative aspects of its material and military assets.

Finally, policymakers in both countries have been highly conscious of the balance of power between them. Such perceptions have profoundly determined their bilateral relations. Pakistanis have been acutely aware of their neighbor's greater potential and actualized power. The problem, though, is that so far few attempts have been made to systematically analyze Indo-Pakistani material, military, and identitive relationships over the forty years in which both countries have interacted.[28] An examination of these relations would inform much of the debate about Indo-Pakistani relations. It would also provide answers to the following questions: Has India had the material and military power to either absorb Pakistan territorially or to reduce the autonomy of Pakistani policymakers? Does India have the material, military and identitive assets and responsiveness to act as a core area? Finally, how appropriate are each of these assets to India's regional goals?

Notes

1. Johan Galtung, "The Politics of Self-Reliance," in *From Dependency to Development,* ed. Heraldo Munoz (Boulder, Co.: Westview Press, 1981), pp. 178-79.
2. A countercore is defined as a nation-state that resists the leadership of a core area. See Jean Barrera, "The Countercore Role of Middle Powers in Process of External Political Integration," *World Politics* 25 (January 1973): 274-87.
3. Daniel Druckman, "Social-Psychological Factors in Regional Politics," in *Comparative Regional Systems: West and East Europe, North America, the Middle East and the Developing Countries*, ed. Werner J. Feld and Gavin Boyd (New York: Pergamon Press, 1980), p. 20.
4. There is a substantial literature of regional integration, particularly among developing countries. See, for example, W. A. Axline, "Underdevelopment, dependence and integration: the politics of regionalism in the Third World," *International Organization* 31 (Winter 1977): 83-105; Lynn K. Mytelka, "The Salience of Gains in Third World Integrative Systems," *World Politics* 25 (January 1973): 236-50; and C. Vaitsos, "Crisis in Regional Economic Cooperation (Integration) among Developing Countries: A Survey," *World Development* 6 (June 1978): 719-69.
5. Karl W. Deutsch et al., *Political Community in the North Atlantic Area* (Princeton, N.J.: Princeton University Press, 1957), p. 5.
6. Ibid., p. 6.
7. This is the argument, for example, of Vaughn A. Lewis, "Evading Smallness: regional integration as an avenue toward viability," *International Social Science Journal* 30 (1978): 57-72.
8. Deutsch, *Political Community*, pp. 40-41.
9. Ibid., p. 40.
10. Barrera, "Countercore," pp. 274-87.
11. The case studies are: (1) The United Arab Republic, 1958-1961; (2) Federation of the West Indies, 1958-1962; (3) Nordic Associational Web, 1953-64; and (4) European Economic Community, 1958-64.
12. Ibid., p. 8n.
13. Ibid., p. 38.
14. Ibid.
15. Ibid., p. 39
16. Ibid.
17. See, for example, Steven L. Spiegel, *Dominance and Diversity* (Boston: Little, Brown & Co., 1972); and Klaus Knorr, *The Power of Nations* (New York: Basic Books, 1975).

18. A good discussion of national power and science and technology is contained in Klaus Knorr, *Military Power and Potential*, (Lexington, Mass.: D. C. Heath, 1970), pp. 73-90.

19. According to Knorr, the *military reputation* of a country refers to "the expectations of other national actors, derived from past experience, that the state concerned has a greater or lesser disposition to resort to military threats when its vital interests are crossed." *The Power of Nations*, p. 9.

20. Yale H. Ferguson, "Latin America," in *Comparative Regional Systems*, ed. Feld and Boyd, p. 339.

21. Etzioni, *Political Unification*, p. 39.

22. Deutsch, *Political Community*, p. 41.

23. Etzioni, *Political Unification*, p. 321.

24. *International Encyclopedia of the Social Sciences*, 1968, s.v. "Power," by Robert A. Dahl. For a justification of the opportunity cost approach and its application to asymmetrical bargaining relations among nations, see Barbara G. Haskel, "Disparities, Strategies, and Opportunity Costs: The Example of Scandinavian Economic Market Negotiations," *International Studies Quarterly* 18 (March 1974): 3-30.

25. Michael Brecher, "Comments on "China's Strategic Alternatives in South Asia", by Wayne Wilcox, in *China in Crisis*, vol. 2: *China's Policies in Asia and America's Alternatives*, ed. Tang Tsou (Chicago: Chicago University Press, 1968), p. 432.

26. Studies of the South Asian regional subsystem include S. P. Varma and K. P. Misra, eds., *Foreign Policies in South Asia*, (New Delhi: Orient Longmans, 1969); P. K. Misra, "Determinants of Intraregional Relations in South Asia," *India Quarterly* 36 (January-March 1980): 68-83; and Leo Rose and Satish Kumar, "South Asia," in Feld and Boyd, *Comparative Regional Systems*, pp. 237-73.

27. For a discussion of other meanings of the term, see Martin Wright, "The Balance of Power," in *Diplomatic Investigations*, eds. Herbert Butterfield and Martin Wright (London: George Allen and Unwin, 1966), pp. 149-75.

28. The countries have been compared according to issue areas, such as military capabilities, nuclear technology, and administrative and political capabilities. But there are few systematic comparisons, an exception being Edward S. Mason, *Economic Development in India and Pakistan* (Cambridge, Mass.: Harvard University Center for International Affairs, 1966).

CHAPTER TWO

PARTITION AND ITS RESULTS

After their independence from Great Britain on 15 August 1947, India and Pakistan repeatedly sought to define new economic and political relations between themselves. Yet they could not begin such relations on a clean slate. Several factors continued to affect their bilateral relations, including the legacies of British colonial rule, the bitter preindependence Congress-League conflict over the destiny of the peoples of the subcontinent, and the traumatic effects of partition.

Partition resulted in an estimated 200,000-600,000 deaths,[1] 12.5 million refugees (at that time the largest single migration of humanity in history),[2] and the division of 1.5 million square miles of territory. Of the two Dominions that came into existence on 15 August 1947, India was the world's second largest developing nation and Pakistan was the world's most populous Muslim nation between the Atlantic Ocean and Indonesia.

Such a far-reaching event culminated from two major historical processes: Hindu-Muslim communal conflict and the rise of Indian nationalism as a challenge to British colonialism in South Asia. Both historical processes became inextricably linked. British imperial policy complicated pre-existing Hindu-Muslim antagonisms. As Britain consolidated its rule in India in the early nineteenth century, it generally supplanted Muslim rulers and looked upon Muslims with suspicion. The Muslims fell behind the Hindus in economic, educational, and hence social and political status. Consequently, when the Congress Party became more vocal in the early twentieth century in demanding liberal-democratic freedoms and self-government, part of the Muslim elite

elite feared that the British *raj*, or rule, would be replaced by a Hindu *raj*.

Muslim leaders founded the Muslim League in 1906 in order to protect Muslim interests. Their demands found favor with the British authorities who were seeking to balance the rising Congress Party. In 1909 Britain granted Muslim demands for protecting minority rights by establishing separate electorates. In the 1930s the Muslim League changed its demands from minority protection to political parity, corresponding to the League's change in perception of itself from an Indian minority to a separate nation.[3] As Mohammed Ali Jinnah argued when the Muslim League first adopted the demand for Pakistan on 22 March 1940, "It is a dream that the Hindus and Muslims can ever evolve a common nationality...The Hindus and Muslims have different religious philosophies, social customs, and literatures. They neither intermarry nor interdine and, indeed, they belong to two different civilizations which are based mainly on conflicting ideas and conceptions."[4]

The Congress bitterly contested the Muslim League's two-nation theory. That theory challenged the Congress's image of itself as a transcommunal political organization. Congress leaders, such as Nehru, believed that the communal problem would be dissolved by the political independence of a united India and by the economic growth and social justice following independence. For Congress leaders, League claims of Hindu-Muslim antagonism were a self-fulfilling prophecy: the more the League talked about such antagonisms, the worse communal relations became.

Try as it could, Congress could neither displace the League nor reduce its hold on Indian Muslims. This hold increased during the Second World War when Britain jailed the Congress leadership for opposing the war effort. Taking advantage of Congress's absence, the League gained official patronage and organizational strength. As a result, by war's end the League was in a stronger position relative to Congress. The test came in the December 1945-January 1946 general elections, which were held to elect members of the Central Assembly, provincial assemblies, and provinces under direct government rule. The League won all thirty Muslim seats in the Central Assembly and

428 of the 492 Muslim provincial seats.[5] The Congress won 57 of the 102 elected seats in the Central Assembly and swept all eight Hindu-majority provinces in India.

The 1945-46 elections thus polarized Indian politics into the Congress and Muslim League camps. The League by itself could not determine India's political and constitutional evolution, but it did have an effective veto over any such developments. The polarization increased in the summer of 1946, when the Muslim League accused Congress of deliberately sabotaging the British government's delicately devised Cabinet Mission Plan. This would have shared power among the communities by allowing the provinces to form voluntary groupings within the framework of a united India. Jinnah accepted the Plan because it recognized the principle of autonomous Muslim provinces and could eventually pave the way for a separate Pakistan. Congress accepted the Plan in principle but made it known that the final Indian constitution would have to be framed by the Constituent Assembly, which it dominated. To the League, this meant the collapse of the Cabinet Mission Plan, whereupon the League decided to take its case directly to the Muslim masses in the form of Direct Action Day. The result, however, was 20,000 people killed or seriously injured in communal bloodshed in the Great Calcutta Killing of August 1946.[6] Communal violence then spread to East Bengal, Bihar, and Punjab. It was aggravated by other social tensions in the country, such as the transition to a peace-time economy, which brought with it the demobilization of veterans and an increase in inflation. It was in such conditions that the three major actors in Indian politics--the British government, the Congress, and the Muslim League--negotiated for India's independence.

Each had its own preferences for the future political order in the subcontinent. Britain had accepted the principle of "responsible self-government" for India as early as 20 August 1917. In 1942, the British War Cabinet, through Sir Stafford Cripps, offered the Indian political parties their own constitution and independence after the war. But although Britain accepted the principle of self-governing India, it still faced the problem of deciding the timing of independence and the form of India's independent government--unitary, federal, one state or two?

The British preferred to leave a united subcontinent because they believed that this would help them to defend Southern Asia. Above all, it was essential that the Indian army and civil service--the twin prides of British rule--remain intact. Thus the British government in London instructed the Cabinet Mission of 1946 and Mountbatten's Mission in 1947 to negotiate with the Indian parties and seek a united India as part of an independence settlement.[7]

The Congress also preferred a united subcontinent. It believed that a united India was the most appropriate territorial and political context in which to implement the goals of the Indian nationalist movement. These goals were growth (such as economic, scientific, and military), equality (such as class, caste, religious, and international), and self-reliance (such as economic, military, political, and cultural). The Congress also believed in secularism as a means to communal harmony. It saw Hindus, Muslims, Sikhs, and other communities as one nationality and part of the same civilization. It therefore opposed the Muslim League's two-nation theory, which rationalized a separate state for Muslims.

The Muslim League preferred to separate as Pakistan. It feared that an undivided independent India would be dominated by the Hindus at the expense of the Muslim community. An independent Pakistan, on the other hand, would allow Muslims to develop their own social, political, and cultural way of life, and it would allow them to escape their resented status of what they saw as "hewers of wood and drawers of water" for the Hindus. Pakistan was to be composed of territories of India where Muslims formed a majority--the Punjab, the North West Frontier Province, Kashmir, Sind, Baluchistan, and Bengal. To ensure that the new country would be economically viable, the League demanded that Assam and the undivided provinces of Punjab and Bengal be included. These last demands clashed with the League's two-nation theory of religion as a basis of nationality because the three provinces contained several non-Muslim majority districts.

In the protracted and often bitter bargaining leading up to independence, each side had to settle for less than its maximum demands. The British realized that the Congress and the League could not agree on a constitutional and political framework for maintaining a united India. But this disappointment was reduced when Congress and the League agreed to stay in the Commonwealth and thereby help defend Southern Asia. The British government realized, too, that it could not impose a solution on the Indian parties, unless it was prepared to substantially raise its coercive apparatus in India. This was unacceptable to the British and the Indian people.[8] Britain's bargaining assets, particularly its control of undivided India's sterling balances, and military, administrative, and technical expertise, could be used, however, to influence the new Dominions to cooperate with each other and with Britain after independence. Generally, though, Britain's power was eroding, and the British government, particularly its representatives on the spot, saw the need for an early withdrawal before law and order deteriorated further. Originally, when Attlee's government announced its plans for Indian independence on 20 February 1947, it had set June 1948 as the deadline for the transfer of power, but as H. V. Hodson notes, "Power to be demitted in the future runs away like sawdust in the present."[9]

Eventually, the Congress reluctantly agreed to partition, given the alternatives: further communal disturbances, a weak central government unable to function in the face of civil disorder, and a possibility that Britain would delay granting independence to India.[10] On the positive side, partition would ensure the security of the minorities in the subcontinent, put an end to conflicts within the central government, make the resulting Dominions united, and would be consistent with democratic procedures and India's interests.[11] Although some Congressmen may have seen partition as irreversible, most refused to believe that it was a permanent parting of the ways for Muslims and non-Muslims. Most believed that Pakistan would be economically, politically, and strategically unviable and that reintegration was inevitable, either in the form of a confederation or federation. Such lingering hopes helped Congress to accept partition.

Finally, the Muslim League obtained a smaller Pakistan than it had hoped for. Mountbatten pointed out to Jinnah the fallacy of the League's demands for a united Punjab, Bengal, and Assam within Pakistan. As Hodson writes, "Time and again, in their early discussions, the Viceroy contended with the unassailable logic, that the arguments which the Muslim leader produced for partitioning India were equally valid for partitioning Bengal and the Punjab, and that if he was to get Pakistan he could not therefore get it on the basis of five undivided provinces."[12] Jinnah reluctantly accepted; the British government would not be moved from its principle of protecting minority rights. As it turned out, the Bengal and Punjab legislatures agreed to divide their provinces along communal lines, and only the Sylhet district of Assam went to Pakistan. Nevertheless, Jinnah accepted a "mutilated, a moth-eaten and truncated Pakistan"[13] as at least being better than no Pakistan at all. At last, he believed, most Muslims in the subcontinent would have their own nation-state and be free from the Hindu domination that would have been their lot in an undivided India.

During the struggle for a political order in the subcontinent, Britain, the Congress, and the League gave very little thought to the nature of future economic, political, and military relations between India and Pakistan. Any talk of such relations was in terms of generalities, such as postindependence cooperation. The major reasons for this were the timing of partition and the basic issues over which partition was fought.

First, as late as mid-1946 it was uncertain whether there would be any partition at all. In May 1946 Jinnah accepted the Cabinet Mission Plan, which would have created an undivided India with strong provinces and a weak central government. But when Congress declared that the Constituent Assembly would decide the future Constitution of India, the League concluded that Congress could not be trusted to make the Cabinet Plan workable. The League therefore decided to press for nothing less than an independent Pakistan.

Before May 1946 the British planned for regional cooperation on an all-India basis--that is, provincial cooperation. The Congress refused to consider cooperation between an independent India and Pakistan because it refused to consider Pakistan. The League could not persuade the other two parties to even consider such planning. Britain and the Congress ruled out any contingency planning for dividing the economic, military, and administrative assets of India. Any planning like this, they felt, would prejudge the political and constitutional issues. For instance, in April 1947, the Finance Minister of the Interim Government, Liaquat Ali Khan, put forward Muslim League proposals to divide the Indian army.[14] The proposals were then discussed by the Defense Committee of the Interim Government on 25 April 1947. Liaquat recognized that his proposals were delicate, given the already perilous law and order situation in the country and the morale of the Indian army. His essential point though was that there had to be some contingency planning for partition. Britain and the Congress refused to plan for the division of the Indian army because they saw the plans as a self-fulfilling prophecy.

A second reason why cooperation was inadequately discussed by the three parties is that the decision to divide India was taken on noneconomic and nonmilitary grounds. India was divided according to a community's religion rather than criteria such as ease of regional communications, trade, and defensibility of territory. What beforehand had been one natural geographic, economic, and strategic unit was now divided into two nation-states. In short, communal factors dominated discussions about partition.

Before independence, several studies of the possible economic effects of partition had concluded that Pakistan would lack industry and would be unable to bear the economic burden of defending the North-West Frontier Province (NWFP).[15] Yet these studies had no effect on the Muslim League's demands for Pakistan. It was fully prepared to sacrifice economic well-being for what it saw as the greater good of political self-determination. True, the Muslim League and its supporters were very defensive about Pakistan's poor economic prospects,[16] but they were confident that autonomous economic decision-making by Muslims would eventually make Pakistan economically viable.

Mountbatten announced his Plan for partition on 3 June 1947. All parties formally accepted it two days later, and 5 June marks the date when systematic planning for partition and post-independence cooperation could begin for the first time. Even then, there was uncertainty about the international boundaries of India and Pakistan. The Plan left it to the provinces and Indian states to determine whether to join the existing Constituent Assembly (established after the 1945-

46 general elections) or to participate in a separate Constituent Assembly, which would in effect serve Pakistan. To divide Bengal and Punjab, the legislative assemblies of these two provinces would meet in two parts--Muslim and non-Muslim members. A simple majority of either part would be needed for the province to be partitioned. If partition was decided upon, the Governor-General would then set up a Boundary Commission to demarcate the new boundaries of the partitioned province. Furthermore, if Bengal and the Punjab decided on partition, referenda would be held in the NWFP and the Muslim-majority district of Sylhet in Assam to see which Constituent Assembly the people of these areas wished to join.

The uncertainty over the international boundaries in Bengal and the Punjab meant that all Congress and League negotiators could do was to maintain existing economic relations and discuss economic and defense cooperation only in generalities. The Bengal and Punjab legislatures decided in favor partition at the end of June. Their decisions triggered those provisions of the 3 June Plan that called for referenda in the NWFP and Sylhet and for boundary commissions for Bengal and the Punjab. Thereupon, Mountbatten appointed the boundary commissions on 30 June. Each was composed of four members and a chairman, with equal representation given to the Congress and the League. Sir Cyril Radcliffe served as the common chairman of the two commissions. They were to meet as soon as possible and submit reports demarcating the boundaries of the two parts of Bengal and the Punjab, using the criteria of contiguous majority areas of Muslims and non-Muslims. The Commissions would "also take into account other factors," although these factors were purposely left vague in the Governor-General's announcement in order to give some discretion to the Commissions. The Boundary Commissions divided along party lines and failed to agree on the boundaries. It was left to Sir Cyril to decide the award, which he generally did according to contiguous Muslim and non-Muslim majority areas, except for some adjustments for the location of waterworks and rail communications. In the Punjab, Sir Cyril's award placed the upper waters of the Chenab, Ravi, and Sutlej rivers in India and the lower waters in Pakistan. The new international boundary separated several Pakistani canal systems from their headworks, which were now located in India. Sir Cyril hoped that both countries would work out cooperative arrangements to minimize the award's disruptive effects on road and rail communications, water resources, and electric power transmission.[17]

At the central government level, and in accordance with the 3 June Plan, Mountbatten established a Special Committee of the Interim Government on 5 June to examine the administrative consequences of partition. The Committee was later replaced by a Partition Council consisting of a Steering Committee and ten expert committees.[18] The expert committees--again containing Congress and League representatives--began work on 21 June, and were given only one month to complete their immense task.

Despite the short deadline, the Partition Council managed to agree on the division of the financial, administrative, military, and other assets of India. The criteria for division varied according to the type of asset--human, nonhuman, fixed, or moveable. The administrative services (the civil service, police, and the military) were divided largely along communal lines. Members of the central civil service were given the option of serving either Dominion; but, because of communal tensions, very few non-Muslims chose Pakistan and very few Muslims chose India. Members of the armed forces were also given a similar choice, with the exception that Pakistan-domiciled Muslims could not choose India and Indian-domiciled non-Muslims could not choose Pakistan. Fixed assets (buildings, telegraphs, and so forth) were awarded to the Dominion they happened to be located in. Moveable assets, such as cash and administrative supplies, were divided according to the administrative needs of each Dominion. Where a Dominion found itself short of a particular asset (fixed or moveable), the other Dominion usually agreed to pay compensation.[19] Thus India agreed to compensate Pakistan for the sixteen army ordnance factories that all happened to fall to India.

Other problems could not be so quickly resolved because Congress and the League representatives either disagreed about their division or because the problems raised long-range policy issues that could only be handled by the responsible governments of the two

Dominions. In these problem areas, such as trade policies, the committees recommended stop-gap measures, or Standstill Agreements, in the hope that India and Pakistan would have peaceful relations after independence and would work out more permanent arrangments in a friendly spirit.

THE RESULTS OF PARTITION

Partition had many far-reaching consequences for the distribution of material, military, and identitive assets between India and Pakistan. And though India received the most assets, behind its inheritance lay several weaknesses.

MATERIAL ASSETS

Economic

The British withdrawal left India the strongest state in South Asia economically. Its area of 1.2 million square miles was approximately three times Pakistan's 360,000 square miles. India was also favored geographically. Whereas its territory was compact and contiguous, Pakistan's was divided into two two parts separated by one thousand miles of Indian land and a three thousand mile sea route. Obviously, communications between the western and eastern wings were difficult and dependent upon Indian goodwill.

Despite such advantages, there were several weaknesses in India's geographical position. It had weak lines of communication between East Bengal and the rest of the northeast sector of the country--Assam, the Northeast Frontier Agency (NEFA), Tripura, Manipur, Cooch Behar, and the Khasi states. The only links with this region were by air or by an inadequate two-feet gauge railway linking West Bengal and Assam through the hilly regions of northern West Bengal state.

India's territorial position was also weak regarding the princely states. Though most of the six hundred or so princely states acceded to the Indian Union by 15 August 1947, their accession was limited. Rushed by events, the Indian Home Minister, Sardar Patel, and his assistant, V. P. Menon, had to draw up a plan by which the states would give up their powers in defense, external affairs, and communications. Left unsolved was the consolidation of their territories and their economic and social integration with the rest of India.[20]

Indeed, some of the most important states-- Hyderabad, Jammu and Kashmir, and Junagadh--failed to accede to either India or Pakistan by independence day. Hyderabad was located in the Deccan peninsula and had an area of 82,000 square miles and an estimated population of 16.3 million.[21] Its strategic importance was that it straddled north-south communications in India. Congress's fears that the aloofness of these princely states would lead to India's balkanization were further heightened by Pakistan's deliberate policy of preventing their accession to India. If these states had not acceded to India, the distribution of material assets would still have overwhelmingly favored India, particularly in population. But India's territorial preponderence over Pakistan would have been reduced and its territorial boundaries greatly complicated.[22]

India received the larger proportion of the subcontinent's natural resources, and especially of those resources essential to industrialization: coal, iron ore, and hydroelectric power potential. Pakistan was left deficient in these natural resources. It had some reserves of petroleum and natural gas, but its coal and iron ore resources were small and of poor quality. Compared to India's estimated reserves of 16.4 billion tons of workable coal, Pakistan had only 166 million tons.[23]

Not that Pakistan was left entirely without natural resources. It received the larger proportion of the irrigated acreage of the Indus Rivers irrigation system as well as the most productive cotton and jute growing areas of the subcontinent. Of a total irrigated area of 23.36 million acres in the Indus Basin, India received 3.84 million acres, or 16.4 percent, and Pakistan received 19.52 million acres, or 83.6 percent.[24] A different trend was recorded for the irrigated acreage of undivided India: India received 68 percent and Pakistan only 32 percent.[25]

And the result? The loss of the most productive agricultural land in the subcontinent to Pakistan left India a food-deficit country. Not only was it faced with food shortages, it also faced competing demands on its reduced acreage: either to grow more food for its rapidly increasing population or to grow cash crops, such as cotton and jute, that it had formerly imported from Pakistan.[26] In contrast, West Pakistan was self-sufficient in foodgrains, and, in years of good harvests, even had some surplus for export.[27]

The division of the subcontinent's human resources favored India. India's population of 337.1 million was four times greater than Pakistan's 75.5 million.[28] Nor was that all. Partition gave India most of the industry of undivided India, and because many of the entrepreneurial and trading classes fled Pakistan at partition, India also had a more skilled labor force than Pakistan.

In general, partition detached the agricultural areas of undivided India from the industrial areas. Some of the provinces that went to India, like Bombay and West Bengal, contained most of undivided India's industries, particularly cotton and jute textiles and consumer goods. Consequently, Pakistan's industrial base at independence was either nonexistent or inadequate for its population. (Table 2.1)

Table 2.1

The Partition of Industry in 1947 (Number of industrial units)

Type of industry	India	Pakistan
Cotton	857	15
Jute	111	0
Sugar	176	15
Iron and Steel	36	0
Cement, limeworks, & potteries	57	8
Papermills	19	0
Glassworks	112	5

Source: O. H. K. Spate, "The Partition of India and the Prospects of Pakistan," *Geographical Review* 38 (1948), p. 22.

For all these reasons, in 1947, India's economic infrastructure--in communications, commerce, finance, education, science, and technology--was more developed than Pakistan's. Whereas India had a merchant marine and ten civil aviation companies, Pakistan had no shipping or civil aviation company.[29] Pakistan's Planning Board described the state of Pakistan's communications system as follows: "The transport system was badly disrupted by partition, especially in East Pakistan where the roads and railways were cut by the new frontiers. Port facilities were inadequate to handle more than a fraction of the traffic required by the new country. Transport facilities between the two Wings were practically nonexistent. The whole transport system had to be reoriented."[30]

Pakistan's few commercial and financial institutions were small compared to their Indian counterparts. They included the Habib Bank, the Muslim Commercial Bank, the Eastern Federal Union Insurance Company, the Habib Insurance Company, and the Muslim Insurance Company. Some of these companies, such as the Muslim Commercial Bank, which began on 9 July 1947, had hardly got off the ground.[31]

Indian and Pakistani educational and research institutions were small in number. India did marginally better than Pakistan in inheriting scientific, engineering, agricultural, medical, and vocational schools. Industrialization of the Indian economy before partition had increased the number of its higher educational institutions.[32] In contrast, Pakistan received only three universities--Dacca, Lahore and Sind--and these had little or no facilities for higher research. They were inadequate for the country's population, and after independence were swamped by new students.[33]

India inherited most of the research institutes of undivided India, including the Council for Scientific and Industrial Research (CSIR) and the Tata Institute of Fundamental Research. The latter was founded in 1945 for nuclear research.

India's economic and scientific assets were larger than Pakistan's only in relative terms. On an absolute basis the assets were small compared to India's growing needs and compared to the level of development in the United States and Britain (table 2.2). Partition of undivided India's economic and scientific assets was thus a partition of scarcity rather than of abundance.

ADMINISTRATIVE AND POLITICAL ASSETS

India inherited more administrative and political assets than Pakistan did. While India had functioning administrative assets at partition, Pakistan had to build its administrative system and other symbols of nationhood literally from scratch.[34] At independence the total actual strength of India's elite adminstrative cadre was 418 while Pakistan's was 96.[35] So it seemed that India inherited the greater share of the elite cadres.

Behind India's inheritance, though, were several weaknesses. First, the number of elite cadres was inadequate for India's administrative needs. After the withdrawal of British officers, India's share of the elite cadres was only 39 percent of the former Indian Civil Service (ICS) and Indian Political Service (IPS).[36] Secondly, the ICS and IPS were generalist services geared to law and order functions rather than economic development. India had a shortage of skilled personnel, particularly in the External Affairs Ministry.[37] Finally, India's share of the elite services--or "steel frame" as they were called --was taxed heavily by the immediate problems of administrative reorganization, refugee movements and rehabilitation, communal violence, other dislocations, and by the government's vacillation in price control policies.

Table 2.2

Comparative Indicators of Economic Development in India, Pakistan, and the United States 1949

Unit/1000 population		India	Pakistan	US[a]
Electricity production	000kwh	13.0	1.9	2,296
Coal consumption	tons	80.0	18.0	3,473
Petroleum consumption	tons	7.8	11.0	1,638
Steel consumption	tons	3.8	1.3	364
Cement consumption	tons	7.2	3.6	229
Locomotives	nos.[b]	22.0	16.0	309
Carrying capacity of railway wagons[c]	tons	10.0	8.8	556
Rail freight	000 ton miles	65.0	n.a.	4,568
Load carrying road vehicles	nos.	0.2	0.2	43
All-weather roads	miles	0.3	0.1	2
Telephones	nos.	0.4	0.2	261

Source: Report by the Commonwealth Consultative Committee on the Colombo Plan, 1950, in *Documents and Speeches on British Commonwealth Affairs 1931-1952*, vol. 2, edited by Nicholas Mansergh (London: Oxford University Press, 1953), p. 1063.

a In most cases figures refer to 1948.
b per million population.
c Indian figures exclude 16,516 wagons for which no carrying capacity is recorded.
n.a. figures unavailable

Even so, India had several advantages over Pakistan in the quality of its political system. The Congress was a mass-party with firmly established roots at the local level. It enjoyed widespread prestige from its leadership of the independence movement. Its talented leaders included such diverse figures as Mahatma Gandhi, the charismatic expounder of civil disobedience and nonviolence; Nehru, the conceptualizer of India's domestic and foreign policies; and Sardar Patel, the Party's organization man and boss. In over forty years of struggle against the British, the Congress had emerged as a disciplined party and as a broad coalition of different social groups and ideologies. Before independence, it had already reached internal consensus on the following: the form of constitutional government (liberal-democratic, parliamentary); the need for representative government in the princely states; the abolition of the *zamindari* system of land tenure (an intermediary landlord class); and, the need for uniformity in India's legal, administrative and economic systems.

Further, when independence came, the Constituent Assembly of India had already been in session since 9 December 1946, during which time it had made progress in framing the Objectives Resolution for the future Constitution.

Pakistan's Muslim League, on the other hand, was an elite party of landowners, local notables, middle-class intellectuals and professionals, all hurriedly thrown together in their struggle against the Congress. Unlike thc Congress, which had strong local roots throughout the former British Indian provinces, the Muslim League's leadership came from areas that were now part of India, particularly from the United Provinces, Bombay, and Bihar. The League's experience of running provincial governments also fell short of the Congress's; the League had never been strong enough to run the key provinces of Bengal and the Punjab. Finally, its economic and social program was less well articulated than Congress's. The League pitched its appeal to all Muslims, and this tended to blur its economic and social reform programs. Pakistan's postindependence political instability can be directly traced to these weaknesses in its political assets.

MILITARY ASSETS

Partition left India with the greater share of the assets of the British Indian armed forces. In personnel, it received approximately two-thirds of the Army, three-quarters of the Royal Indian Navy

(RIN), and four-fifths of the Royal Indian Air Force (RIAF) (appendix 2).

In addition, India received all sixteen ordnance factories of the British Indian armed forces, a share of the training establishments, sixteen battalions of the famed Gurkha rifles, and various units of the armed forces of the former princely states.

Besides its manpower, Pakistan's military assets included an infrastructure of fortifications in the NWFP; two famed *martial races* of the former Indian Army (the Pathans and Punjabi Muslims); all of the training, permanent air stations, and workshops of the RIAF; and several other training establishments, including the Staff College at Quetta.[38]

Balancing Pakistan's assets were a number of liabilities. East Pakistanis had no martial tradition and were underrepresented in the new Pakistani armed forces. There was no complete Muslim battalion in the former British Indian Army whereas there were complete Hindu and Gurkha units. And Pakistan had not received its share of the military equipment of the British Indian army from the new Indian government. The Joint Defense Council, which administered the division of the Army, had awarded Pakistan 165,000 tons of equipment, but on independence day these were only paper assets. Finally, Pakistan's geography made military planning and coordination difficult between the two wings. As Ayub Khan was later to say, the geographical separation of East and West Pakistan and Pakistan's lack of defensive depth were a "soldier's nightmare."[39]

That India got the bulk of the Indian armed forces should not obscure the fact that its military assets were also limited. In the first place, army units had to be reorganized into a coherent fighting force with clear lines of authority and communication. It is true that the problems of reorganization were much worse for Pakistan, since it had no complete Muslim units, but the new Indian army also had to form integrated units containing all communal groups and castes. Secondly, the Indian armed forces' officer corps was very small. On independence day no Indian officer held a rank higher than brigadier, and no Indian officer had ever had experience of strategic planning.[40] Like Pakistan, India was forced to rely on British officers after independence until its officer corps could be complelety indigenized. Thirdly, India inherited generally obsolete military equipment for its three services. To be sure, this was much better than Pakistan's, but India's defense production base was narrow, incapable of producing sophisticated weaponry, and depended upon British personnel and expertise. Finally, the Indian government put competing demands upon the Indian army, which had to fight in Kashmir, aid in the safe transfer of refugees from Pakistan, and carry out its normal duties of aiding civilian authorities and patrolling India's lengthy borders.

IDENTITIVE ASSETS

India and Pakistan had just undergone a bitter partition caused by conflicting values and symbols of religion and nationality. Partition, though, could not erase some of the underlying common values and interests shared by their peoples.

Both countries were part of the same civilizational area and shared many religious, cultural, ethnic, and linguistic similarities. The Urdu, Punjabi, and Bengali languages were spoken on both sides of the border. There were, too, some tangible reminders of the shared history, if not values, of both countries. Moghul monuments like Taj Mahal and Fatepur Sikri were located in India, as were centers of Islamic learning like the Deoband school and Muslim Aligarh University. Pakistan's historical and religious inheritance included the famous Kali temple in Karachi and several Sikh shrines, including Nankana Sahib in the Sheikpura district of Lahore. Thus both countries remained interdependent in culture and religion after 1947.

India and Pakistan also had two other major identitive assets. First, they inherited common values from their former colonial master, Britain. Similar administrative and legal systems, the use of the English language by their elites, and similar outlooks among the English-trained officer corps formed some of the identitive assets from this source. The Indian and Pakistan elites also shared a distrust of communism as an ideology and as a way of life for their peoples.

A second set of identitive assets originated from the similar economic problems faced by India and Pakistan. Both were developing countries with low per capita income, capital investment, and productivity. Their populations were inadequately fed, housed, and clothed and suffered from the problems of overpopulation such as large-scale unemployment and underemployment. In addition, both India and Pakistan had experienced colonialism. As newly-independent states both sought to preserve their sovereignty and to end colonialism and racism elsewhere in the world. This was, then, an identity of the poor and disadvantaged.

CONCLUSION

Although India received the greater share of the material and military assets of undivided India, it received several liabilities as well. Materially, most of the natural resources, skilled manpower, industry and research institutes went to India. But these assets were small on a per capita basis, and India was left weak agriculturally. Militarily, India gained the bulk of the armed forces, but, like its material assets, these were inadequate for India's needs as an independent state. In identitive assets, the conflict between India and Pakistan over religion and nationality could not overshadow several shared cultural, relgious, and ideological values and symbols. After independence the task for Indian and Pakistani governments was to build up their assets and use them for power and influence.

Notes

1. Sarvepalli Gopal, *Jawaharlal Nehru: A Biography*, vol. 2: *1947-1956* (London: Jonathan Cape, 1979), p. 13.

2. India, Dominion, Ministry of Information and Broadcasting, *After Partition* (Delhi: Publications Division, 1948), p. 50.

3. The League's demands for parity with the Congress are discussed in Nicholas Mansergh, "The Partition of India in Retrospect," *International Journal* 21 (Winter 1965-66): 1-19.

4. Presidential Address to the All-India Muslim League at Lahore 22 March 1940, in K. Sarwar Hasan, ed., *The Transfer of Power: Documents on the Foreign Relations of Pakistan* (Karachi: Pakistan Institute of International Affairs, 1966), p. 16.

5. S. R. Mehrotra, "The Congress and the Partition of India," in *The Partition of India: Policies and Perspectives, 1935-1947*, ed. C. H. Philips and Mary Doreen Wainwright (London: George Allen & Unwin, 1970), p. 217.

6. H. V. Hodson, *The Great Divide: Britain--India--Pakistan* (London: Hutchinson & Co., 1969), p. 166.

7. Attlee's Directive to Mountbatten of March 1947 stated: "It is the definite objective of His Majesty's Government to obtain a unitary Government for British India and the Indian States, if possible within the British Commonwealth...You should take every opportunity of stressing the importance of ensuring that the transfer of power is effected with full regard to the defense requirements of India. In the first place, you will impress upon the Indian leaders the great importance of avoiding any breach in the continuity of the Indian Army and of maintaining the organization of defense on an all Indian basis. Secondly, you will point out the need for continued collaboration in the security of the Indian Ocean area for which adequate provision might be made in an agreement between the two countries. At a suitable date His Majesty's Government would be ready to send military and other experts to India to assist in discussing the terms of such an agreement." For the full text, see Hodson, *Great Divide*, pp. 545-47.

8. Ibid., pp. 202-3.

9. Ibid.,p. 203.

10. In an interview nine years after partition, Nehru discussed the reasons why Congress accepted partition. An undivided India would have constant communal turmoil. "It would be a very weak India, that is, a federal India with far too much power in the federating units. A larger India would have constant disintegrating pulls." Michael Brecher, *Nehru: A Political Biography*, abr. ed. (London: Oxford University Press, 1961), p. 145.

11. Ibid., p. 144.

12. Hodson, *Great Divide*, p. 216.

13. Quoted in Jamil-ud-din Ahmed, *Some Recent Speeches and Writings of Mr. Jinnah*, vol. 2 (Lahore: Ashraf, 1947), p. 578.

14. Accounts of Liaquat Ali Khan's proposal to divide the Indian armed forces are contained in John Connell, *Auchinleck* (London: Cassell, 1959), pp. 872-80; and Chaudhri Muhammed Ali, *The Emergence of Pakistan* (New York: Columbia University Press, 1967), pp. 130-33.

15. See, for example, Lord Pethick-Lawrence, "Viability of Pakistan," in *The Transfer of Power, 1942-47*, vol. 1, ed. Nicholas Mansergh (London: Her Majesty's Stationery Office, 1976), pp. 951-63; and Taya Zinkin, "Note on Pakistan," Ibid., pp. 801-5.

16. See, for example, Anwar Qureshi, "The Economic Basis of Pakistan," *Asiatic Review* 43 (April 1947): 160-65.

17. Hasan, *Transfer of Power*, p. 374.

18. The expert committees were (1) Organization, Records and Personnel (2) Assets and Liabilities (3) Central Revenues (4) Contracts (5) Currency, Coinage, and Exchange (6) Economic Relations (Controls) (7) Economic Relations (Trade) (8) Domicile (9) Foreign Relations, and (10) Armed Forces. India, Ministry of Information and Broadcasting, *After Partition*, pp. 19-20.

19. Details of the partition process can be found in "Partition of India," *India Quarterly* 44 (October-December 1948): 313-23.

20. V. P. Menon, *The Story of the Integration of the Indian States* (Bombay: Orient Longmans, 1961), pp. 91-94.

21. C. N. Vakil, *Economic Consequences of Divided India* (Bombay: Vora & Co., 1950), p. 74.

22. If Hyderabad, Jammu and Kashmir, and Junagadh had not acceded or otherwise have been absorbed by India, India would still have been left with a population of 310 million, or about three times Pakistan's population. If the three states had remained independent, India would still have been three times larger than Pakistan. If these states had acceded to Pakistan, India would have been only double the area of Pakistan. This analysis is based on the area and population data in Vakil, *Economic Consequences*, pp. 73-74.

23. Ibid., p. 186.

24. N. D. Gulhati, *Indus Waters Treaty: An Exercise in International Mediation.* (Bombay: Allied Publishers, 1973), p. 454.

25. Vakil, *Economic Consequences*, p. 157.

26. Ibid., pp. 30-31.

27. Ibid.

28. Ibid., pp. 73-74.

29. Ibid., pp. 418-26.

30. Pakistan, Planning Board, *The First Five Year Plan, 1955-60* (Draft), vol. 2 (Karachi: Government of Pakistan Press, 1956), pp. 329-30.

31. M. A. H. Ispahani, "Factors Leading to the Partition of British India," in *Partition of India*, eds. Philips and Wainwright, pp. 358-59. See also, Hanna Papanek, "Pakistan's Big Businessmen: Separatism, Entrepreneurship and Partial Modernization," *Economic Development and Cultural Change* 21 (October 1972): 1-32.

32. Jagdish N. Bhagwati and Padma Desai, *India: Planning for Industrialization* (London: Oxford University Press, 1970), p. 52.

33. M. Razuiddin Siddiqi, "Scientific Education and Research in Pakistan," in *Science and the Human Condition in India and Pakistan*, ed. Ward Morehouse (New York: Rockefeller University Press, 1968), pp. 77-87.

34. Several eye-witnesses vividly testify to the meagerness of Pakistan's administrative resources. One author recalls that in the whole of the Foreign Office in Karachi in 1947 there was only one typewriter. Vincent Sheean, *Nehru: The Years of Power* (London: Gollancz: 1960), quoted in S. M. Burke, "The Management of Pakistan's Foreign Policy," in *Pakistan: The Long View*, ed. Ralph Braibanti et al. (Durham, N. C.: Duke University Press, 1977), p. 340. Ayub Khan, who became General Officer Commanding in East Pakistan, describes the lack of resources in East Pakistan when he assumed command in 1947: "The provincial government, with which I came in frequent contact, was newly formed and poorly staffed. But worse still, it was politically weak and unstable. There was no army...We had very poor accommodation; at Headquarters there was no table, no chair, no stationery--we had virtually nothing at all; not even any maps of East Pakistan. Gradually we started to organize ourselves." *Friends Not Masters* (London: Oxford University Press, 1967), p. 22.

35. Ralph Braibanti et al., *Asian Bureaucratic Systems Emergent from the British Imperial Tradition* (Durham, N. C.: Duke University Press, 1966), p. 646.

36. Ralph Braibanti, "Public Bureaucracy and Judiciary in Pakistan," in *Bureaucracy and Political Development*, ed. Joseph LaPalombara (Princeton, N. J.: Princeton University Press, 1963), p. 365.

37. Warren F. Ilchman, "Political Development and Foreign Policy: The Case of India," *Journal of Commonwealth Political Studies* 4 (November 1966), p. 222.

38. A. L. Venkateswaran, *Defense Organization in India* (Delhi: Publications Division, 1967), p. 48.

39. Quoted in A. R. Siddiqi, "Years of Indo-Pakistan Armed Conflicts," *Defense Journal* (Islamabad) 4 (1978), p. 3.

40. The preindependence exclusion of Indians from strategic planning for the Royal Indian Air Force is related by Air Marshal M. S. Chaturvedi, *History of the Indian Air Force* (New Delhi: Vikas, 1978), pp. 54-56.

CHAPTER THREE

INDIA AND PAKISTAN RECOVER: 1947-54

Indian and Pakistani leaders were dissatisfied with partition. They viewed the terms of the partition settlement as a second-best solution. After 1947, both countries had to make the best of the assets and the liabilities that they had inherited. Their priorities were to increase their material and military assets and reduce the liabilities resulting from partition.

MATERIAL CAPABILITIES, POWER AND INFLUENCE

Economic

Between 1947 and 1954, India had a better economic growth rate than Pakistan, particularly per capita income. India's GNP increased by 13.9 percent, while Pakistan's was about half of that (7.8 percent).[1] The proportions of national income generated by the agricultural, industrial, and service sectors remained relatively constant in both countries. Pakistan registered some increases in its manufacturing sector, but care must be taken in interpreting these changes because they occurred from an extremely low initial manufacturing base. As one economist notes, "Pakistan entered the world with an 'abnormally' low amount of industrial capacity and industrial production for a country of her size, income level, and resource base. A substantial portion of the rapid industrial growth and import substitution that took place, especially in the 1950s, was a readjustment to an economic infrastructure commensurate with her basic economic characteristics."[2]

Further, the types of industrialization in India in Pakistan are as important as their magnitudes. Pakistan's impressive "catching-up" in this period was in light industrial and consumer goods industries, such as cotton and jute textiles, leather, sugar, cement, and paper. By contrast, Indian industrialization covered a much more diversified base. It included coal, iron and steel, heavy machinery, and power, which contribute more to the infrastructure of a modern economy and hence add to a country's material and military power and influence.

Industrial growth in India and Pakistan during this period occurred against a background of slow agricultural growth in both countries. In Pakistan an emphasis on growing cash crops, the Korean War boom of 1950-52, and the government's policy of holding down agricultural prices, all led to poor agricultural performance. Yields of food crops actually declined, and, with a rising population, Pakistan soon became a net food importer. India's agricultural performance was as dismal. For though agricultural growth was historically high and actually outpaced India's population growth, it was insufficient to generate more than a modicum surplus, either for sustaining industrialization or for export, and India too became a net food importer.[3] India's food crop yields did increase compared to Pakistan, but most of its increased agricultural production resulted from an expansion of cultivated acreage and not of rising agricultural productivity.[4]

In summary, the growth of Indian and Pakistani national income points to three major conclusions: First, industrial and agricultural production levels recovered from the disruption of partition. Both economies readjusted to their new economic resource bases. Secondly, the Indian economy performed much better than Pakistan in growth rates and type of industrialization. Finally, the industrial changes had very little structural impact on both economies because agricultural growth was stagnant. Industrialization affected only a small sector of the economies, which continued to be predominantly agricultural.

The partition of the subcontinent reduced India's economic power and influence. Before 1947, the regions of the British Indian Empire were economically complementary. Those areas that were later to become Pakistan supplied raw materials, such as jute, cotton, and wheat, for the industrial areas of India, which in turn provided consumer and industrial goods to these primary producing areas. Partition separated these natural economic regions into two, often antagonistic, political units. This is shown in the trade and water disputes between the two countries.

Trade. Theoretically, partition would not have created any economic problems if both countries had agreed to replace the de facto customs union at partition (that is, the Standstill Agreements) with a more permanent customs union. This failed to come into being for three major reasons: First, other disputes, especially Kashmir and the flight of refugees, politicized the trade disputes. This led, secondly, to a desire among many Pakistanis for an independent economic system, one that would be free from Indian pressures. Finally, as in many customs unions, the problem of equity arose. In October 1947, the Pakistani government pointed out that although Pakistan produced roughly 73 percent of the total jute crop of the subcontinent, most of the jute and jute manufactures were exported from Calcutta. As a result India received over 90 percent of the foreign exchange earnings from jute while growing only 27 percent of the subcontinent's jute.[5]

The Indian government replied that such claims of equity should be settled as part of an overall permanent agreement among the two Dominions on customs revenues, with the possibility of retroactivity to deal with Pakistan's claims for jute." A matter such as this," it said, "will have to be considered comprehensively over the whole field of import, export and Central Excise duties in relation to common economic and fiscal policies and the absence of any customs or trade barriers, or in other words in the light of a Customs and Excise Union and all that such a Union implies."[6] At several Inter-Dominion conferences, the Indian government clearly proposed a customs union with Pakistan. Pakistan's government demurred because it feared that Pakistan would be the junior partner in this customs union.[7]

While the dispute about equity was taking place, the Standstill Agreement on trade broke down. The Indian government charged Pakistan with the first major infraction of the Agreement, arguing that the Sind provincial government had restricted the free flow of several commodities that were intended for export to India.[8] A further infraction occurred in November 1947 when Pakistan imposed export duties on raw jute from East Bengal. The Standstill Agreement then collapsed in the next two years as India and Pakistan imposed export and import duties on each other's goods.

The biggest disruption of Indo-Pakistani trade followed Britain's decision in September 1949 to devalue the pound sterling. India followed suit and devalued the rupee, but Pakistan kept the old exchange rate for its rupee.

India's devaluation and Pakistan's refusal to follow had far-reaching consequences for their bilateral relations. First, it led to a further delinking of their economies. The stronger Pakistani rupee (100 Pakistani rupees to 144 Indian rupees) meant that India had to pay more for its imports of cotton, jute and other raw materials from Pakistan. Because India was the major buyer of these goods, the precipitous fall in demand for them led to a decline in Pakistan's jute and cotton prices and to increased smuggling of jute into India. To enforce the exchange rate and to maintain the price of Pakistani goods, the Pakistani government set up a Jute Control Board. Pakistan withheld the supply of 1.2 million bales of jute that had already been purchased by Indian traders before the September devaluation. It also restricted the movement of goods between India and Pakistan. Significantly, it held up railway equipment with which India intended to build the Bengal-Assam railway. India retaliated by stopping the supply of coal to Pakistan in December. The result of this trade war was a complete halt to Indo-Pakistan trade from September 1949 to April 1950.

A second consequence of the devaluation dispute was that both countries increased their search for alternative markets. Pakistan's direction of trade moved away from India, and Britain became Pakistan's largest trading partner (appendix 1). India and Pakistan realized, however, that they were too closely interdependent to make a sudden break from each other. The economic effects were just too severe. A trade agreement on 25 April 1950 brought the trade war to an end. Further trade agreements in February 1951, August 1952, and March 1953 eased the delinking of the two economies but at lower volumes of trade than before devaluation.

A final consequence of devaluation was that it worsened the political relations between the two countries. Its effects went beyond the economic sphere. It led to distress both among the jute farmers of East Bengal, who saw a decline in their crop prices, and among the jute mill workers of West Bengal, who were laid off because of shortages of raw material supplies. In turn, these hardships increased communal tensions in both provinces and led to increased refugee movements out of East Bengal. The Pakistan government accused India of waging a trade war against it; India replied that Pakistan's difficulties arose from the normal operations of supply and demand. It also added that Pakistan's minimum prices and restrictions on the movement of goods to India interfered with the normal operation of supply and demand in the jute industry.[9]

Water Disputes. Some Pakistanis also interpreted East Punjab's shut-off of water to Pakistan in April 1948 as a coercive and punitive act by India. The origins of this dispute lie in the 1947 partition of not only India and the Punjab but also the Indus Rivers basin. Sir Cyril Radcliffe's Punjab Boundary Award in August 1947 gave India the upper waters of the eastern tributaries of the Indus--the Chenab, Ravi, and Sutlej. (The Beas tributary remained wholly within India.) Pakistan found itself the lower riparian of these tributaries. Because India occupied most of the disputed territory of Jammu and Kashmir, Pakistan also found itself to be the lower riparian for the Jhelum tributary and the main Indus River. In making the Punjab award, Sir Cyril mostly took into account the communal distribution of population in the province. But he also expressed the hope that "where the drawing of a boundary line cannot avoid disrupting unitary services as canal irrigation, railways, and electric power transmission, a solution may be found by agreement between the two states for some joint control of what has hitherto been a valuable common service."[10]

East and West Punjab did agree to maintain the water supplies for the portions of the Indus River system that they shared. Both signed a Standstill Agreement on 20 December 1947 to last until 31 March 1948. But that was all their cooperation. In the interim period they made no progress toward permanent arrangements for sharing the waters, despite frequent requests from the East Punjab government to do so.

On 1 April 1948, the day after the Standstill Agreement expired, the East Punjab government shut off the waters to the Central Bari Doab Canal (C.B.D.C.) in Pakistan. The shut-off lasted several days, and came before the *rabi* (spring) growing season. It directly threatened the livelihood of West Pakistani farmers served by the C.B.D.C.

Why did East Punjab's government discontinue the water supplies? Some suggest that this coercion was meant to apply pressure on Pakistan on the issue of Kashmir.[11] The problem though with this explanation is that it implies coordination between the Indian central government and the East Punjab government. Swaran Singh, the Minister in the East Punjab government responsible for Irrigation in 1947-49, disputed this, saying "The government of East Punjab was responsible for the decision. It was myself and the Chief Minister through an internal process of consultation. There was no consultation in advance with the government of India because it was not thought to be necessary."[12]

Although the decision to cut off the water was unrelated to other Indo-Pakistan disputes, it was clearly coercive. At the time of this decision, the East Punjab government strongly felt that it was entitled to the exclusive use of the waters of the eastern tributaries, particularly since large parts of East Punjab were without canal irrigation. According to N. D. Gulhati, "The East Punjab government felt that if, in the absence of a formal agreement, it did not discontinue, at least temporarily, the use of the C.B.D.C. for the benefit of West Punjab, the latter might acquire some sort of legal right on U.B.D.C. [Upper Bari Doab Canal], namely its continued use for the benefit of C.B.D.C."[13]

East Punjab's actions forced the West Punjab government to negotiate. In mid-April the Chief Engineers of both provinces met at Simla, the East Punjab capital, and reached temporary agreement on the resupply of water and the payment by Pakistan of royalty charges for the supply of water. On 8 May 1948, the two Punjabs and also the two Dominion governments made another agreement. This skirted the legal claims of both sides, but introduced the principle of replacement. India would progressively reduce its supplies to Pakistan to enable the West Punjab government to tap alternative sources. The West Punjab government also agreed to pay the Reserve Bank of India an amount of money that the Indian Prime Minister specified to be Pakistan's water bill.

In August 1950, Pakistan repudiated the May 1948 agreement and refused to pay its water bill. It charged that the May 1948 agreement had been made under duress. The evidence shows otherwise. First, the Pakistan government made the charge a full two years after the agreement; in the meantime it had said nothing to India or the world about coercion. Secondly, Pakistan eventually (and voluntarily) paid the disputed sum of money to India when both countries concluded their dispute under the Indus Waters Treaty of 1960. Finally, F. J. Berber, the West German international lawyer who gave India legal advice in the dispute, noted that East Punjab resumed supplies of water to Pakistan before the 8 May agreement.[14]

As in other economic disputes with Pakistan, India could not influence Pakistan's policy on the use of the Indus Waters. By 1950 bilateral negotiations had failed to settle the dispute, and Pakistan began to mobilize international support for its legal position on the use of the eastern tributaries. Under the 8 May agreement, India had asserted the principle of replacement as a solution to the dispute--Pakistani canals formerly fed from India would receive waters from the main Indus River and its western tributaries via a series of new link canals. But India's ability to pay for the replacement canals was limited. The Indian government also argued that the continued supply of water to Pakistan was a sacrifice on India's part because it was prevented from developing the arid parts of East Punjab and Rajasthan as long as Pakistan had not tapped alternative water supplies from the west. Pakistan ignored India's sacrifices, and not surprisingly, for Pakistan was only concerned with that part of the Indus Basin that had come under its control at partition.

A new phase in the dispute opened in 1951 following the intervention of David E. Lilienthal, a former chairman of the Tennessee Valley Authority (TVA) and the United States Atomic Energy Commission. In an influential article called "Another Korea in the Making," Lilienthal argued that India and Pakistan could devote their economic resources more profitably to the functional development of the Indus Waters Basin, perhaps along the lines of America's multi-state T.V.A. He argued that functionalist integration would make both countries less vulnerable to communist subversion.[15] Lilienthal's suggestions influenced the President of the World Bank, Eugene Black, who wrote to Nehru and Liaquat Ali Khan in September 1951, promising the good offices of the World Bank to resolve the dispute along functionalist lines. Both Prime Ministers accepted Black's offer because they saw it as a way to break the deadlock.

Indian and Pakistani representatives met at Washington in May 1952 and agreed to prepare detailed proposals for a comprehensive settlement treating the Indus Basin as one functional unit. But these efforts failed. The Indian and Pakistani proposals for sharing the waters were too far apart for any compromise. Pakistan insisted on receiving as much water from the eastern tributaries as possible, and such demands were unacceptable to India. For the next two years there was deadlock as both sides disputed the other's legal, political,and technical claims. By the end of 1953, the World Bank reluctantly concluded that the only solution to the dispute was one in which India and Pakistan became independent in water supplies. On 5 February 1954, the Bank proposed that India receive the entire use of the eastern tributaries and Pakistan the western tributaries. In the interim India would pay Pakistan for the cost of the replacement works.[16] India accepted the Bank proposal in principle on 25 March 1954. The Pakistan government insisted on clarifications of the proposal and on guarantees of its existing water supplies from India. The Bank proposal followed the logic of the 8 May 1948 principle of replacement, but it took the principle of division much further and gave up any hope of a functionalist solution to the dispute. The Bank Proposal also promised Pakistan reduced dependence upon India for water supplies. It was therefore consistent with the Pakistan government's long-term policy of economic independence.

A general conclusion about Indo-Pakistan economic relations between 1947 and 1954 is that both countries acted unilaterally at a time when their economies were still interdependent. Neither side could escape the consequences of the other's actions. Both countries had to agree on short-term bilateral trade and water agreements to ease the problems of sudden de-linking. The long-term trend, however, was toward increasingly independent economies.

Nuclear Energy

As in other areas of national life, such as communications, economics, finance, and trade, India and Pakistan placed their scientific and technical institutions in order after partition. India received most of the scientific, technical, and educational institutions, even though these were too small in number, type, and quality for India's needs as a large developing nation. Consequently, the first priority of Indian and Pakistani governments was to expand the number of institutions, increase the stock of skilled manpower, establish national networks of research, and coordinate research between government, industry, and higher education. One such area of science and technology was the peaceful application of nuclear energy.

Both governments realized the potential importance of nuclear science and technology for economic modernization. But India had two particular advantages over Pakistan in nuclear research: first, it inherited the Tata Institute for Fundamental Research; and, secondly, Nehru and Dr. Homi Babha, Indian's leading nuclear scientist, articulated a clear policy of Indian nuclear energy development. Despite other economic needs, and despite the American, British, and Canadian policy of restricting information on the peaceful uses of nuclear energy, Nehru was determined that India would not be left out in developing this advanced technology.

The Indian government's Industrial Policy Resolution of 6 April 1948 demarcated the public and private sectors of Indian industry and made atomic energy development a government monopoly. In August 1948 the government established an Atomic Energy Commission under the Department of Scientific Research. The AEC was to be an advisory and policymaking body responsible for all aspects of nuclear science and technology, including surveying for atomic minerals, researching peaceful applications of nuclear energy, and training personnel. As a later chairman of the AEC notes, the work of the AEC between 1948 and 1954 was "restricted to the survey of radioactive minerals, setting up plants for processing monazite and limited research in the area of electronics, methods of chemical analysis of minerals and the recovery of valuable elements from available minerals."[17] Another aim of the AEC was to acquire skilled manpower for nuclear research.

Pakistan made no progress in nuclear energy in this period. This was partly because it inherited meager scientific and educational resources and partly because the Pakistan government gave higher priority to applied research for raising economic productivity. Also, the peaceful applications of nuclear energy were as yet unclear in this period and the lead in this area was taken by developed countries like the United States, Canada, Britain, and the USSR. Still, as Pakistan consolidated its economic and social systems, and as the peaceful applications of nuclear energy became clearer and more feasible, Pakistani policymakers gave increasing thought to creating a Pakistan Atomic Energy Commission.[18] Pakistan's Industrial Policy Resolution, which like India's was published in April 1948, made no mention of atomic energy, but it did place strategic industries under governmental control and regulation.

The first phase of Indo-Pakistan relations corresponds to changes not only in Pakistan's external alliances but also to international developments in nuclear energy. On 8 December 1953, the Eisenhower administration proposed its "Atoms for Peace" program for sharing nuclear science and technology for peaceful purposes. The rest of the 1950s thus promised greater nuclear development for India and Pakistan.

Political

One of the most significant differences in material assets between India and Pakistan was in political development. Both countries did very well in reorganizing their administrative systems. Pakistan did particularly well considering its initial obstacles--disjointed administrative units, fewer civil servants, and lack of administrative facilities. But India improved on Pakistan's performance by preserving the continuity of leadership, developing political parties and electoral systems, creating a strong center of political authority, adopting a constitution, and extracting resources for economic development.

Leadership. It is often pointed out that Pakistan suffered a grevious blow after independence when Mohammed Ali Jinnah, the *Quaid-e-Azam* (Great Leader), died on 11 September 1948. Jinnah had always taken care to present himself as a symbol of the nation above any purely sectional interest; and so after independence he became the Governor-General of the new Dominion as well as the de facto Prime Minister. His death removed one of the unifying links in Pakistan's polity. Power passed to Liaquat Ali Khan, Jinnah's lieutenant and the only person who could even approximate Jinnah's authority. Unfortunately, a Pathan assassinated Liaquat on 16 October 1951.

India's political system also suffered severe losses of leadership in this period. A Hindu extremist assassinated Mahatma Gandhi on 30 January 1948. Sardar Patel, the Home Minister and strongman of the Congress party organization, died in December 1950. Thus both countries lost leaders at the very time when they could least afford to do so. But of the two countries, India was the more fortunate. From 1947 to 1954, while Pakistan had three Prime Ministers, Nehru served continuously as India's Prime Minister. The continuity of Indian leadership gave India's domestic policy greater coherence than Pakistan's. A strong Prime Minister was able to begin economic planning, consolidate the political integration of the country, formulate a constitution, and control the military and civil service.

Political Parties and Electoral Systems. The continuity in India's political system resulted not only from Nehru's preeminence but also from the Congress Party's success in establishing itself as the dominant party in independent India. The Congress successfully changed from an independence movement to a governing party, although not without some struggles between its organizational and parliamentary wings. Unlike the Muslim League in Pakistan, the Congress was prepared to test itself in electoral battle. Nehru was willing to experiment, take risks, and push democracy in India, instead of waiting for some imaginary day when the proper conditions for democracy in India would arrive. India's first general election was held in the winter of 1951-52, based on universal adult suffrage. Congress captured 74.4 percent of the seats in the Lok Sabha, the lower house of Parliament. In the state elections of 1952 it won 68.4 percent of the 3,283 state assembly seats.[19]

The Muslim League emerged from partition weaker than Congress in leadership, organization, and experience of government. Pakistan's major social groups--the Bengalis, West Pakistanis and Muslims from India--had been thrown together hurriedly into Jinnah's Pakistan Movement. They had little experience of working together politically. With a weak party machinery and in an atmosphere of Pakistan under siege from India, Jinnah placed more emphasis on controlling Pakistan through the bureaucracy rather than the party machinery.[20]

The League steadily lost ground in popular support. It was undercut by the central leadership and had few opportunities to test its programs in competitive elections. No national elections were held on the basis of universal adult suffrage; there were only provincial elections, and in these the League did badly. In East Pakistan a United Front of the Awami League and the Krishak Sramik Party (KSP) replaced the Muslim League. Not only was the Muslim League unresponsive to East Pakistani regionalism, it also had a poor organizational structure and lacked mechanisms for resolving intraparty disputes. So with no national party or leadership, political power in Pakistan passed by default to the only institutions capable of maintaining national unity--the armed forces and the bureaucracy.

Political Integration. Congress established a strong center of political authority in India and successfully integrated the Indian princely states. By independence day, most Indian states had acceded to the Indian Union on the three subjects of defense, foreign relations, and communications. Only Junagadh, Jammu and Kashmir, and Hyderabad remained aloof from the Indian Union. All three states were bitterly contested by India and Pakistan.

The Junagadh and Hyderabad disputes were settled when Indian troops took over these states in November 1947 and September 1948 respectively. In Junagadh and Hyderabad, the rulers were Muslims and the populations were mainly Hindu. The religions of the rulers and the ruled were the exact opposite in Jammu and Kashmir: the Maharajah of Jammu and Kashmir was Hindu while seventy percent of his subjects were Muslims. Kashmir was the largest of the Indian states (85,885 square miles) and also one of the most territorially compact. And, unlike Junagadh and Hyderabad, it adjoined both India and Pakistan. The ruler knew that if he acceded to either Dominion he would probably lose his throne; as a Hindu ruler he would be an anomaly in Pakistan, and in India his privileges would be curtailed by the new democratic government. So he vacillated. The most that he did by independence day was to sign a Standstill Agreement with Pakistan.

The immediate cause of the Kashmir dispute between India and Pakistan is controversial. The state government of Kashmir claimed that invaders from Pakistan were operating in the Poonch district of the state. Later, the state government accused Pakistan of violating the Standstill Agreement. In particular, it charged Pakistanis with disrupting food supplies, other essential items, and the state's postal, banking, and communication links with Pakistan.[21] Pakistan's government denied these charges. It countered that Muslims were being killed in Kashmir by both state troops and non-Muslim refugees from West Pakistan. To the charge of violating the Standstill Agreement, the Pakistan government replied that "the difficulties that have been felt by your Administration have arisen as a result of widespread disturbances in East Punjab and the disruption of communications caused thereby, particularly by the shortage of coal." It added, "these difficulties have been felt actually by the West Punjab government themselves."[22]

The historical evidence is clear that a revolt against the state government broke out in the Muslim Poonch district over the imposition of taxation. The district's residents included many ex-servicemen who had fought in the British Indian Army in the Second World War. They strongly resisted Kashmiri state troops, evacuated their families to Pakistan, and then set up an "Azad" (Free) Kashmir government. At this stage, news of alleged atrocities against their fellow Muslims reached Pathan tribesmen in the NWFP. They began to invade Kashmir from Pakistan.

The Maharajah thereupon appealed to the Indian government for help. The Indian government replied that it was legally unable to help unless he acceded to India, which he did on 26 October 1947. The tribesmen, meanwhile, pillaged the Kashmir countryside before making their way to Srinagar, the state capital. This delay allowed the Indian army to repel the tribesmen only a few miles from Srinagar.

The Pakistan government refused to accept Kashmir's accession to the Indian Union. It was unable, though, to commit its regular troops to Kashmir because the acting Commander-in-Chief of the Pakistan Army, General Gracey, refused to accept such orders from Jinnah without first consulting the Supreme Command Headquarters in Delhi headed by Field-Marshal Auchinlek. (Supreme Command Headquarters, directed by the Joint Defense Council, was a temporary body for dividing the British Indian Army and reconstituting it into the armies of the two new Dominions.) The British government disbanded Supreme Command Headquarters in November 1947, leaving Pakistan free to throw its regular troops into Kashmir, which it did in April 1948 after Gracey had warned the Pakistan government of an imminent Indian offensive against Azad Kashmir. An undeclared war broke out between the two Dominions. Fighting continued throughout 1948, until both countries accepted a cease-fire on 1 January 1949.

In contrast to Junagadh and Hyderabad, India failed to solve the Kashmir dispute decisively by military force. When the fighting stopped, India held most of the state's territory and population, including the important Vale of Kashmir, all of Ladakh and Jammu and parts of Poonch. Pakistan held the western part of Poonch and the northern parts of the state, which included the small feudal states of Baltistan, Gilgit, Nagir, and Yasin.

Both governments began to integrate their parts of Kashmir into their political systems. New Delhi had several advantages in this. Nehru was a close friend of Sheikh Abdullah, the popular leader of the state government. Abdullah's political ideas and programs--democracy, secularism, social and economic reform, and economic planning--were miniature versions of Congress's all-India programs. Shortly after Kashmir's accession, he became the State Prime Minister and announced plans for democratic elections, land reform and a new state constitution. Abdullah's National Conference Party won all 75 seats in the state Constituent Assembly elections of October 1951. As part of the constitution-making for the state, he then negotiated with the central government in July 1952 on the division of powers between the state and center. The ensuing "Delhi Agreement" established the Indian Constitution's precedence over the state constitution. It allowed Kashmir some autonomy in residuary powers, in regulating permanent residents in the state, and in the center's application of emergency powers to Kashmir.

Behind this apparently successful integration lay several weaknesses for India's central government. Nehru's friendship with Abdullah did not prevent the latter from insisting on autonomy for the state. The Delhi Agreement between the two leaders left many important federal issues to be resolved in later discussions. Moreover, Abdullah ran a divided state and government. The October 1951 state elections were hardly a democratic learning experience for Kashmiris; of the 75 seats, 43 National Conference candidates were elected unopposed, and the opposition parties, particularly the Hindu Praja Parishad, accused the National Conference of intimidation and electoral fraud.[23] Abdullah's policies of land reform, state regulation of commerce and industry, and state autonomy generated opposition from the Hindu minority, which wanted complete integration with India. In 1952 the Praja Parishad, supported by Hindu communal parties in India, launched a campaign for full integration. This disrupted Kashmir's economic and social system and polarized Hindu-Muslim relations in the state. Abdullah was forced to concede limited autonomy within the state to Jammu and Ladakh. But this failed to satisfy the opposition, and Abdullah began to fear that the Hindu campaign would lead to Kashmir's total absorption into India. When he hinted at Kashmir's independence, he was replaced by those members of the state government who wanted continued association with India. In May 1954 his successor, Bakshi Ghulam Mohammed, and the central government implemented the Delhi Agreement by applying the Indian Constitution to Kashmir. Kashmir still had more autonomy than any other Indian state.

By giving Kashmir autonomy, the Indian government sought to counter Pakistani and other international charges that it was absorbing Kashmir into the Indian Union against the wishes of Kashmiris. Still, Kashmir's integration with India between 1947 and 1954 followed the broad pattern of other princely states. In the first stage, the states signed instruments of Accession, handing over responsibilities in defense, foreign affairs and communications to the center. In the second stage, the center rationalized the states' territories and began to establish popular governments. In the final stage, the center integrated the princely states financially and administratively with the rest of India. All internal customs barriers were abolished in India.

Pakistan had fewer princely states than India but found it much more difficult to integrate them. Wilcox suggests five reasons for this: the diversity of the Pakistani states, many of which contained tribal populations; Pakistan's weak central governments; protection of the rulers under the interim Constitution; Pakistani anticipation of adverse international opinion; and, finally, provincial rivalries, which delayed radical change.[24]

Wilcox's first reason is partly correct. Pakistan's western border states did contain fiercely independent tribal populations, but India's princely states were as diverse as Pakistan's, if not more so. The diversity in India was one reason why India's central political elite adopted different strategies of integration. Some Indian states were amalgamated with the provinces; others were grouped to form unions of states; and problem states were directly adminstered from New Delhi. The fourth reason (international opinion) also fails to explain Pakistan's relative performance because India also took international opinion into account in its Kashmir policy. The other three reasons, though, do accurately explain Pakistan's poorer integrative performance. As Wilcox points out, the League's pre-partition policy of encouraging princely state autonomy was a double-edged sword: once Pakistan became independent the princes insisted that the central government fulfill its promises of state autonomy.[25]

Constitutional Development. Congress's dominance in the Indian Consituent Assembly allowed it to frame a Constitution for India, which went into effect on 26 January 1950. The Constituent Assembly proceedings were marked by consensus on the federal and parliamentary frameworks, the guaranteeing of individual rights, and the broad economic, social, and political objectives to be followed by future governments. The consensus was due to the fact that the Congress had already hammered out its programs before independence.

Pakistan had no such running start by independence day. The political elite was divided by disputes over the nature of the Islamic state, the electoral representation of minorities, and regional representation at the center. The latter dispute caused much of the constitutional and political deadlock. The Bengalis were the majority of Pakistan's population but the West Pakistani political elite, particularly the Punjabis, believed that either East Pakistan should be subordinated to the western wing or that both wings should have equal representation in the central legislature. The Reports of the Basic Principles Committee of the Constituent Assembly met opposition from both West and East Pakistan. By May 1954, Pakistan still did not have a constitution. Instead, the modified Government of India Act of 1935 served as the interim constitution.

Economic Planning. Indian and Pakistani success in economic planning and mobilizing resources depended on their ability to create strong centers of political authority and viable political systems. In India, where the roots of planning can be traced to the independence movement, the government established a Planning Commission in March 1950 chaired by the Prime Minister. The Indian government adopted five-year economic planning for several reasons. First, the Congress Party had already accepted an extensive role for the state in creating administrative uniformity, in democratizing India, and in raising the living standards of the Indian masses. Secondly, India's poverty was so large and the Indian capitalist class so small that the Congress realized that some sort of central economic planning would be needed to direct investment in essential areas like heavy industry, transport, communications, and agriculture. Finally, Nehru was particularly impressed by Soviet five-year economic planning. He saw it as a possible way to increase production in India as rapidly as possible and to raise India to the status of a regional and world power. India's democratic framework and predominantly capitalist system precluded the methods of Soviet command planning, but Nehru was convinced that long-range economic planning would mobilize India's material potential and would set goals for all Indians to follow.

India's First Five-Year Plan (1951-56) began on 1 April 1951. It grouped together several existing development projects into one framework. In order of priority, the major outlays were in irrigation and power, transport and communications, social services and rehabilitation, agriculture and community development, and industry.[26] By May 1954 the Plan had been operating for three years and had successfully raised investment and national income.

In Pakistan uncertainty over the political framework hampered long-range planning and development. The government established a Development Board in early 1948. Two years later the Board drew up a Six Year Development Program (1951-57). Like India's First Plan, this was essentially a collection of existing projects, but unlike India's Plan, it failed to set any social and economic objectives. Nor did it take stock of Pakistan's physical or human resources. The government began a more determined effort at planning on 18 July 1953, when it established the Pakistan Planning Board. The Board was responsible for drawing up a systematic national plan of development to commence on 1 April 1954. Planning had little support from weak central governments, and so the start of the First Plan was delayed from April 1954 to April 1955.

The contrasting political stability of India and Pakistan had a marked impact on their responsiveness. The tasks of recovering from partition and consolidating their political systems were immense for the elites of both countries. But there is no evidence that the Indian elite was too absorbed in these tasks to pay much attention to communications from Pakistan. For one thing, the Indian elite managed to control the Indian political system: it reorganized the administrative machinery, integrated the princely states, rehabilitated the refugees, quelled the communist rebellion in Telengana, and began economic planning. Moreover, some of these domestic tasks were carried out by Patel and the Indian civil service, and not by Nehru, who found time to devote to foreign policy. Finally, the correspondence between the Indian and Pakistani leadership shows that both governments spent much time and effort in attempting to resolve their disputes. Almost every communication contains an appeal to resolve the disputes so that the governments could then go on to pay more attention to their internal development.

This is not to argue that the Indian leadership was entirely responsive in its negotiations with the Pakistan government. Communal tensions in India in 1952-53 narrowed Nehru's room for maneuver over Kashmir. Communal groups like the Jan Sangh, Akali Dal, Hindu Mahasabha, RSS, and the Jammu Praja Parishad agitated for Kashmir's full integration into India and the replacement of Nehru as Prime Minister. These agitations, plus Abdullah's independent line in Kashmir, all weakened Nehru's negotiating position with Pakistan at a time when the Pakistan government was flexible but itself weak. According to one of Nehru's biographers, "The Pakistan authorities, declaring that to them Kashmir was the only really difficult problem, made 'quite plaintive and almost pathetic' appeals for a settlement; but because of the internal situation Nehru was in no position to offer terms. He could only assert that the status quo should be accepted with minor modifications."[27] A Kashmir settlement at this time raised several costs for Nehru. It threatened to increase communal passions in the subcontinent at a time when the Abdullah government hinted at independence and when Nehru could not impose his orders through the Home Ministry.[28]

Domestic political instability made Pakistani governments less responsive to their Indian counterpart. Indeed, some Indian scholars suggest that internal political weaknesses forced the new Pakistani governments to use India as a whipping boy to keep Pakistan's heteregenous society united. Thus, it is argued that the Pakistan government, and particularly the NWFP government, deflected the unmanageable Pathan tribesmen to invade Kashmir in order to keep them occupied and from directing their energies against the new Pakistan government.[29] It is also argued that the Pakistan government raised the threat of India in East Pakistan to prevent that province from coming under further Indian economic and cultural influence.[30]

Although these arguments are difficult to prove, they can be evaluated. First, there is no doubt that communal memories, tensions, and suspicions all set limits to what Pakistan's governments were able to do--they could neither ignore the Kashmir issue nor give unjustifiable concessions to India. Secondly, it would be unfair to blame the failure of a Kashmir settlement on Pakistan alone. That failure was just as much the result of India's unresponsiveness. Finally, if it is true that Pakistan's domestic political weaknesses caused confrontation with India, it is equally true that the government's policy of confrontation with India (for example, over the princely states) caused domestic political weaknesses.

To sum up: India had a clear lead over Pakistan in political development in the immediate postindependence period. The Indian political system's initial advantages reinforced its stability and integration. By contrast, the weaknesses of Pakistan's political system in leadership, clearly articulated programs, and federalizing parties can be traced to Pakistan's meager political assets at independence. The political conditions in which India and Pakistan could have settled their differences and reinforced each other's political integration were thus absent.

MILITARY CAPABILITIES, POWER AND INFLUENCE

India had many defense objectives after independence. It had to consolidate the armed forces and defense production establishments. The officer corps had to be nationalized. India also had to start strategic planning befitting a sovereign state, and increase the efficiency of the armed forces. Defense planners hoped that some of the savings from increased efficiency would go to finance the more capital-intensive air force and navy.[31]

Like India, Pakistan also had to adjust to life as a sovereign nation by reorganizing its armed forces. Pakistan, however, was at a greater disadvantage than India in increasing its military capabilities. First, its military inheritance at partition was smaller than India's. Its industrial, scientific, technical, and skilled manpower base was also less developed than India's. Secondly, its officer corps was smaller, less experienced, and hence more dependent upon British officers. Finally, the officer corps was regionally imbalanced (East Pakistanis were underrepresented) and was politically divided over the civilian government's Kashmir policy and rate of promotions.[32] These disadvantages were partly offset by the military's ideological faith in defending the new state of Pakistan and by its mistaken belief that Muslims were better soldiers than Hindus. Even though Indian governments rejected the British theory of martial races, the Pakistani governments and military still adhered to it, with disastrous results for Pakistan's own political integration and relations with India. Two mistakes in particular were fatal: Pakistan failed to see that Hindus were just as good soldiers as Muslims (the famed Gurkhas were Hindus) and that Pakistan needed a nationally representative army.

While India increased its military assets over Pakistan (appendices 2-7), the following factors delayed the military modernization of both countries: a shortage of foreign exchange, an arms embargo imposed by the United States and Britain during the 1948-49 Kashmir War, and difficulty in purchasing arms from abroad. A global increase in Cold War tensions and the outbreak of the Korean War in June 1950 meant that the Western powers had few modern arms to provide India and Pakistan. The major achievements of both countries in this period, then, were confined to rationalizing their military organizations, nationalizing officer corps, and establishing new training schools. The major difference between the two countries was that the Indian government began a limited program of long-range defense production. In short, both countries laid the organizational foundations of their national military power, even if the weapons and equipment were inadequate or absent.

The growth in Indian military assets clearly gave the Indian government an advantage in its bargaining relations with Pakistan. But Indian and Pakistani governments disagreed about the exact use that India made of these superior military capabilities. On several occasions, Pakistani governments accused India of using its military resources to punish and coerce Pakistan. It alleged that India withheld Pakistan's share of partition military assets in order to punish Pakistanis for demanding and receiving their own separate state. The Indian government denied these charges.[33]

The Indian government did use its military assets to coerce Pakistan. It used force or the threat of force to challenge Pakistan's action's in Junagadh, Hyderabad, and Kashmir and to force Pakistani governments to ensure the safety of non-Muslims in East Pakistan. On 3 March 1950, Nehru warned Pakistan that he would adopt "other methods" if necessary if Pakistan remained unwilling to peacefully solve the refugee problem from East Pakistan.[34] The next year India concentrated its troops along West Pakistan's borders after Pakistan had mobilized its own troops on the Kashmir border. With its larger military force, India held the advantage, and the Pakistan government refrained from going to war.[35]

The Indian government also used its military assets to influence Pakistan to create a common defense of the subcontinent. Indian leaders, including the Defense Minister, Baldev Singh, and senior officials of the Ministry of Defense made frequent statements about the need for Indo-Pakistan defense integration.

As the largest South Asian country, India inherited the British role of maintaining the strategic unity of the subcontinent. Of course, independent India was a different regional leader than Britain. The Congress's anticolonial struggle made the new Indian government emphasize equality and independence among formerly colonized nations. The Indian government had to avoid appearing to dominate South Asia, lest this seemed like a new imperialism. Geostrategic factors gave Indian governments no choice but to define India's security perimeter as the borders of South Asia. When communist Chinese troops invaded Tibet in October 1950, Nehru drew India's security perimeter to include the northern borders of Nepal.[36]

Nor were such perceptions of the strategic unity of South Asia confined to Indian leaders. Pakistan's Foreign Minister, Sir Zafrullah Khan, and Governor-General, Khwaja Nazimuddin, recognized the security interdependence of both countries. But this integration could only begin once the major disputes were settled between India and Pakistan. Pakistan's Foreign Minister noted that "East and West Pakistan constitute the flanks of the land mass of the Indian sub-continent...The security of India so far as land-based operations is concerned is thus tied up with the security of Pakistan. A strong, stable, friendly and cooperative Pakistan is essential to the security of Inida. In a word Pakistan is the Warden of the Marches of the Indian sub-continent."[37]

With the Kashmir dispute still unresolved, Pakistani governments saw India as the main security threat. There were other security threats, too. In 1947 the Afghan government renewed its demands for a separate Pathan state--*Pakhtoonistan*--to be carved out of Pakistan's NWFP. Tribesmen from Afghanistan frequently raided Pakistan in 1948 but were contained by Pakistan's armed forces. Facing many demands on its small defense resources, Pakistani governments had to carefully allocate defense resources between its two wings and between its two major security threats--India and

Afghanistan. As it turned out, they gave more resources to West Pakistan and to meet the Indian threat. Afghanistan was seen as less of a threat; it was smaller in population than Pakistan, less well-armed, and there were common bonds of religion and culture between Pakistan and Afghanistan. Consequently, Pakistan withdrew almost all of its regular forces from its Afghan borders in order to meet the perceived threat from India.

India and Pakistan remained wary of their two communist neighbors--the USSR and China. The increase in tensions between the Soviet bloc and the West in 1950 gave impetus to Indian attempts to sign a No-War Pact with Pakistan. But generally, Indian leaders discounted a direct communist attack against the subcontinent. Even after the Chinese occupation of Tibet in October 1950, the Indian government still saw Pakistan as the major military threat to India. Home Minister Sardar Patel feared China's ultimate intentions, but Nehru downplayed a Chinese military threat.[38] So, in the absence of a common perceived external threat to the subcontinent, the only thing that India and Pakistan could agree on was that the other country was the major threat to its security.

Indian and Pakistani leaders were aware of the high opportunity costs of their military conflict and tension for their economic and social development. Such private and public statements appear frequently and in different contexts, which suggests that the perceptions of high opportunity costs were indeed genuine.[39] But Indian and Pakistani desires for national independence outweighed these costs. For New Delhi the financial costs of defending Kashmir and the rest of India from Pakistan were large but acceptable given the alternative of losing Kashmir. In any case, part of the large defense expenditures arose not from India's defense against Pakistan, but from larger objectives of becoming a regional power in South Asia and the Indian Ocean. For Karachi the economic costs of high defense expenditures, which were consistently greater per person than India's, did indeed divert resources from economic and social development, but national independence had higher priority. Behind the Pakistan government's cost calculations lay a more general objective of preserving Pakistan's autonomy as an Islamic state.

IDENTITIVE CAPABILITIES, POWER AND INFLUENCE

Partition resulted in greater social cohesion in India than in Pakistan. Whereas India's population was 86.6 per cent non-Muslim and 13.4 percent Muslim, Pakistan's population was 73.1 percent Muslim and 26.9 percent non-Muslim.[40] Ironically, the proportion of majority and minority communities in Pakistan closely resembled that of undivided India.

Partition was not, therefore, a surgical solution to the communal problem in the subcontinent. The minorities remaining in India and Pakistan were so large that they could not be ignored by either the majority community in the new state or by the other state. The refugee movements created a group of discontented people in both countries who brought with them bitter memories of treatment at the hands of the opposing religious communities. Communal hatreds increased in India and Pakistan. Some sections of the press in both countries urged retaliation against the other country.

The existence of large minorities in both countries, the tragic and historically unprecedented communal warfare and refugee movements, the deadlock in settling evacuee property claims between India and Pakistan, and the Indian government's refusal to accept the two-nation theory all ensured that religious and cultural factors would remain obstacles to improved identitive ties after independence. Indeed, an increased rate of refugee movements from East Pakistan to India between 1950 and 1952 brought the two countries close to war on several occasions. For this reason Nehru warned the Pakistan government that he would "adopt other methods," if necessary, if it remained unwilling to solve the refugee problem peacefully.

Fortunately, war was averted, largely because neither side wanted it. The two Prime Ministers met in New Delhi and signed the Nehru-Liaquat Pact on 8 April 1950. This agreement went further than the two previous Inter-Dominion agreements, held in May and December 1948, in attempting to safeguard the physical security and rights of the minority communities. They further agreed to "Take prompt and effective steps to prevent the dissemination of news and mischevious opinion calculated to rouse communal passion by press or radio or by any individual or organization," and "Not permit propaganda in either country directed against the territorial integrity of the other or purporting to incite war against them..."[41]

The Nehru-Liaquat Pact of 1950 temporarily eased communal conflict and tensions between India and Pakistan. It was, however, only a limited agreement to prevent relations from getting any worse. Mutual suspicions between India and Pakistan were too strong and the number of disputes between them was too large for the Pact to have any lasting impact in improving identitive ties. Refugee movements continued in 1951, and another war scare arose when the Indian government began massing its troops on the West Pakistan border. Again, the aim was to coerce Pakistan to resolve the refugee problem, as well as the Kashmir problem.

Despite a 1953 agreement to allow greater pilgrim travel and to maintain religious shrines in each country,[42] identitive ties remained weak. Some politicians and sections of the press in India and Pakistan continued to vilify the other country, and their activities were noticed by the governments of both countries. Identitive ties further weakened when India and Pakistan introduced a visa passport system for travel between the two countries.

The common values resulting from colonialism and the continuing links with the Commonwealth restrained the conflict between India and Pakistan but were not enough to promote integration. Initially, Britain's greatest effect on Indo-Pakistan relations was to restrain both sides and prevent a deterioration of their bilateral relations. Immediately after independence, Indian and Pakistani room for maneuver was limited by the presence of British personnel in the armed forces and administrative services of the two Dominions. Pakistan's British Commander-in-Chief, General Douglas Gracey, restrained Jinnah from using military force in Kashmir in October 1947. In late 1948, when war had already broken out in Kashmir, British officers pointed out the dangers of a wider war to both Dominions.[43]

Other than this influence, Britain and the Commonwealth had only a slight effect in ameliorating Indo-Pakistan conflicts. The main reason for this is different Indian and Pakistani conceptions of the role of the Commonwealth as a mediator in bilateral disputes. Although Nehru saw the Commonwealth as "an additional link and channel of communication with Pakistan,"[44] he did not see it as a supranational body that should solve the disputes between India and Pakistan. Instead, those disputes would have to be settled by the two countries themselves. For this reason, Nehru opposed Pakistani attempts to place the Kashmir dispute on the formal agenda of Commonwealth conferences, such as the Commonwealth Prime Ministers' Conference held in London in January 1951. He was, however, quite prepared to discuss the dispute in informal sessions with Pakistani and other Commonwealth leaders.[45]

Unlike India, the Pakistan government did not see the Commonwealth as a means for increasing its links with India. Instead, its policy was to progressively reduce those links and to emphasize its status as an independent nation equal to India in international law. As an example of this policy of separation, Jinnah objected to Mountbatten remaining the common Governor-General of both Dominions. According to Chaudhri Muhammed Ali, "Pakistan would have a severe ordeal to face in its early years. Only a strong faith in their destiny as an independent nation could sustain the people through the trial and tribulations ahead of them. There must, therefore, be a viable act of cleavage between India and Pakistan. If the Quaid-i-Azam himself became the Governor-General of Pakistan, he would be a living symbol of Pakistan's independent status."[46] Jinnah saw the Commonwealth as an arbitration body where Pakistan could present its side of the disputes with India and receive satisfaction in settling the disputes. In short, Pakistan sought to mobilize support in the Commonwealth against its larger neighbor.

The result of these two conceptions was that neither side was satisfied with the Commonwealth's role in resolving Indo-Pakistan disputes. In a testimony to the Commonwealth's impartiality, both sides accused it of favoring the other. As early as 19 December 1947 a disillusioned Jinnah said, "I feel Great Britain is treating Pakistan with indifference...Britain and the other Dominions are in a position to use moral persuasion to help settle differences between members of the Commonwealth. It appears that His Majesty's Government are so far shirking their responsibility in this respect."[47] Nehru also criticized Britain's position in the Kashmir dispute. He reacted strongly against what he saw as undue British and American pressure on India to settle the Kashmir dispute.[48]

INDIA'S POLICIES AS A CORE AREA

To Pakistani governments, India's resources in the period 1947-54 were all directed towards undoing partition and reabsorbing Pakistan. Certainly, the struggle over the princely states, the division of the assets of the British Empire in India, the immense violence and refugee movements accompanying partition may all be interpreted in this light. But was this Indian policy? Logically, three hypotheses are possible explaining India's policies towards Pakistan in this period: indifference, conflict, and integration.

Indifference

The first hypothesis is that the Hindus of India wanted to be rid of the "troublesome" Muslims once and for all. In this view, if the Muslims wanted their own state, however nonviable and absurd in geography, then they were welcome to it. Evidence of this view comes from Sardar Patel's famous statement that when one has a diseased limb (that is, according to him, Pakistan and the Muslims), one amputates it.[49] The various proposals of Hindu extremists that there be an exchange of Muslims and Hindus between India and Pakistan also tends to support the view that some Indians wanted total separation between the two countries.

Although this may have been the policy of some Hindu extremists, it does not square with Congress's desire for regional and defense integration after independence. Before 15 August 1947, Congress passed frequent resolutions affirming the unity of the subcontinent. Hence Pakistan could not be a matter of total indifference to the Congress. This is shown in the eloquent resolution passed by the Working Committee of the Congress on 14 June 1947:

> Geography and the mountains and the seas fashioned India as she is, and no human agency can change that shape or come in the way of her final destiny. Economic circumstances and the insistent demands of international affairs make the unity of India still more necessary. The picture of India we have learnt to cherish will remain in

> our minds and our hearts. The A.I.C.C. [All-India Congress Committee] earnestly trusts that when the present passions have subsided, India's problems will be viewed in their proper perspective and the false doctrine of two nations in India will be discredited and discarded by all.[50]

Conflict

The second hypothesis, and the one held publicly by most Pakistani leaders, is that the Indian government intended to destroy Pakistan from the outset. The following evidence is adduced to support this hypothesis.[51] First, Congress leaders advanced partition the original date of June 1948 to August 1947 because they knew that this would work to the economic, administrative, and military disadvantage of the fledgling Pakistan. Secondly, many sections of the Indian population terrorized Muslims in East Punjab province, the princely states of East Punjab, the United Provinces, Delhi, and in other parts of India. The aim was to break the economic and political power of the Muslims in the subcontinent. Thirdly, India used force in the princely states of Junagadh, Hyderabad, and Kashmir in order to prevent the establishment of any Muslim-dominated state in the subcontinent. Fourthly, India's particular military interest in Kashmir lay in controlling the upper waters of the Indus Rivers system, gaining territorial access to the troubled NWFP and Afghanistan, and thereby encircling West Pakistan. The Punjab Boundary Award, which gave India direct access to Kashmir, was part of India's grand strategy. Finally, India denied Pakistan its rightful share of the assets of British India.

The evidence shows that the Indian government had no intention of destroying and reintegrating Pakistan. First, the speed-up of the partition process was the work of Mountbatten and not, as Chaudhri Mohammed Ali suggests, of the Congress through its agent V. P. Menon. Many years later, Mountbatten himself made it clear that Nehru preferred the original partition date of June 1948.[52] Moreover, an advanced partition date worked to India's as well as Pakistan's disadvantage, considering the many complex decisions to be taken during partition.

Secondly, the view that Indians were intent on destroying Pakistan fails to distinguish between the government of India and its people. It assumes a rational-actor model of Indian behavior by attributing a singleness of purpose to many different groups--Sikhs, Hindu extremist organizations, the government of India and the princely states, the Congress, the Chief Engineers of the Punjab, and Indian traders. This view also fails to take into account the Congress Party's opposition to communal violence. Wilcox notes that Indian policy towards Pakistan at this time reflected divisions within the Indian leadership.

> The president of the Congress Party, Maulana Abul Kalam Azad, was for reconciliation, as was Gandhi; Nehru as prime minister was struggling with Sardar Vallabhai Patel, the deputy prime minister, for control of the government, and Patel stood for a hard line toward Pakistan. Lord Mountbatten, the residual British guarantor of the partition, had a special voice with Nehru in his role as governor-general of India. Thus, what appeared to Pakistan's tenuous political elite as willful sabotage and unremitting hostility was the product of a complex, confused interplay, within the Indian government, of competing leaders and priorities.[53]

The Pakistani view also ignores the sufferings of Hindus, Muslims, and Sikhs alike during the partition upheavals.

Pakistani views of expansionist Indian aims in the princely states are also incorrect. As is true of other partition disputes, the Congress and the League saw the accession of the princely states differently. Before the transfer of power, the Congress fought hard to have British paramountcy over these states transferred to the new Dominion of India. Its arguments were threefold: first, these states had never historically been sovereign in international law before British paramountcy: secondly, when British power ended none of the princely states would be able to defend itself or conduct its external relations; and thirdly, the rulers lacked popular support and had to be integrated into a democratic India. The Muslim League, on the other hand, argued that when the British left, they took paramountcy with them; the princely states were free to accede to either Dominion or they were free to become sovereign states.

India did achieve relative military success in Junagadh, Hyderabad, and Kashmir. But Pakistan's views of an expansionist India neglects two important factors: first, Indian material and military weaknesses at the time, and second, the Indian leadership's widespread fear of the balkanization of India. By encouraging this balkanization in Junagadh and Hyderabad, the Pakistani government only heightened the Indian government's territorial insecurities. In India memories were still fresh of Muslim League demands for the whole of Punjab, Bengal, and Assam to be included in Pakistan and connected to each other by a land corridor across northern India.

India's strategic encirclement of Pakistan by a series of actions leading from the Punjab Boundary Award to the control of Kashmir is also doubtful. In the first place, the Punjab Boundary Award was unsatisfactory to both India and Pakistan. In the second place, Indian military operations in Kashmir were limited and defensive. Once India gained the bulk of the state's territory, it was quite prepared to maintain the status quo.[54] Finally, this grand strategy makes little military sense. If the Indian government had wanted to destroy Pakistan, the best way to have done so would have been to invade West Pakistan across the Punjab plains. It could also have invaded East Pakistan with very little opposition from the regular Pakistani Army. And why did India build the expensive Assam Railway connecting West Bengal with the relatively isolated northeast part of India, if it expected to territorially absorb East Pakistan? That India did not invade when it had the military advantage shows that it had no aggressive designs against Pakistan.

Finally, the view that the Indian government denied Pakistan its fair share of the partition assets and that it did its utmost to make Pakistan unviable is incorrect. Rather, the evidence shows that India *helped* Pakistan become viable. The Indian government helped to set up the Pakistan government headquarters at Karachi; it provided the necessary administrative machinery to enable the Pakistan government to run smoothly, such as duplicating files and loaning temporary personnel; it helped Pakistan to ease its transitional difficulties by providing industrial goods, coal, and other raw materials, and funds to Pakistani scholars stranded abroad and to Pakistani staff in India; and it provided adequate financial resources to Pakistan.[55] The Indian government favorably treated Pakistan in dividing the liabilities of British India. It gave Pakistan 17.5 percent of these liabilities and a moratorium of four years before sharing the burden of debt. After that, Pakistan would have fifty-four years to pay the liabilities.[56] In other words, the Indian government agreed to give Pakistan more of the assets and less of the liabilities of British India than was justified by Pakistan's relative population size.

The Indian government did temporarily withhold the military supplies and cash balances due to Pakistan, but this must be seen in the context of Indo-Pakistan conflict over Kashmir. Indian decision-makers purposely linked the transfer of these assets to Pakistan's behavior in Kashmir. The aim was to prevent their use against India in Kashmir and to gain leverage over Pakistan. In a letter to Liaquat Ali Khan on 5 January 1951, Nehru's point was that "Payment has been deferred because we cannot, while operations against Jammu and Kashmir are being conducted from bases in Pakistan, with Pakistan's contrivance and assistance, reasonably be expected to make available funds which might be used to intensify military cooperation against us."[57]

Integration

The final hypothesis of Indian policy toward Pakistan is that Congress was willing to agree to partition because it believed that Pakistan would be unviable and would therefore have to return to India either in the form of a regional integration scheme, a confederation or a federation. This is the most accurate interpretation of Indian policy. The policy relied on the key assumption that Pakistanis would see the errors of their ways and would then voluntarily cooperate with India. It also implicitly assumed that India was a core area, that it had the material and military assets to form a security-community with Pakistan. Tragically, the events of 1947-48 invalidated these assumptions. The communal conflict at partition, the struggle over the princely states, the canal waters dispute, and the disputes over Pakistan's share of the cash balances and military assets of undivided India all produced an atmosphere of interstate suspicion and hostility.

In such an atmosphere any talk of confederation, economic cooperation or integration only increased Pakistani suspicions of India's policies. Cooperation was seen as reintegration, the nemesis of Pakistan's leadership. Nehru recognized these Pakistani fears, observing on many occasions that perhaps a cooling-off period between the two sides was necessary before they eventually discussed regional integration. For instance, in 1947, he wrote, "I have no doubt that sooner or later India will have to function as a united country. Perhaps the best way to reach that stage is to go through some kind of partition now."[58] Nehru's policy was to calm Pakistani fears and to produce an "atmosphere of security" in which both sides could perceive their common interests in defense and economic and social development. To this end, he discouraged propaganda in India calling for the reintegration of Pakistan. In mid-1948 he even went so far as to say that should Pakistan want to reintegrate, India would not agree.[59] This was a calculated attempt to calm Pakistani fears about Indian policy towards reintegration. It is also shows the Indian government's responsiveness to Pakistani wishes to set up a separate, independent and viable state.

Another example of Indian responsiveness was Nehru's offer of a No-War Pact with Pakistan, the first formal attempt by India to establish a pluralistic security-community between the two countries. Discussions on this began in late 1949. Nehru proposed a short declaration, patterned on the Kellogg-Briand Pact of 1928, to improve the psychological atmosphere: "The Government of India and the Government of Pakistan, being desirous of promoting friendship and goodwill between their peoples, who have many common ties, hereby declare that they condemn resort to war for the settlement of any existing or future disputes between them.[60]

Liaquat welcomed this, but added that "To attain this object, it is essential that there should be tangible action to match the spirit of the declaration, since peoples and Governments are judged by their actions rather than their words."[61] Nehru wanted to start from the general declaration and then descend to the particular disputes between the two countries. Liaquat's position was the reverse: to start with the particulars and then ascend to the general. He feared that such an *a priori* declaration would reduce Pakistan's bargaining position in the disputes. Ultimately, the No-War Pact discussions failed because of these mutually exclusive positions and disagreement over the particular disputes and mechanisms for resolving them.

The Indian government's ability to persuade Pakistan to sign a No-War Pact was limited for two major reasons: India's material and military weaknesses and the Pakistani government's determination to mobilize domestic and foreign resources in order to resist Indian dominance in the subcontinent. The Pakistan government was unwilling to discuss regional economic and military integration as long as several disputes, notably Kashmir, remained outstanding. It believed that any recognition of India as a core area would mean Pakistan's capitulation on these disputes. After independence Pakistan sought Commonwealth support against India. It soon became disillusioned with what it saw as the Commonwealth's, and particularly Britain's lack of interest.

The Pakistan government then turned to its neighbors in the Middle East for support. As one writer aptly puts it, this was a policy of marrying its cultural and security interests.[62] The Pakistan government believed that fellow Muslims would support Pakistan, which after all had been established to preserve and promote Islam. To mobilize support, the government made direct diplomatic contact with Middle Eastern states. It also supported the Palestinian cause, decolonization in North Africa, and pan-Islamic cultural and economic integration.

Pakistan's efforts failed. The Middle Eastern countries were jealous of their national sovereignty and lukewarm to the idea of cultural and economic integration. Attempts at permanent institutional integration failed. The international Islamic conferences that were held in Pakistan in November 1949 and February 1951 were attended by unofficial participants. Another reason for failure was that secular, modernizing regimes such as Nasser's Egypt were suspicious of Pakistan's appeals to pan-Islamic solidarity. Relations with these regimes became even more strained after 1952 as Pakistan moved steadily closer to an alliance with the United States.

Having been rebuffed by the Commonwealth and the Middle East, Pakistan's government concluded that it could ensure it security only by an alliance with a stronger military and economic power. Negotiations for a strategic alliance between Pakistan and the United States began in 1951. The Pakistan Army, under Ayub Khan, was especially interested in a military alliance because it would increase its military resources. For the Pakistan government as a whole, the expected benefits of the alliance were: first, increased security against India, which had only recently coerced Pakistan in the "war scares" of 1950 and 1951; and, second, the enlistment of a powerful ally in support of Pakistan's claims in Kashmir.

Pakistani and American officials negotiated during 1953-54 on the terms of United States-Pakistan military assistance agreement.[63] The United States made it clear that it saw the agreement as part of a much larger regional defense system linking pro-Western Southeast Asian nations with a proposed Middle Eastern defense system. It therefore encouraged Pakistan to sign a bilateral treaty of military cooperation with Turkey in April 1954 as the first step to the Middle Eastern defense system.

Why did Pakistan conclude a military alliance with the United States when it was also negotiating with India over Kashmir? It is unlikely that the military assistance was meant to force a military solution to the dispute. Pakistani leaders realized the weaker position of their country in any military showdown with India. More likely, they saw assistance as a way to improve their bargaining power with India. In January 1954, Prime Minister Mohammed Ali told an American correspondent that although the military agreement might strain relations with India "...I am convinced that ultimately it would make a settlement easier. At present, we can't get a settlement, mainly because Nehru isn't much interested in a fair settlement. When there is more equality of military strength, then I am sure that there will be greater chance of settlement."[64]

If the Pakistan government believed that military assistance would improve its bargaining position, it must also have realized that it had a number of associated costs, particularly increased hostility from the Soviet Union, China, and especially India. A more satisfactory explanation of Pakistan's contradictory policy--alliance with the United States and negotiations with India--is that it reflected differences within the Pakistan government. The Pakistan Army also favored a military alliance because the additional resources would help it in the bureaucatic politics with the civilian regime.[65]

Pakistan's agreement with the United States in May 1954 was a turning-point in South Asia's intraregional relations. It marked the end of the first phase of Indo-Pakistan relations, one in which Pakistani governments had to fend for themselves against India. Nehru had sought to insulate South Asia and the developing world in general from the military and political rivalries of the Western and Eastern blocs. Pakistan's alliance with the United States threatened India's regional dominance and its foreign policy of nonalignment. One immediate effect, as Nehru pointed out, was to widen the areas of disagreement between India and Pakistan and to bring to an end the tentative steps toward a Kashmir settlement that both countries had made since 1953.[66] In the longer run it complicated the power relations between them and increased external involvement in South Asia.

Notes

1. U. S., Agency for International Development, *Gross National Product: Growth Rates and Trend Data, June 1966* (Washington, D.C.: AID, 1968), p. 10.
2. Stephen R. Lewis, Jr. *Pakistan: Industrialization and Trade Policies* (London: Oxford University Press, 1970), p. 15.
3. Pakistan, Planning Board, *The First Five Year Plan (Draft)*, vol. 1, p. 10.
4. Edward S. Mason, *Economic Development in India and Pakistan* (Cambridge: Harvard University Center for International Affairs, 1966), p. 11.
5. Extract from Aide-Memoire, 13 October 1947 in *India 1947-50: Select Documents on Asian Affairs,* vol. 2: *External Affairs* ed. S. L. Poplai (London: Oxford University Press, 1959), p. 280.
6. Ibid., p. 281.
7. Ibid., p. 276.
8. Ibid., p. 272.
9. White Paper on Indo-Pakistan Trade, in Poplai, ed., *India 1947-50*, vol. 2, pp. 278-79.
10. Award of the Chairman of the Punjab Boundary Commission, 12 August 1947, in K. Sarwar Hasan ed., *The Transfer of Power: Documents on the Foreign Relations of Pakistan* (Karachi: Pakistan Institute of International Affairs, 1966), p. 374.

11. Aloys Arthur Michel, *The Indus Rivers: A Study of the Effects of Partition* (New Haven and London: Yale University Press, 1967), pp. 196-97.

12. Interview with Swaran Singh, San Francisco, California, 4 September 1983. N. D. Gulhati, India's Chief negotiator of the Indus Waters Treaty of 1960, writes: "It must be stated here that the action taken by the East Punjab Government to cut off, even temporarily, the supplies of the C.B.D.C. in West Punjab without prior approval of, or reference to, the Central Government did not command much sympathy from many sections in India. Seventeen months after the incident, I well recall an occasion when Prime Minister Jawaharlal Nehru, during the course of a discussion, castigated East Punjab Government and its engineers, in no ambiguous terms, for "having taken the law into their own hands." *Indus Waters Treaty: An Exercise in International Mediation* (Bombay: Allied Publishers, 1973), p. 64.

13. Gulhati, *Indus Waters*, p. 63.

14. F. J. Berber, "The Indus Waters Dispute," *Indian Year Book of International Affairs*, no. 6 (1957), p. 51.

15. David E. Lilienthal, "Another Korea in the Making?" *Collier's* 128 (4 August 1951), pp. 22-23, 56-58.

16. The terms of the Bank Proposal and the initial reaction of the parties are contained in Gulhati, *Indus Waters*, pp. 134-61.

17. H. N. Sethna, "India's Atomic Energy Program--Past and Future," *International Atomic Energy Agency Bulletin* (hereafter IAEA Bulletin) 21 (October 1979), p. 2.

18. The key individuals included Abdul Qayyum Khan, Chaudhri Muhammad Ali and Ghulam Muhammed. Shirin Tahir-Kheli, "Pakistan," in *Nuclear Power in Developing Countries*, ed. James E. Katz and Onkar S. Marwah (Lexington, Mass.: D. C. Heath, 1982), p. 262.

19. W. H. Morris-Jones, *The Government and Politics of India* (Bombay: B. I. Publications, 1974), pp. 184-86.

20. Khalid Bin Sayeed, *The Political System of Pakistan* (Boston: Houghton Mifflin Co., 1967), pp. 62-64.

21. Telegram of the Prime Minister of Jammu and Kashmir addressed to the Governor-General of Pakistan, 18 October 1947, in K. Sarwar Hasan, ed., *The Kashmir Question: Documents on the Foreign Relations of Pakistan* (Karachi: Pakistan Institute of International Affairs, 1966), pp. 49-50.

22. Ibid, p. 52.

23. Josef Korbel, "The National Conference Administration of Kashmir, 1949-54," *Middle East Journal* 8 (Summer 1954), p. 287.

24. Wayne A. Wilcox, *Pakistan: The Consolidation of a Nation* (New York and London: Columbia University Press, 1963), pp. 212-13.

25. Ibid.

26. India, Planning Commission, *First Five Year Plan*, part 1 (New Delhi: Manager of Publications, 1954), p. 70.

27. Sarvepalli Gopal, *Jawaharlal Nehru: A Biography*, vol. 2: *1947-1956* (London: Jonathan Cape, 1979), p. 132.

28. Ibid., pp. 122-28.

29. Sisir Gupta, *Kashmir: A Study in India-Pakistan Relations* (Delhi: Asia Publishing House, 1966), pp. 117-19.

30. M. V. Lakhi, "The Two Wings," *Seminar* 117 (May 1969), p. 18.

31. H. M. Patel, "Balance of Hopes and Fears--A Review of the Past Five Years," *United Service Institution of India Journal* (hereafter USIIJ) 82 (July-October 1953), p. 145.

32. Most of the officers were from the Punjab and, to a lesser extent, from the NWFP. East Pakistanis were underrepresented; by July 1955 they made up only 1.56 percent of army officers, even though East Pakistanis were about 55 percent of the population. Rounaq Jahan, *Pakistan: Failure in National Integration* (Dacca: Oxford University Press, 1972), p. 25.

33. Letter to Prime Minister of Pakistan, 5 January 1948, in M. Rafique Afzal, ed., *Speeches and Statements of Quad-i-Millat Liquat Ali Khan, 1941-51* (Lahore: Research Society of Pakistan, University of the Punjab, 1967), p. 40.

34. Jyoti Bhusan Das Gupta, *Indo-Pakistan Relations 1947-1955* (Amsterdam: Djambatan, 1958), p. 226.

35. Ayub Khan, the Commander-in-Chief of the Pakistan Army, claimed that he dissuaded Prime Minister Liaquat Ali Khan from going to war over these troop concentrations. Mohammad Ayub Khan, *Friends Not Masters* (London: Oxford University Press, 1967), p. 40.

36. Jawaharlal Nehru, *Speeches*, vol. 2: *1949-53* (Delhi: Publications Division, 1954), p. 179.

37. Zafrullah Khan, "Pakistan's Place in Asia," *International Journal* 6 (Autumn 1951), p. 267.

38. Nehru to Patel, 18 November 1950, in Durga Das, ed., *Sardar Patel's Correspondence*, vol. 10, (Ahmedabad: Navajivan Publishing House, 1974), pp. 342-47.

39. See, for example, Liaquat Ali Khan's letter to Nehru, 14 February 1950, in Afzal, ed. *Statements of Quaid-i-Millat*, p. 590; and Mohammad Ali of Bogra's letter to Nehru, 29 March 1954, in Hasan, *Kashmir Question*, pp. 355-56.

40. Vakil, *Economic*, p. 71.

41. The text of the Agreement is contained in the Indian Commission of Jurists, *Recurrent Exodus of Minorities from East Pakistan and Disturbances in India* (New Delhi: Indian Commission of Jurists, 1965), appendix 3.

42. M. S. Rajan, *India in World Affairs: 1954-56* (Bombay: Asia Publishing House), p. 476.

43. Kavic, *India's Quest*, pp. 33-34.

44. S. C. Gangal, "India and the Commonwealth," in *India's Foreign Policy*, ed. Bimal Prasad (New Delhi: Vikas, 1979), p. 333.

45. S. R. Mehrotra, "Nehru and the Commonwealth," in *Indian Foreign Policy: The Nehru Years*, edited by B. R. Nanda (Honolulu: The University Press of Hawaii, 1976), p. 40.

46. Chaudhri Muhammad Ali, *Emergence of Pakistan*, pp. 175-76.

47. Quoted in Siddiqi, *Pakistan Seeks*, pp. 73-74.

48. Gopal, *Jawaharlal Nehru*, vol. 2 (London: Jonathan Cape, 1979), pp. 27-28.

49. Michael Brecher, *Nehru: A Political Biography*, (London: Oxford University Press, 1961), p. 134.

50. Quoted in V. P. Menon, *The Transfer of Power in India* (Princeton, N. J.: Princeton University Press, 1957), p. 384.

51. This catalog of alleged Indian hostility is based upon Ali, *Emergence of Pakistan*, pp. 123-24; and the letter of the Minister of Foreign Affairs of Pakistan, Sir Zafrullah Khan, addressed to the Secretary-General of the UN, 15 January 1948, in Hasan, *Kashmir Question*, pp. 114-36.

52. Gopal, *Jawaharlal Nehru*, vol. 2, p. 356.

53. Wayne Wilcox, "India and Pakistan," in *Conflict in World Politics*, ed. Steven L. Spiegel and Kenneth N. Waltz (Cambridge, Mass.: Winthrop Publishers, 1971), p. 251.

54. Fazal Muqeem Khan recognizes India's material and military weaknesses at the start of the Kashmir War. "It was quite wrong," he writes, "to believe that India would launch an attack on West Punjab if Pakistan stepped into Kashmir. India could only have done so at her own peril, having her own troubles, in some ways more serious than those of Pakistan. The Indian states issue was yet to be settled. Some of their rulers were extremely ambitious and the smallest reversal which India might suffer would have been enough to start a disintegration in her political system. In fact at that stage India had more to lose from war than Pakistan." *Story*, p. 93.

55. India, *After Partition*, pp. 114-22.

56. Vakil, *Economic Consequences*, pp. 495-96.

57. Nehru to Liaquat Ali Khan, 5 January 1948, in Afzal, ed. *Statements of Quaid-i-Millat*, p. 587.

58. Nehru to K. P. S. Menon, 29 April 1947. Quoted in Gopal, *Jawaharal Nehru*, vol. 1, p. 343.

59. Gopal, *Jawaharlal Nehru*, vol. 2, p. 33.

60. India, Ministry of External Affairs, *Correspondence between the Prime Ministers of India and Pakistan on the subject of the "No War Declaration." Part I & II* (New Delhi: Manager, Government of India Press, 1950), p. 13.

61. Ibid, p. 4.

62. Siddiqi, *Pakistan Seeks*, p. 87.

63. For accounts of the origins of the United States-Pakistan agreement, see Selig Harrison, "India, Pakistan and the US: Parts I, II, and III," *New Republic* (August 10, 24 and September 7 1959); James W. Spain, "Military Assistance for Pakistan," *American Political Science Review* 48 (September 1954): 738-51; and William J. Barnds, *India, Pakistan, and the Great Powers* (New York: Praeger, 1972), pp. 83-106.

64. "Why Pakistan Wants U.S. Aid," *U.S. News and World Report*, 15 January 1954, p. 35.

65. Barnds, *Great Powers*, pp. 102-103.

66. Nehru to Mohammad Ali, 9 December 1953, in Hasan, *Kashmir Question*, p. 345.

CHAPTER FOUR

"DEFENSE AGAINST WHOM?": 1954-62

Pakistan's military alliance with the United States altered the economic and military balance between India and Pakistan. It allowed Pakistan to build up its material and military assets to a far greater extent than was possible from its existing domestic resources. Pakistan's aim in seeking this external aid was to improve its bargaining power with India. But the alliance had a number of regional and international consequences that reduced Pakistan's initial advantages.

The Soviet Union reacted to the military alliance by increasing its material aid to India and Afghanistan. It extended its diplomatic support to India's position on Kashmir and Afghanistan's position on Pakhtoonistan. The Eisenhower administration, realizing that India was too important a country to neglect in containing international communism, continued America's policy of economic aid to India. After 1954, the administration gave India increased material assistance, mostly in the form of PL-480 and PL-665 commodity aid.[1] Finally, India made diplomatic and military efforts to match western aid to Pakistan. It became receptive to Soviet economic assistance and purchased advanced combat aircraft from Britain and France.

The Indian government's policy was still to promote regional integration with Pakistan, but this came to have less priority as India paid more attention to its internal development and to its foreign policy goals of nonalignment and warding off a growing military threat from communist China. In contrast to the first period of Indo-Pakistani relations, when there was relatively little external involvement, the period between 1954 and 1962 is marked by greater external involvement in South Asia. This must be taken into account in assessing the balance of power between India and Pakistan.

MATERIAL CAPABILITIES, POWER AND INFLUENCE

Economic

In the second phase of Indo-Pakistani relations, the Indian government was more successful in building up its economic assets. India was more politically stable and had a much better material base, particularly in industries. Hence, the government could plan and implement its economic and social development policies. India's Second Five Year Plan, which began on 1 April 1956, was more ambitious than the first one. It aimed at laying the infrastructural foundations of India as a major industrial power. Mining, iron and steel, aluminum, machine tools, railway locomotives, chemicals, and electric power, all took priority. Pakistan's First Five Year Plan was supposed to begin on 1 July 1955, but failed to gain strong support from the many governments that were in office from May 1954 to the military takeover in October 1958. Those governments lacked effective authority to extract domestic resources for economic and social growth. No political party emerged to blunt Pakistan's many regional, religious, and class divisions. The governments of the day were more preoccupied with short-term political survival than with long-term economic planning. This changed when the military took over in 1958. With political stability restored, the new regime gave a high priority to Pakistan's economic and social development. Pakistan noticeably improved its agricultural and industrial growth rates relative to India.

India had a better record of increasing its national income in this period.[2] Its industrial growth was broad-based and in sectors adding to material and military strength--heavy industry, tranport, coal and iron-ore mining, chemicals and so forth. Overall industrial production and particular industries registered impressive growth rates. Pakistan also had impressive growth rates, and these could no longer be attributed to its low initial base of industrialization.[3] But, apart from the development of basic infrastructure, such as power, railways, ports and roads, most of this growth was in consumer goods industries, which added little to Pakistan's material and military power.[4] For instance, during the Second Plan, India increased the capacity of its existing steel plants and built three new ones. Pakistan lacked adequate resources to build any steel plants. It imported most of its steel, and most of its small domestic steel production came from smelting scrap.[5]

Pakistan continued with its import substitution industrialization in consumer and light goods. A major reason was that Pakistan's economy still had to be diversified. Pakistan faced the choice of either importing consumer and light goods or of diversifying its predominantly agricultural economy. Another reason why it chose the former was that consumer and light goods used relatively simple technologies. Finally, self-sufficiency in these areas freed foreign exchange for imports of capital goods.[6]

The achievements in industrial growth in both countries were offset by less impressive growth rates in agriculture. This was mainly because their elites had an urban bias and preferred to allocate more resources to industry. Pakistan's total foodgrain production showed no increase during the First Plan, 1955-60. To cope with the resulting food shortage, it had to increase food imports, and this placed a further strain on the economy as the country's foreign exchange reserves were reduced. One casualty was that imports of items needed for industrialization, such as raw materials and machinery spare parts, had to be curbed.

India's agricultural performance was as disappointing as Pakistan's where self-sufficiency and productivity were concerned. First, the growth rate of agricultural production fell below national requirements. Two disastrous harvests in 1957-58 and 1959-60 forced the Indian government to increase food imports.[7] Like Pakistan, India also had to spend scarce foreign exchange on food imports. These imports, plus an increased demand for the machinery and raw materials needed for industrialization, caused India's international liquidity to plummet from US $1.8 billion in 1954 to US $512 million in 1962.[8] In the same period, Pakistan's international liquidity increased slightly from US $364 million to $382 million.[9]

Second, the growth of agricultural productivity in India was too slow to boost India's economic assets relative to Pakistan in this period. As Mason points out, "an examination of the Indian record in the 1950's suggests that an expansion in the cultivated area and number of workers employed in agriculture had more to do with output expansion than did increase in output per acre. Neither country, during the 1950's, accomplished a significant increase in productivity per man or per acre."[10]

India's economic growth did not give it an overwhelming margin of economic power over Pakistan. If anything, India's economic power was reduced. Pakistan's industrialization made it even less dependent on Indian goods and services. On 31 January 1958, Pakistan became self-sufficient in electricity production and no longer purchased it from India.[11] On 18 May 1959, the Industries Minister announced that Pakistan had become self-sufficient in cotton textiles, jute manufactures, woollen goods, hosiery, shoes, cigarettes, matches, soap, paints, vegetable ghee (clarified butter), paper, cement, sugar, and other light industries and consumer goods.[12]

Between 1954 and 1962, Indo-Pakistani bilateral trade formed a small part of their total world trade. India's exports to Pakistan took a smaller share of India's world exports compared to the period from 1947 to 1954. A similar decline was recorded for India's imports from Pakistan (appendix 1). Pakistan's world trade became increasingly integrated with the Middle East, Western Europe, and North America. The United States emerged as Pakistan's largest trading partner (appendix 1).

In principle, despite increasing self-sufficiency brought about by import substitution industrialization, and despite a static volume of bilateral trade, both countries continued to be economically complementary. Pakistan still needed Indian coal and building and forestry products for East Pakistan; India needed Pakistan's cotton and jute. A series of trade agreements between 1955 and 1962 provided for the exchange of these products. The foreign exchange difficulties of both countries also enhanced their complementarity. Increased bilateral trade in local currencies would have allowed both countries to conserve their scarce foreign exchange.[13]

Nonetheless, in practice, political and economic obstacles hindered the expansion in bilateral trade. Pakistan was reluctant to increase trade with India as long as the Kashmir issue was unresolved, and it sought to insulate East Pakistan from Indian influence. The government constructed jute mills in East Pakistan in order to remove dependence on Indian mills. At the same time, both countries were increasingly absorbed in their own internal economic development and conducted their economic planning in a self-centered fashion.

The Indus Waters dispute showed the limits of India's economic power and influence over Pakistan. As noted in chapter three, on 5 February 1954 the World Bank attempted to break the impasse between India and Pakistan by presenting its own plan for the development of the Indus Basin. It essentially gave up the idea of a functionalist solution--that is, a plan based on engineering rather than political principles. Instead, it divided the Indus Basin into two halves: Pakistan would get the entire flow of the western rivers, and India the entire flow of the eastern rivers. In addition, Pakistan would have a transitional period to build link canals from the western rivers to irrigation systems that had formerly been fed from the eastern rivers in India. In short, the Bank recognized that the only solution to the dispute was one in which both countries became independent in water supplies.

The Indian government accepted the Bank proposal in principle on 22 March 1954. But Pakistan held out, hoping to extract further concessions from both India and the Bank on water allocations and financing for replacement canals and development projects. Quite simply, Pakistan was able to hold out because its bargaining position had improved the moment it had allied with the United States.[14] In comparison, India's only economic sanction was to threaten to divert the eastern waters in order to force Pakistan to speed up its replacement. Yet even this option was limited by India's acceptance of the Bank's mediation. By cutting off the water, India would be reneging on its informal commitment to the Bank that it would not upset the status quo while the Bank was mediating. India also depended on the Bank for much-needed development aid. Thus India was in a bind: it was impatient to use the eastern waters to irrigate East Punjab and Rajasthan, but it could not seriously cut off water to Pakistan without substantial international costs. At most New Delhi could risk threatening to withdraw the water by a certain deadline. Yet, Pakistan's government ignored these threats. It took no action whatsoever to speed up work on the replacement canals in the face of a threatened cut-off from India. Why? N. D. Gulhati, India's chief negotiator of the Indus Waters Treaty, writes that Pakistan hoped to mobilize international support to nullify India's coercive economic power.[15]

If India's economic power was limited, so too was its economic influence. India could finance the new link canals in Pakistan but lacked the money to finance the much costlier development projects on Pakistan's western rivers. When the Bank and several western powers offered Pakistan financing for these development projects, the Pakistan government became more willing to settle the dispute with India.[16] Under the financial settlement Pakistan received $541.2 million in grants and an additional $150 million in loans for the development projects. India simply lacked such resources to offer to Pakistan.

Representatives of India, Pakistan and the World Bank signed the Indus Waters Treaty in Karachi on 19 September 1960. The Treaty specified the water allocations to both sides, established the transitional period for Pakistan to replace waters from the eastern rivers, provided funding arrangements and the institutional mechanisms for bilateral consultations, and stipulated guarantees and emergency provisions to safeguard water supplies. Overall, the Treaty did little to improve relations between India and Pakistan. It was limited to one issue area (water development), and it was really a means of separating Indian and Pakistan water supplies. Ironically, though it closed a bitter dispute in Indo-Pakistani relations, it made the two countries more independent of each other.

In summary, India began an ambitious industrialization policy under the Second Five Year Plan (1956-61). It succeeded in raising industrial production, particularly in heavy industry. By comparison, Pakistan's natural resource base was too narrow to emulate this industrialization. Instead, it conducted a strategy of import substitution in light and consumer goods industries. Both countries paid relatively little attention to each other in their economic planning. India was absorbed in its own economic development program; besides, Pakistan was unwilling to expand bilateral trade. India's economic power and influence were limited.

Nuclear Energy

Despite India's lead over Pakistan in scientific manpower and economic resources, both countries were at a similar stage of development: both had to build the scientific and organizational base for their nuclear energy programs. After 1953, they benefitted from the spread of scientific and technological information from the "Atoms for Peace" program, the UN Conference on Peaceful Uses of Atomic Energy, and from the declassification of nuclear power information by the United States, Britain and Canada. This proliferation of knowledge was especially helpful to Pakistan, the weaker state scientifically, technologically and economically.

The Indian government's official policy was to build a self-sufficient nuclear program for peaceful purposes. It began work on all phases of the nuclear fuel cycle: exploration of nuclear materials, mining, milling, fuel fabrication, heavy water production, construction of research reactors, fuel reprocessing, and waste treatment and storage. In August 1954, the government established a Department of Atomic Energy (DAE) to administer India's nuclear energy program. In 1955 it set up an Atomic Energy Establishment at Trombay, near Bombay, which had a scientific and technical staff of about 200.

The DAE made tangible progress in developing nuclear energy in this period. By 1961 the size of the Atomic Energy Establishment had increased to 1,300 scientists, technicians, and researchers, all organized into 15 divisions.[17] The DAE successfully carried out research; the *Aspara, Cirus, and Zerlina* research reactors went critical in 1956, 1960, and 1961 respectively. Finally, the cabinet and the Planning Commission gave the DAE approval to build commercial nuclear power stations. To demonstrate the economic and scientific feasibility of nuclear power in India, the government ordered an enriched uranium light water plant from General Electric of America on a turn-key basis. By 1962 India had successfully established the physical and human base for developing nuclear energy.

In 1955, Pakistan's government set up an advisory committee of scientists to consider the development of nuclear energy. In 1956 the government upgraded the committee to the Pakistan Atomic

Energy Commission (PAEC) and gave it the task of administering all aspects of nuclear energy development. The PAEC's objectives at this stage were threefold: first, to build a cadre of scientists, technicians, and other trained personnel; secondly, to build research facilities; and, thirdly, to survey Pakistan's natural resources for radioactive materials. Pakistan's existing material assets were inadequate for these objectives, and so the cadres were trained abroad. The International Atomic Energy Agency (IAEA) also helped by setting up a 5 MWe swimming-pool research reactor at Islamabad. By the end of 1962 Pakistan had made progress in its nuclear energy program. First, the cadre of skilled personnel had completed their training abroad.[18] Second, the government had established the Pakistan Institute of Nuclear Science and Technology (PINSTECH) at Islamabad and a Nuclear Training and Research Center at Lahore. Third, work on the site of the research reactor in Islamabad was at an advanced stage. Finally, mineral surveys uncovered radioactive materials in the sands along the ocean beach at Cox's Bazaar in East Pakistan.[19]

Overall, Pakistan's progress in nuclear energy was slower than India's. This was not only because India had a head start and had larger resources, but also because the Indian AEC had more powers than its Pakistani counterpart and was less subject to the examination of its programs by non-technical persons.[20]

Political

The political development of India and Pakistan continued to diverge after 1954.

Nehru and the Congress Party gave India political stability in the 1950s. India's liberal-democratic parliamentary system had taken root. The size of the electorate increased in the 1950s, as did the number of elective seats at the state and local level. In the 1957 general election the Congress improved its dominant political position both at the center and at the state level. Congress increased its share of the popular vote from 45.0 to 47.8 percent and its share of Lok Sabha seats from 74.4 to 75.1 percent.[21]

But there were drawbacks. Most of all, increased political participation worked, in the short-term, against a strong center of political authority in India. Different linguistic groups in the 1950s demanded the redrawing of state boundaries to correspond to linguistic divisions. Major agitations took place in Bombay city and province and in the Punjab. The demands were so intense and sustained that Nehru was forced to grant the States Reorganization Act of 1956, which redrew state boundaries and created 14 states according to the major linguistic divisions of India. Bombay and the Punjab remained undivided; their linguistic groups failed to agree on a satisfactory division of the provinces. In the long-run, states reorganization strengthened Indian federalism and the Center's authority. It did away with several artificially-drawn states and created new ones. These became symbols of regional loyalty and provided opportunities for education, income, and hence status for the linguistic groups.

India's federalism was aided by the further political and economic integration of Kashmir into the Indian Union. On 17 November 1956, Kashmir's State Assembly adopted a Draft Constitution, which affirmed that the State "is and shall be an integral part of the Union of India."[22] In the next four years, the Indian Constitution was progresively applied to Kashmir. The integration took place under the chief ministership of Bakshi Ghulam Mohammed. Although not as popular as his predecessor, Sheikh Abdullah, Bakshi managed to stay in power through a combination of patronage, rigged elections, corruption, and political support from the Center.

Indian political stability allowed continuity in economic and social planning. The Second Five Year Plan went into operation in 1956, followed by the Third Plan in 1961. In the 1960s, however, Nehru's domestic political dominance weakened. Parliament increasingly attacked his China policy. The Congress's grass-roots organization deteriorated. The Congress suffered its worst electoral setback since independence in the 1962 general election, although it kept its large majority in the Lok Sabha.

Pakistan's political system followed an opposite course: from severe political instability in 1954-58 to relative political stability in 1958-62 after the October 1958 military coup. Unlike India, Pakistan by 1954 had failed to frame a constitution acceptable to all the major economic, social, and political groups. A coalition of Punjabis and *muhajirs* (migrants from India) dominated the political system and sought to maintain this dominance by neutralizing the political power of other ethnic groups in Pakistan: the Bengalis, Sindhis, Pathans, and Baluchs.

Pakistan lacked a national political party and leaders with a national outlook. This being so, Pakistan's parliamentary system was left to unstable party coalitions. The Muslim League, which had lost electoral support in the East Pakistani provincial elections of March 1954, now found its support eroding in the western wing as well. It had to compete with the new Republican Party, founded by Dr. Khan Sahib in 1956. Thereafter, Pakistani party politics degenerated into opportunistic in-fighting among the political parties. The parties increasingly lost touch with the Pakistani people, who were given few opportunities for electoral participation. Apart from provincial elections, no national election based on universal adult suffrage was ever held. As Prime Minister Suhrawardy wrote in 1957, "...whatever our weaknesses of the past, they certainly have not been attributable to overdoses of democracy, for we have yet to try to full dosage."[23]

Prime Minister Chaudhri Muhammad Ali's government did manage to complete a Constitution. The 1956 Constitution--Pakistan's first since independence--promised greater democracy for the nation. It retained the parliamentary system and was based on universal adult suffrage. Pakistan's first general election was to be held in March 1958, but political instability led to its postponement to February 1959. It never took place. The military seized power in October 1958.

Political instability, weak civil institutions, an increase in the strength of the armed forces, and a severe economic crisis, all partly explain the takeover.[24] Other causes were the personal ambitions of Pakistan's President and the corporate interests of the armed forces. The takeover was their joint attempt to forestall elections. Mirza feared that he would be replaced as President after the election, while the army feared that the elections would lead to a Bengali-dominated majority in the central legislature, a majority that would reduce defense expenditures.[25]

The military takeover had a number of significant political consequences. President Mirza and General Ayub Khan on 7 October

1958 abrogated the 1956 Constitution, dismissed the central and provincial governments, dissolved the (unrepresentative) national Parliament and the provincial assemblies, abolished all political parties, and placed Pakistan under martial law.

The military then consolidated its rule. It removed Mirza and repressed other politicians and "anti-social" groups that it associated with the old political system. This done, it turned to a reform program. A series of commissions recommended numerous reforms in land reform, education, administrative reorganization, and the legal system. To carry out its vision of a reformed Pakistan, the military government sought to nurture the country's political institutions under military guidance. The two key parts of this *guided democracy* were *basic democracies* and a new constitution. Basic democracies were a system of local government and an indirect means of electing the President and the national and provincial assemblies. The 1962 Constitution was a centralizing constitution with extensive powers given to the President, who served as the linchpin of the new political system. It provided for a weak unicameral legislature and judiciary and no justiciable civil rights. It banned political parties and gave Pakistan a federal system but with no exclusive provincial powers. The Constitution came into force on 7 June 1962, replacing martial law.

How did political developments in India and Pakistan affect their responsiveness?

Nehru was often absorbed in domestic policy issues such as states reorganization and economic and social development. So, obviously, he could not pay full attention to relations with Pakistan, especially since he was both Prime Minister and Foreign Minister. The attention hypothesis, however, does not fully explain India's indifference towards Pakistan. Despite Nehru's preoccupations with domestic policy, the External Affairs Ministry had sufficient guidelines on relations with Pakistan. Moreover, Nehru remained as active as ever in foreign policy and continued to give a high priority to the nonaligned movement and to relations with China.

If the Indian government was unresponsive to Pakistan's demands on Kashmir in this period, it was because Nehru feared that any settlement harmful to India's interests there would lead to India's overall disintegration. Plainly, once the Pandora's box of Kashmir was opened, Nehru lacked confidence in India's ability to remain politically integrated and free from communal conflict.[26] Of course, Pakistan governments argued that this was a mere excuse for Indian footdragging over Kashmir, but the fact remains that India's political integration was still not fully assured in this period--witness the agitations over states' reorganization or the secessionist movement in Nagaland.

The chances of a Kashmir settlement were further narrowed by Pakistan's internal instability and inflexibility on Kashmir. Indeed, there appears to be a relationship between the two. Thus, when Pakistan negotiated with India over Kashmir between 1954 and 1956, no Pakistani government was sufficiently strong to opt for flexibility on Kashmir. Instead, unable to command stable parliamentary majorities from disciplined mass parties, the governments of the day were often led by the press, volatile public opinion, and party factions who used the anti-India issue to bring down officeholders.

Even so, the effect of Pakistan's instability on its responsiveness should not be exaggerated. Firoz Khan Noon, Prime Minister from 1957 to 1958, faced opposition from the Muslim League but still sought peaceful relations with India. As he later wrote in his memoirs, "My statement in Parliament after aggressive speeches by the Opposition parties who asked for military action in Kashmir, that if Pakistan wanted war with India she would have to find another Prime Minister, had a very good effect in India and created a congenial climate."[27]

As a result, both governments met to settle their disputes. In September 1958, the Prime Ministers agreed to exchange enclaves of territories on the eastern borders of India and Pakistan. The issue of the western borders, particularly the marshy area known as the Rann of Kutch, was left for further discussion. Unfortunately, the military takeover in Pakistan in October 1958 ended this promising turn of relations. Thus, although Pakistani governments were sometimes willing to improve relations with India, they were unable to implement their policies.

The military takeover restored political coherence in Pakistan. In the upshot the previous class of Pakistani politicians disappeared. In their place emerged an elite whose loyalty to Pakistan's territorial integrity and national sovereignty was beyond question. As he showed in approving the settlement of the Indus Waters dispute and in offering a joint defense of South Asia, Ayub was clearly in political control and in a strong position to negotiate with India.

Military rule strengthened Pakistan politically towards India, but the military government nonetheless tended to misperceive the relative bargaining power of the two countries. Specifically, Ayub viewed India as a cumbersome mixture of social groups ready for social and political disintegration. One foreign journalist writes that "In a conversation with General Ayub Khan, then president of Pakistan, in February 1960, the latter made it plain that he did not expect India to survive as a united country and that, sooner or later, some even would occur that would trigger the balkanization of the country, cutting down what was left of India to a size that would be more to the taste of Pakistan."[28] In contrast, Ayub saw a united Pakistan on the verge of a new era of economic and social growth under military rule. Time, he calculated, was on Pakistan's side.

Was Ayub really as strong in bargaining with India as he seemed in the martial law period, 1958-62? Plainly, he failed to appreciate the strength of Indian federalism or how liberal democratic and parliamentary institutions contributed to India's political integration. As for Pakistan's apparent stability, he miscalculated. It was transient, based only on martial law and the exclusion of important social groups from the political system--the urban middle class, the Bengalis, and ethnic minorities in West Pakistan. Furthermore, Ayub still had to find ways to legitimize military rule, which meant that he had to be cautious over the Kashmir issue. Whereas a solution could be found over the Indus Waters, Ayub was too weak at home to neglect Pakistan's claims to Kashmir--the most emotional issue in Pakistani life that no government could ignore, even if it wanted to do so.[29]

In summary, between 1954 and 1962, India's civilian-controlled political system witnessed an expansion of political participation by new social groups--linguistic, caste, regional and class--and an erosion in the political dominance of Nehru and the Congress Party. In the short term both trends weakened central authority there. But by making Indian democracy more socially broad-based and more critical of the elite's domestic and foreign policies, they strengthened India's political system. In contrast, Pakistani stability after October 1958 was due to martial law. The military barred the pre-1958 political elite from political participation, hoping instead to foster a new political elite to operate Pakistan's guided democracy. On Kashmir, Pakistan's demands were unacceptable to India for they threatened Indian social stability. Though Pakistan's responsiveness increased after the military coup in October 1958, it was limited to secondary issues between India and Pakistan.

MILITARY CAPABILITIES, POWER AND INFLUENCE

By early 1954, India and Pakistan had increased their military assets substantially since independence. India still had more manpower, equipment, and training facilities, but Pakistan was less militarily vulnerable than it had been in 1947. The Pakistan military had increased its force levels and had improved its organization and training.[30] American military aid significantly helped in these endeavors. The improvement was across-the-board. There were more soldiers, better organization, tougher training, and improved morale. All three services benefitted. One harmful effect: an arms race between the two countries began after 1954, although India's military assets also grew to offset increased diplomatic and military hostility with China after 1958.

Armies

The Indian government increased the size of the army to handle the secessionist movement in Nagaland and the Chinese military threat along India's Himalayan borders. The government added only two infantry divisions (appendix 3), which suggests that it was relying on diplomacy to solve the border dispute with China.

Despite its numerical superiority over Pakistan, the Indian army had several weaknesses. The officer corps was short of manpower, although such shortages were much worse in Pakistan. An increased intake of officer cadets in 1960 had no impact on the Indian army's effectiveness because of the long training time for new officers. A severe foreign exchange shortage in 1957-59 prevented the army from modernizing its weapons and equipment. The government concentrated financial resources on economic and social development at military expense. Worse, civilian intervention in promotions and operational decisions further reduced the army's morale. Abroad, the Indian government's policy of nonalignment projected a pacific image of India in international affairs. Not surprisingly, then, many Indian soldiers saw themselves out of the mainstream of national and international life.[31]

By contrast, Pakistan's military aid from the United States and other western countries improved the skill, morale, organization, and leadership of the Pakistani Army. The size of the army did not increase to any appreciable extent, but Western aid did enable Pakistan to bring some of its infantry and armored units up to full strength (appendix 3).

Military assistance also allowed Pakistan to offset India's advantages in manpower by improvements in firepower. Foreign arms transfers to the Pakistan Army were far greater than to India and included M-4 Sherman tanks, modern M-47 and M-48 tanks, plus a large number of M-113 armored personnel carriers. This new equipment was an immediate tonic for the morale of the army.[32]

Air Forces

Between 1954 and 1962, the Indian Air Force (IAF) modernized its combat and transport squadrons, began training its pilots for jet aircraft, established new training schools, and increased self-sufficiency in most stages of training. In organization, the IAF created a new Eastern Command with headquarters at Calcutta.

Aircraft transfers to India were greater than to Pakistan. This was true not only of combat aircraft, but also of supporting aircraft--transports, trainers, helicopters, reconnaisance aircraft, and so forth. India also received some superior-quality aircraft; for example, its Hunter F.56s had greater range, speed, and maneuverability than Pakistan's F.86 Sabres.

The Pakistan Air Force (PAF) had some advantages of its own. First, it received 14 F-104 Starfighters, which were front-line NATO aircraft at the time. Secondly, it received Sidewinder and Falcon missiles and modern types of bombs. Finally, unlike India, which had more diverse sources of aircraft suppliers, the PAF's aircraft were either from the United States or the United Kingdom. This simplified the PAF's training and logistical operations. The PAF's combat aircraft strength tripled from 1953 to 1962 (appendix 5). This expansion was accompanied by a steadily increasing level of skill and training. The PAF's training facilities acquired American training aircraft and knowledge of modern fighter tactics.[33] On 5 January 1959, President Ayub Khan opened the PAF Staff College in Karachi.

The Navies

Because of severe foreign exchange shortages in 1957 and 1958, the Indian government had to abandon its large-scale naval modernization program. Instead, a less ambitious naval expansion followed. Foreign naval transfers to India replaced existing inventories. The Indian Navy acquired a Majestic class light aircraft carrier from Britain, which it commissioned on 4 March 1961. This significantly altered the balance of naval power between India and Pakistan.

While the Indian Navy continued to maintain its close ties with the Royal Navy, two developments reduced their intimacy: India became increasingly self-sufficient in naval training, and the indianization of the Indian Navy continued. On 22 April 1948 Vice-Admiral R.D. Katari became the first Indian Chief of the Naval Staff. Indianization was fully completed in April 1962 when the Indian government appointed an Indian as Chief of Naval Aviation at Naval Headquarters in New Delhi.[34]

Like its sister services, the Pakistan Navy benefitted from American military aid. Naval strength increased with the addition of one light cruiser in 1956 and several destroyers from 1956 to 1958. The number of minesweepers, tugs, and replenishment craft also increased significantly. United States aid also allowed Pakistan to improve its naval training institutions and to construct a floating dock, various repair facilities and a naval base at Chittagong in East Pakistan. The navy's training improved as it participated in several regular exercises with SEATO and CENTO members. In all, the Pakistani Navy maintained its relative position with the Indian Navy--not least because foreign aid allowed the government to strengthen this capital-intensive service.

Defence Production

Any change in the relative defense production capabilities of India and Pakistan depended on the economic growth of each. Since India more successfully industrialized than Pakistan in this period, its defense production capabilities increased faster too. Nonetheless, India's actual defense production fell short of its potential.

After an initial period in which it indianized and reorganized from 1947 to 1954, the Indian government began many new programs of defense production. Almost always, the aim was to make India self-sufficient, or, if that was not immediately possible, to give India the eventual capacity to be self-sufficient. Defense production plants began work on indigenously producing transport vehicles, medium tanks, semi-automatic rifles, electronic equipment, naval vessels, and aircraft.[35] India's progress in aircraft production reflected its overall progress in defense production. The government began new programs for manufacturing light, training, combat, and transport aircraft (appendix 7). Several conclusions emerge. First, India was capable of designing and producing light aircraft for a variety of civilian and military uses, such as transport, air observation, and communications. Second, in more advanced aircraft India relied on licensed agreements which specified assembly and, at a later stage, full production within India. Production of these aircraft was by no means small. Thirdly, India was still at an early stage in designing and developing indigenous aircraft like the HJT-16 Kiran and the HF-Marut. Both of these planes had design and development problems, particularly in engine thrust.[36] Finally, India made a number of license agreements late in this period (the MiG-21 fighter and the French Alouette III helicopter) with production coming onto line only after 1962.

Overall, from 1954 to 1962 India initiated the major weapons systems of the 1960s--the Vijayanta medium tank, Gnat fighters, MiG-21s, and Leander-class frigates. Its defense production was still at a learning stage, and there were shortages of skilled manpower, physical plant, and modern equipment. The industrial base, while growing, was still too narrow to support advanced defense industries.

Pakistan's defense production was smaller, less diverse, and less ambitious than India's. It was geared to producing clothing, small arms, ammunition, and other stores for the army. Western military assistance allowed the army to improve the storage and distribution facilities for its weapons and equipment. It also allowed the PAF and Pakistan's Navy to improve their maintenance plants. Although Pakistan's defense production was small, it was adequate for its peace-time needs. The evidence for this comes from two sources. From 1959 onwards Pakistan had the capacity to export small arms, ammunition, and other stores.[37] And in 1960 the United States gave Pakistan a loan to convert some of the idle industrial capacity at the Wah ordnance factory to production of civilian items.[38]

Three factors slowed India's rate of activating its military assets in this period. It sensed a low threat from Pakistan. Its industrial and defense production policies emphasized long-term investment and long gestation times. And it had severe foreign exchange shortages, resulting, as mentioned earlier, from increased imports under the Second Five Year Plan.

The Indian government still saw Pakistan as its major security threat, but it believed that it could contain this threat comfortably. It responded to western military and economic aid to Pakistan by attempting to match its acquisitions of arms, especially combat aircraft. Nor did western assistance to Pakistan deflect the Indian government from its policy of building up its military and material assets and potential. It believed that in the long-run this policy would do more to strengthen India's military power and influence than short-run arms purchases from abroad. In short, it saw military power and influence to be dependent on the growth of India's material power. Nehru explicitly stated his theory of power as follows: "The equation of defense is your defense forces plus your industrial and technological background, plus thirdly, the economy of the country, and fourthly, the spirit of the people."[39] Military expenditures were only part of this defense equation and grew in real terms from $503 million in 1954 to $582 in 1960. Thereafter, they jumped sharply as Sino-Indian relations worsened, reaching a level of $862 million in 1962. Pakistan's military expenditures increased from $170 million in 1954 to $205 million in 1960 and then dropped to $192.5 million in 1962.[40]

India could afford to concentrate on its internal economic development as long as its saw no immediate security threat from its neighbors. But Sino-Indian relations deteriorated sharply after the Tibetan revolt against China in early 1959. Several thousand Tibetan refugees fled to India, including the Dalai Lama, who was granted asylum in India in April 1959. The Chinese government saw this as an hostile act by New Delhi. Thereafter border skirmishes between the two countries intensified. The Indian government responded by boosting its military expenditures, particularly in the border regions. The aim was to take precautionary measures against a Chinese attack but not to build up the military assets in the region to such an extent as to provoke this attack.[41]

Pakistan's government was as concerned as India's by the rise of Chinese military power along India's northern borders. On several occassions between May 1959 and January 1960, Ayub offered India a joint defense of the subcontinent provided that both countries settled the Kashmir. Once that dispute was resolved, both countries could disengage their troops from their common borders and deploy them to face external threats to the subcontinent. Both sides could also concentrate on their internal economic and social development instead of being engaged in a costly arms race. Ayub Khan, like his predecessors, was using a formidable counter in the bargaining relationship with India--pointing out to India the opportunity costs of their continued conflict.

Those opportunity costs had certainly increased for India as Sino-Indian relations deteriorated. But Nehru still did not see them as being sufficiently high to accommodate Pakistan, and he therefore rebuffed Ayub's offer. First, Ayub's offer had been conditional on resolving the Kashmir conflict. Nehru's basic position on Kashmir had remained unchanged since Pakistan's acceptance of western military aid in 1954. If anything, his bargaining position had worsened since then. Sino-Indian hostilities led to increasing scrutiny of his foreign policy in Parliament and among informed public opinion. This limited his ability to compromise with Pakistan. Those sections of the Indian military that favored Ayub's offer of joint defense were uninfluential in India's security policy-making. The Defense Minister, Krishna Menon, saw Pakistan and not China as India's number one enemy. For another thing, Nehru believed that accepting Ayub's offer would provoke China militarily and harm India's expanding ties with Moscow. Nehru hoped that China would adhere to the "Five Principles" of bilateral relations--respect for each other's territorial integrity and sovereignty, non-aggression, noninterference in each other's internal affairs, equality and mutual benefit, and peaceful coexistence. He believed that ultimately China would not settle its border dispute with India by force. The desire not to provoke China and the USSR accounts for Nehru's reply of "defense against whom?" to Ayub's offer. Finally, and rather unconvincingly, Nehru argued that acceptance would put India into the western camp since Pakistan was a member of CENTO and SEATO. He failed to realize that Ayub was offering an informal understanding, not an alliance.

Some critics contend that Ayub made his proposal in bad faith and in order to exploit India's military weaknesses compared with China.[42] Others argue that Nehru rejected the proposal out of hand.[43] In other words, it is argued that the joint defense offer was neither carefully proposed by Ayub nor disposed of by Nehru. Are these arguments that belittle the importance of Ayub's offer sound? The evidence is otherwise. First, Ayub's offer involved domestic costs within Pakistan, particularly among those sections of the regime and public opinion who felt that he had offered a security relationship to India without gaining any tangible results in Kashmir.[44] Such an offer, then, could not have been made carelessly. And secondly, the Indian cabinet did condider Ayub's offer.[45] Even though the cabinet may have only endorsed Nehru's earlier public dismissal, the Indian decision-making on this subject shows that Nehru's rejection was carefully reasoned.

India's rejection of Ayub's offer occurred when Ayub was reassessing the value of Pakistan's alliance with the West. This reassessment was came about as a result of the policies of the great powers in Asia.

After May 1954, the United States emerged as the major supplier of economic and military aid to South Asia. The United States saw Pakistan as an important ally in containing communist power. In conjunction with Britain and other western powers, it integrated Pakistan more closely into regional alliances in the Middle East and Southeast Asia. Pakistan's strategic value to the United States was reduced by two factors. First, Pakistan's government insisted that its alliance with the west was intended to counter not only communist but also Indian "aggression." Secondly, the United States realized that Pakistan by itself could not act as a barrier against Soviet and Chinese expansion in South Asia. For that purpose, India--with its greater demographic, material, and military weight--was needed. Also China was challenging India militarily and politically in the late 1950s and early 1960s. So, although the United States gave Pakistan military and economic aid, it also gave India economic aid. India was the largest recipient of United States global economic aid at this time.

Pakistan's government, naturally, was displeased. It criticized American aid to India, arguing that it rewarded India's nonalignment policy and slighted the military and diplomatic efforts of America's faithful allies.[46] Pakistan's disillusionment increased as the United States and other western powers stepped up their military aid to India when Sino-Indian relations deteriorated after 1960. Pakistan's government felt that it was being sacrificed and that the aid to India would be used against Pakistan.

Pakistan rightly pointed out that western aid strengthened India. American aid to India released far larger amounts of foreign currency for other purposes than did American aid to Pakistan. In addition, India received aid from both the United States and the Soviet Union, whereas Pakistan received very little aid from the Soviet bloc between 1954 and 1962.[47] Nonetheless, there were still some important differences in the foreign aid given to India and Pakistan. First, economic aid to India, while large in an absolute sense, was smaller on a per capita basis than the economic aid to given to Pakistan.[48] Secondly, as Selig Harrison pointed out, the economic aid to India strengthened a liberal democratic system, whereas aid to Pakistan strengthened a military regime.[49] Finally, even with large western economic aid, and with a more sympathetic American administration after 1960, India was unable to receive the weapons that she wanted from the United States. The United States repeatedly turned down Indian requests to buy supersonic combat aircraft and related weapons, such as Sidewinder air-to-air missiles.[50] In short, the Pakistan government wrongly saw economic aid to India as interchangeable with military aid.

So by the end of the 1950s, Pakistan's foreign policy had to take into account a firm Indian stand on Kashmir, increasing Sino-Indian tensions, and increased western support to India. These all forced it to reassess its relations with the USSR and China. As a smaller power, Pakistan's objective was to improve its relations with these two neighboring giants without sacrificing its security ties to the United States. Ayub hoped that an emphasis on bilateral relations would increase Pakistan's diplomatic maneuverability and avoid entanglement in the rivalries between India and China, the USSR and China, and the United States and USSR.

Until 1962 Pakistan had little success in improving relations with China. Beijing felt threatened by several Pakistani policies. It opposed Pakistan's participation in western pacts (particularly SEATO), Pakistan's 1959 bilateral defense pact with the United States, its proposal for joint defense with India, its support for Taiwan, and, finally, Pakistan's support for China's exclusion from the United Nation. China ignored Ayub's offer to demarcate their common borders because it still had not precluded settling the border dispute with India by diplomacy.[51] But then, suddenly, Sino-Pakistan relations improved after 1961. Pakistan reversed its diplomatic position on China's membership in the United Nations. At the same time China realized that a diplomatic solution to the Sino-Indian border dispute was becoming less likely. In March 1962, Pakistan and China agreed to begin negotations to demarcate the border between Xinjiang province and Pakistan-held Kashmir. These negotiations began on October 13, a week before the outbreak of the Sino-Indian border war.

Throughout the period from 1958 to 1962, the USSR remained cool to Pakistan's desire for improved relations. It viewed Pakistan as a base for America's containment policy (the ill-fated Gary Powers' U-2 mission had orginated from Peshawar air force base in West Pakistan). Also India was now doubly important for the USSR. It was a large developing country and an influential member of the nonaligned movement. India could also help the USSR contain Chinese power once Sino-Soviet relations worsened after 1959. The Soviets did not side with their fellow communists in the Sino-Indian border dispute; instead, they strengthened India by providing economic aid and transport aircraft suitable for use in the Himalayas. In August 1962 both countries signed a license agreement to produce MiG-21 aircraft in India. Nevertheless, the Soviets were still very cautious about providing military aid that could be used by India against the Chinese. In fact, up to 1963, they continued to provide some military aid to China. They did not want to foreclose the possibility of a settlement with China.

The Sino-Indian dispute had the most impact on Indo-Pakistani relations. At stake in the dispute were China's territorial control of Tibet, India's defense of its Himalayan borders, and the demarcation of the Sino-Indian border, a border inherited from the colonial past and unacceptable to China for ideological and strategic reasons. The border reminded China of its unequal status under western domination and it prevented China from consolidating its control of Tibet. In 1955 China began work on a road from Xinjiang province to western Tibet in order to integrate Tibet and its population more fully into the People's Republic. One problem: the road passed through Indian territory in the Aksai Chin part of Ladakh. The Indian government responded, as noted earlier, by increasing its military strength in the Himalayas. The aim was not to provoke China, but this is exactly what happened. Nehru's "Forward Policy" sought to challenge Chinese territorial claims by physically occupying the disputed areas and evicting Chinese troops where necessary. China's warnings of retaliation were ignored. Nehru simply did not believe that the Chinese would attack in force to settle the border dispute.

China had some strategic assets in the Himalayas which India did not--the control of the high ground, a larger available military force with better training in mountain warfare, better organization and supplies, more effective use of intelligence, and better civilian and military leadership in strategy and tactics.[52] This superior force attacked on 20 October 1962 and routed the Indian military. China unilaterally declared a ceasefire on 20 November 1962.

The political, military, and psychological consequences of the war were immense. India had been humiliated by a larger Asian power; its domestic and foreign policies were brought into question; and Nehru's domestic and international prestige suffered the sharpest setback in his fifteen years as Prime Minister. Pakistanis, too, saw the war as a turning-point--India had been taught a lesson and Chinese power had been clearly demonstrated in the Himalayas. The 1962 war marks a watershed in India's domestic and foreign policies and in Indo-Pakistani relations.

To sum up: from 1954 to 1962 Pakistan reduced the relative gap in military assets between it and India. India maintained its absolute superiority over Pakistan but lacked the military assets to fight a possible two-front war against Pakistan and China. Both India and Pakistan used their military assets differently. India sought to deter Pakistan and China from upsetting the territorial status quo. Pakistan sought to increase its diplomatic bargaining power and to influence India to settle the Kashmir issue by offering to jointly defend the subcontinent. Although both had adequate military resources to deter each other, the military balance of power between them was upset by changes in the Sino-Indian military equation. India's reputation for military power suffered a severe setback in the defeat of 1962.

IDENTITIVE CAPABILITIES, POWER, AND INFLUENCE

A number of issues continued to confound Indo-Pakistani relations and to narrow their identitive ties. These included refugee movements from East Pakistan to India, evacuee property, cultural differences, and the status of Kashmir. The latter dispute blocked progress by India and Pakistan toward regional economic and defense cooperation. Two other major issues drew the countries further apart--the 1956 Pakistan Constitution, which declared Pakistan an Islamic Republic, and the October 1958 military coup in Pakistan, which strained relations with the civilian, democratic government of India.

Refugee movements from East Pakistan increased in 1954 and steadily rose in the next two years until they reached a peak in February and March 1956.[53] The movements then slowed after the Indian government imposed entry restrictions and after the Pakistani government took measures to improve the security of Hindus in East Pakistan. Both countries made progress on the issue of evacuee property. Intergovernmental discussions took place in March 1955 to settle moveable property claims, that is, shares, securities, insurance policies, bank accounts, safety deposit lockers, personal effects, and so forth. Both governments signed a Moveable Evacuee Property Agreement on 1 November 1955, which established procedures for transferring moveable property to the other country. The two countries implemented the agreement over the next four years.[54]

In 1960 India and Pakistan tried to improve mutual press coverage. The Indo-Pakistan Information Consultative Committee met in New Delhi in April of that year and issued a joint communique urging the press of both countries to observe restraint in publishing news about the other country. The Committee also formulated a 12-point code of behavior for the Indo-Pakistani press.[55] That such a code had to be developed shows that identitive ties in this area were weak.

There is also very little evidence that the Pakistani government intended to widen cultural ties with India. What evidence there is shows that the government preferred to narrow those ties. For instance, in late 1961 a Pakistan Film Fact Finding Committee recommended that all Indian films be banned from Pakistan for the next five years in order to develop Pakistan's small film industry. Ayub's government accepted its recommendations on 13 January 1962 and imposed an immediate ban on Indian films.[56] Later, the government had to modify this ban to allow the screening of films that had already been imported. The government's actions did nothing to reduce the popularity of Indian films, particularly of Bengali-language films in East Pakistan.[57]

Pakistan's 1956 Constitution increased the political similarities with India in one respect: Pakistan shed its Dominion status and joined India in becoming a republic. The differences, however, outweighed the similarities. The preamble declared Pakistan an Islamic Republic, even though the meaning of that term was not fully specified or implemented in the 1956 Constitution. India reacted to the document by continuing to deny the validity of the two-nation theory. For Nehru, Pakistan's political instability and lack of economic and social development could ultimately be traced to the Pakistani leaders' belief in the two-nation theory, a theory which he believed contributed to their rootlessness.[58]

The military takeover in Pakistan in October 1958 further reduced identitive ties. Initially, Nehru slammed the new regime as "a naked military dictatorship," which, of course, did not endear him to the new regime.[59] Still, the consequences of this regime change for Indo-Pakistani identitive relations should not be exaggerated. Indian and Pakistani conceptions of religion, politics, and nationalism were already so far apart that the military takeover only added to the pre-existing basic disagreements between the two countries. The contrast in regime types was not the root cause of those disagreements. And, while Nehru preferred liberal-democratic governments in South Asia, he was pragmatic enough to accept authoritarian regimes.[60] Ayub's government was also in a far stronger position to strengthen identitive ties with India, if it had chosen to do so. Gone were the old, politically insecure Pakistani politicians who had made conflict with India a major weapon against their domestic political opponents. Ayub's government was more secure domestically and thus in a far stronger position to negotiate with India. Nor could the Pakistani military, the symbol of nationhood, be accused of "selling out" to India.

An analysis of Indo-Pakistani relations from 1954 to 1962 shows the growth of few identitive ties. Some partition disputes were settled, such as moveable property, but new disputes arose to reduce identitive ties. Identitive ties were not independent factors in improving or worsening Indo-Pakistani relations. The major obstacles to improved relations continued to be Kashmir and external intervention in South Asia.

CONCLUSION

The period from 1954 to 1962 saw a continuation of the previous themes of Indo-Pakistani relations: India's attempts to indigenously develop its national power and Pakistan's attempts to mobilize external material and military aid to make up for shortfalls in domestic resources. India's aim was self-sufficiency; Pakistan's autonomy relative to India. Both countries had varying degrees of success in these efforts. India successfully began heavy industrialization but still depended on foreign assistance for its industry and agriculture. Pakistan's industrialization was sufficient for it to act as an economic countercore in South Asia, but the industrialization did not add much to Pakistan's material or military power. Pakistan, though, narrowed the gap with India in two areas: in activated military power after 1954 and in the stability of its political system after the military coup in October 1958. These changes were insufficient to force India to accommodate Pakistan on Kashmir. India's material and military capabilities grew faster than Pakistan's, but its responsiveness to Pakistan was limited by domestic economic and political weaknesses and by Pakistan's costly demands for settling the Kashmir dispute. These stalemated bilateral relations were also affected by changes in the international system. Growing Sino-Indian conflict led to increased western and Soviet aid to India. It also made Pakistan reassess its alliance with the west and Pakistani policies towards China. Above all, the Sino-Indian War marked an important system change in South Asian politics. The Chinese showed India's military power to be weak, at least in the Himalayas, and the Pakistani government believed that India's reputation for military power had suffered a severe blow.

Notes

1. America's total foreign aid between 1954 and 1962 was $42.4 billion. Out of this India received $2.4 billion (5.7 percent) and Pakistan $1.4 billion (3.2 percent of the total). Syed Ali Husain, "Politics of Alliance and Aid: A Case Study of Pakistan (1954-1966)," *Pakistan Horizon* 32 (First and Second Quarters 1979), p. 26.

2. India, Central Statistical Organization, *Basic Statistics relating to the Indian Economy* (Delhi: Manager of Publications, Government of India Press, 1970), p. 1.

3. Joseph S. Stern and Walter P. Falcon, *Growth and Development in Pakistan* (Cambridge: Harvard University Center for International Affairs, 1970), pp. 9-10.

4. One economist hypothesized that Pakistan's import substitution industrialization strategy based on consumption goods failed to provide savings for further economic growth. What was needed was a strategy based on intermediate and capital goods. John H. Power, "Industrialization in Pakistan: a case of frustrated take-off?" *Pakistan Development Review* 3 (Summer 1963): 191-207. The Pakistan Planning Commission reached the same conclusion in drawing up the Third Plan. See *The Third Five Year Plan 1965-70* (Karachi: Manager of Publications, 1968), pp. 3, 447-48.

5. Pakistan, Planning Commission, *The Second Five Year Plan: 1960-65* (Karachi: Manager of Publications, 1961), p. 247.

6. Pakistan, *Planning Board, The First Five Year Plan 1955-1960 (Draft)*, vol. 2 (Karachi: Manager of Publications, 1956), p. 222.

7. In drafting the Second Plan, the Indian Planning Commission estimated that 6 million tons of food would be imported; the actual total imported in the Second Plan was 20 million tons. *Third Five Year Plan* (Delhi: Government of India Press, 1961), p. 109.

8. International Monetary Fund, *International Financial Statistics* vol. 16 (Washington, D.C.: IMF, 1963), p. 142.

9. Ibid., pp. 204-7.

10. Edward S. Mason, *Economic Development in India and Pakistan* (Cambridge: Harvard University Center for International Affairs, 1966, p. 11.

11. W. Nelson Peach, Mohammed Uzair, and George W. Rucker, *Basic Data of the Economy of Pakistan* (Karachi: Oxford University Press, 1959), p. 91.

12. Aslam Siddiqi, *Pakistan Seeks Security* (Lahore: Longmans Green, 1960), p. 63.

13. In the three-year agreement signed on 22 January 1957, both governments undertook "to explore all possibilities for expansion of trade between the two countries on the basis of mutual advantage, recognizing the needs and requirements of each other for foreign exchange in the context of developing their economies and having regard to the present disequilibrium in their trade and payments position." *Asian Recorder* 3 (26 January-February 1957), pp. 1273-74.

14. Aloys Arthur Michel, *The Indus Rivers: A Study of the Effects of Partition* (New Haven, Conn.: Yale University Press, 1967), pp. 240-41.

15. Niranjan D. Gulhati, *Indus Waters Treaty: An Exercise in International Mediation* (Bombay: Allied Publishers, 1973), pp. 310-17.

16. The initial external funding for the Treaty was (US) $742.2 million, made up of the following contributions in grants and loans (in millions): United States $515.0, World Bank $103.0, Britain $58.4, West Germany $30.2, Canada $22.1, Australia $15.5, and New Zealand $2.7. Out of this Pakistan received $691.2 million and India $56 million. In addition, India contributed $173.8 million. Michel, *Indus Rivers*, pp. 248-51. For the text of the Treaty, see Gulhati, *Indus Waters*, pp. 376-411.

17. India, Planning Commission, *Third Plan*, pp. 626-28.

18. Shirin Tahir-Kheli, "Pakistan," in *Nuclear Power in Developing Countries*, ed. James Everett Katz and Onkar S. Marwah (Lexington, Mass: D.C. Heath & Co., 1982)), pp. 263-64.

19. Pakistan, Planning Commission, *Third Plan*, pp. 502-3.

20. This comparison was made by the then head of the PAEC, Nazir Ahmed, "The Pakistan Atomic Energy Commission," *Pakistan Quarterly* 8 (Winter 1958), pp. 52-53.

21. W. H. Morris-Jones, *The Government and Politics of India* (Bombay: B. I. Publications, 1974), p. 184.

22. Quoted in Sisir Gupta, *Kashmir: A Study in India-Pakistan Relations* (Delhi: Asia Publishing House, 1966), p. 374.

23. H. S. Suhrawardy, "Political Stability and Democracy in Pakistan," *Foreign Affairs* 35 (April 1957), p. 425.

24. For Ayub's explanations of the coup, see *Friends Not Masters* (London: Oxford University Press, 1967), pp. 56-85. See also Wayne Wilcox, "The Pakistan Coup d'Etat of 1958," *Pacific Affairs* 38 (Summer 1965): 142-63; Khalid Bin Sayeed, "Collapse of Parliamentary Democracy in Pakistan," *The Middle East Journal* 13 (Autumn 1959): 389-406; and K. J. Newman, "Pakistan's Preventive Autocracy and its Causes," *Pacific Affairs* 32 (March 1959): 18-33.

25. Sayeed, *Political System*, p. 92.

26. Gupta, *Kashmir*, p. 345.

27. Sir Malik Firoz Khan Noon, *From Memory* (Lahore: Ferozsons, 1969), p. 285.

28. Amaury de Riencourt, "India and Pakistan in the shadow of Afghanistan," *Foreign Affairs* 61 (Winter 1982-83): 419-20.

29. The improvement in Indo-Pakistan relations after the signing of the Indus Waters Treaty was brief. On 6 October 1960, Ayub made a strong speech in Azad Kashmir reaffirming Pakistan's claims in Kashmir. Gupta, *Kashmir*, p. 344.

30. A good first-hand comparison of the Indian and Pakistani armies at the beginning of the 1954-62 period is given in Field Marshal Sir John Harding, "The Indian and Pakistani Armies of Today," *Asian Review* 51 (July 1955): 175-87.

31. Margaret MacMillan, "The Indian Army since Independence," *South Asian Review* 3 (October 1969), pp. 53-54.

32. Fazal Muqeem Khan, *The Story of the Pakistan Army* (Lahore: Oxford University Press, 1963), pp. 159-60.

33. John L. Fricker, *Battle for Pakistan: The Air War of 1965* (London: Ian Allan, 1979), p. 33.

34. A. L. Venkateswaran, *Defense Organization in India* (Delhi: Publications Division, 1967), pp. 153 and 217.

35. Ibid., pp. 301-2.

36. Kavic, *India's Quest*, p. 137.

37. Siddiqi, *Pakistan Seeks*, pp. 59-60.

38. *Asian Recorder* 8 (28 May-3 June 1962), p. 4604.

39. Jawaharlal Nehru, *Speeches*, vol. 3: *March 1953-August 1957* (Delhi: Publications Division, 1958), p. 40.

40. Stockholm International Peace Research Institute, *Yearbook 1972* (New York: Humanities Press, 1972), pp. 88-89.

41. Kavic, *India's Quest*, p. 61.

42. See, for example, G. S. Bhargava, *South Asian Security after Aghanistan* (Lexington, Mass.: D. C. Heath & Co., 1983), p. 12.

43. Kavic, *India's Quest*, p. 70.

44. Zulfikar Bhutto later claimed that it was his views on the Indian threat that forced Ayub to reconsider his policies towards joint defense and the Sino-Indian border conflict in Ladakh. It is unlikely that Bhutto by himself was influential in reversing Ayub's policies. Bhutto was a junior member in a military-dominated cabinet, and Ayub was in firm control of the military at that time. Bhutto's correspondence with Ayub on this matter is contained in Zulfikar Ali Bhutto, *The Third World: New Directions* (London: Quartet Books, 1977), pp. 110-17.

45. Interview with Swaran Singh, San Francisco, California, 4 September 1983.

46. Khan, *Friends Not Masters*, pp. 129-39.

47. Husain, "Politics of Alliance," p. 29.

48. John W. Mellor, *The New Economics of Growth: A Strategy for India and the Developing World* (Ithaca, N. Y.: Cornell University Press, 1976), pp. 218-20.

49. Selig Harrison, "India, Pakistan and the US--Part III," *The New Republic*, 7 September 1959, p. 12.

50. Kavic, *India's Quest*, pp. 105-6.

51. Ayub, *Friends Not Masters*, p. 163.

52. The military balance between India and China in the Himalayas is discussed in Leo E. Rose, "Conflict in the Himalayas," *Military Review* 43 (February 1963): 3-15.; K. Subrahmanyam, "1962: The Causes and the Lessons," *International Studies* 11 (October 1969): 149-66; and "Nehru and the India-China Conflict of 1962," in *Indian Foreign Policy: The Nehru Years*, ed. B. R. Nanda (Honolulu: University Press of Hawaii, 1976), pp. 102-30; and Yaacov Vertzberger, "India's Strategic Posture and the Border War Defeat of 1962: A Case Study in Miscalculation," *The Journal of Strategic Studies* 5 (September 1982), pp. 376-88.

53. M. S. Rajan, *India in World Affairs: 1954-56* (London: Asia Publishing House, 1964), pp. 478-85.

54. *Asian Recorder* 1 (29 October-4 November 1955), p. 493.

55. *Asian Recorder* 6 (21-27 May 1960), p. 3324.

56. *Asian Recorder* 8 (5-11 February 1962), p. 4412.

57. *Asian Recorder* 8 (19-25 March 1962), p. 4484.

58. Nehru, *Speeches*, vol. 3, p. 364.

59. Jawaharlal Nehru, *India's Foreign Policy: Selected Speeches, September 1946-April 1961* (New Delhi: Publications Division, 1961), p. 494.

60. Nehru's regime preferences and pragmatism in South Asia are discussed in S. D. Muni, "India's Political Preferences in South Asia," *India Quarterly* 31 (January-March 1975): 23-35.

CHAPTER FIVE

FROM WAR TO WAR: 1963-65

The 1962 Sino-Indian War forced India to reorder its priorities. The basic goals of growth, equity, and self-sufficiency remained as sacrosanct as ever. The government, though, reassessed India's security environment and the relative importance of material and military factors in attaining domestic and foreign policies. Nehru's original policy had been to concentrate on economic assets and then, in turn, increase India's military strength. After 1962, the government saw that India lacked the breathing-space to concentrate on the former. India's foreign policy had to have sufficient military strength to back it up in order to avoid a repeat of 1962.

As the shock of the 1962 War receded, the Indian government drew a number of strategic lessons from the war. It concluded, first of all, that China would remain hostile to India in the future and that military preparations would be needed to defend India's northern borders. Secondly, as Sino-Pakistani relations improved, the government concluded that military threats were likely from both countries. Indian strategic planning therefore had to take account of possible joint military threats from China and Pakistan. Thirdly, India's policy of nonalignment became less idealistic and more hard-boiled as the Indian government attempted to back up its foreign policy with appropriate policy instruments. Fourthly, the government concluded that Soviet friendship was essential. India had become dissatisfied with the level, type, and use of western military aid during and immediately after the 1962 War. It saw the aid as inadequate and unsuitable for India's military needs. Worse, it reduced India's international autonomy. Friendship with the USSR would provide India with much-needed military assistance, would reestablish India's nonalignment, and would help to counter Chinese and Pakistani power. Finally, the government concluded that the Himalayan buffer states (Bhutan, Nepal, and Sikkim) had greater bargaining power now that their strategic importance to India had increased. Consequently, India had to be more responsive to these states.

To wipe out the humiliation of 1962, to preserve India's autonomy in South Asia and the international system, and to apply the lessons of 1962, the Indian government began systematically to mobilize India's military potential. Pakistan could not ignore the consequences of this build-up, which threatened to change substantially the balance of power.

MATERIAL CAPABILITIES, POWER, AND INFLUENCE

Economic

Pakistan's economy grew at a faster rate than India from 1963 to 1965 (table 5.1). Mason notes that Pakistan's relative performance was the result of: the type of economic development strategy followed; improved agricultural performance brought about by changes in governmental policies; and differences in the amount of foreign aid to India and Pakistan.[1]

Table 5.1

India and Pakistan: Comparative Economic Growth, 1963-65
(in constant 1962 prices)

	1963	1965	Net change	Percent change
GNP (US $million)				
India	38,220	39,650	1,430	3.7
Pakistan	9,065	9,990	925	10.2
PER CAPITA GNP (US $)				
India	82	81	-1	-1.2
Pakistan	83	87	4	4.8

Source: United States, Department of State, Agency for International Development, *Gross National Product: Growth Rates and Trend Data* (Washington, D.C.: AID, 1966), Table 3b, p. 10.

The economic development strategies adopted by India and Pakistan in their five-year plans partly explain the differences in their economic growth rates in this period. When the Sino-Indian War broke out in October 1962, India was eighteen months into its Third Five-Year Plan (1961-66) and Pakistan midway into its Second Five-Year Plan (1960-65). India's Third Plan continued the development of heavy industry begun in the Second Plan (1956-61) and targetted a 70 percent increase in industrial production. The Indian Planning Commission set ambitious production targets for steel ingots, aluminum, machine tools, and installed power capacity.[2]

Mason attributes India's slower rate of growth of output in the 1960s to this program of heavy industrialization, which was characterized by "a long gestation period between initial investment and capacity operation of the included facilities and a high ratio of investment to output...The type of industrialization favored by Pakistan, on the other hand, had, characteristically, a much shorter gestation period and a much lower capital-output ratio. The results were visible in a very high rate of growth of industrial output in that country."[3]

In Pakistan, planning only really began in earnest in the Second Plan period (1960-65). As in the First Plan, the emphasis remained on increasing production in small- and medium-sized industries in jute, cotton products, and consumer goods rather than in heavy industry. Given Pakistan's scarce economic resources, the Planning Commission's strategy was to invest in industries giving high, immediate yields rather than small yields over a longer period of time.[4]

By mid-1965 the Pakistan Planning Commission held that the time was ripe to start a program of heavy industrialization. The economic gains from import substitution of consumption goods had been almost exhausted, Pakistan's domestic market could support intermediate and capital-goods industries, and, finally, heavy industrialization would increase Pakistan's economic self-reliance. The Third Plan (1965-70) increased allocations for basic metal and metal products industries, machinery and transport equipment, and petro-chemicals. This strategy was postponed because the September

War forced Pakistan's government to reorder its military and development expenditures.

The Pakistan government's increased emphasis on raising agricultural production in the Second Plan and good harvests also account for Pakistan's larger GNP growth rates in the period from 1963 to 1965. The new economic policies, which actually began in 1960, gave a greater role for market mechanisms, greater incentives to producers, and increased amounts of agricultural inputs, such as seed, fertilizer, plant protection, and water supplies. Such policy reforms can be traced to two factors: the emergence of a military government representing the rural middle class, which wanted land reform and greater agricultural inputs and incentives; and, second, American economic advice, which emphasized market incentives in agriculture.

By contrast, India's agricultural production stagnated between 1962 and 1967. A good monsoon led to bumper harvest in 1964-65, but this was followed in 1965-66 by a severe drought, which caused foodgrain production to fall by a disastrous 20 percent.[5]

Finally, Pakistan's larger GNP growth rate is also explained by differences in net foreign resource transfers to India and Pakistan. Between 1963 and 1965 Pakistan received twice the net foreign resources per person than did India.[6]

Pakistan's superior rate of economic growth had important consequences for the distribution of economic assets between India and Pakistan. High economic growth rates from 1960 to 1962 and 1965 to 1966 increased the confidence of Pakistan's government. Ayub saw Pakistan's success as an example for other developing nations to follow. His aim was to contrast Pakistan's predominantly free enterprise system with what he saw as India's cumbersome social democratic planning. In short, Pakistan's economic growth increased its ability to act as an economic countercore in South Asia.

By the beginning of 1963, Indo-Pakistani bilateral trade was a small part of their overall world trade. It was small because of the partition upheaval, the subsequent trade and political disputes, and the domestic economic planning for self-sufficiency. Nevertheless, traces of the former asymmetrical trading relationship remained (appendix 1). The Indian market was more important to Pakistan than Pakistan's market was to India. Pakistan's exports to India were mainly food and raw materials; most of India's exports to Pakistan were coal, iron and steel manufactures, machinery and building materials.[7]

Besides Pakistan's desire to avoid dependence on the Indian economy, other factors reduced bilateral trade. First, Pakistan's import substitution industrialization made both economies less complementary. Pakistan produced goods that it had formerly imported from India, and, indeed, competed with India in international markets in some of these goods, particularly jute manufactures and cotton piece goods.[8] Second, part of the foreign aid to India and Pakistan was tied aid, which required the purchase of goods and services from the donor. The effect was to move the Indian and Pakistan economies further apart. Finally, to cement political ties and to indicate its preferred regional alignments, Pakistan sought to increase its trade with underdeveloped export markets, such as China, Iran, and Turkey. After 1963 China became the most important buyer of Pakistan's raw cotton and an increasingly important buyer of its raw jute and jute manufactures.[9] On 21 July 1964, Pakistan, Iran, and Turkey established the Regional Cooperation for Development (RCD) in order to increase cooperation amongst these CENTO members in trade, travel, communications, and technical assistance.

Pakistan's economic growth increased its ability to act as economic countercore. But India still remained responsive to regional cooperation in South Asia. In 1964 the Indian Ministry of External Affairs established the Indian Technical and Economic Cooperation Program (ITEC) to supervise India's foreign aid program. This showed that the Indian government was increasingly aware of aid as an instrument of India's foreign policy.[10]

In summary, Pakistan's better economic growth resulted from high, immediate yields in consumer and light industries, better agricultural growth, and larger per capita foreign aid than India. These factors reduced India's economic power and correspondingly increased Pakistan's power as an economic countercore. Trade between the two countries stagnated and was overshadowed by trade with other, more preferred, countries. India's weaker economic growth, however, had little effect on the Indian government's responsiveness to economic cooperation. An important development in India's emergence as a core area was the creation of ITEC to oversee Indian foreign aid programs.

Nuclear Energy

Both countries made progress in training nuclear scientists, in establishing research centers, and in concluding agreements with foreign suppliers in nuclear power plants.

On 8 August 1963, Indian and American government officials reached agreement on building an enriched uranium boiling water reactor (BWR) at Tarapur, near Bombay. The supplier was General Electric Company of America, and construction of the reactor began in October 1964. The aim of this turn-key project was to show as quickly as possible to domestic and foreign audiences that nuclear power was both technologically and economically feasible in India. The cost, though, of this quick acquisition of nuclear technology was dependence on the United States for enriched uranium and spare parts.

The first stage of the Bhabha profile for eventual Indian nuclear self-sufficiency (natural uranium heavy water reactors producing plutonium for use in the second stage) actually began in December 1963 when the Indian and Canadian governments signed an agreement to build CANDU (Canadian Deuterium Uranium) reactors at Kota, Rajasthan. Canada agreed to train Indian scientists, engineers, and contractors in building and operating these reactors.

Other developments that increased India's self-sufficiency in the nuclear fuel cycle included the completion and formal opening of a chemical separation plant at Trombay in January 1965 and the government's decision to set up a Nuclear Fuel Complex at Hyderabad to produce nuclear fuel elements.

Pakistan's nuclear power program, although more modest than India's, made steady progress after 1962. In 1963 the PAEC, with the help of the IAEA set up a swimming-pool-type research reactor at PINSTECH. During the Second Five-Year Plan (1960-65), the PAEC trained some 350 nuclear scientists and engineers.[11] Finally, the PAEC began plans to build a 70 MWe nuclear power station at Rooppur in East Pakistan and a 132 MWe station at Karachi.[12] Overall, Pakistan still lagged considerably behind India in developing nuclear energy.

Political

The Indian and Pakistani political systems were a study in contrasts in this period. Pakistan had greater continuity in political leadership than India. Ayub attempted to consolidate the military's hold on Pakistan's political system by establishing his concept of guided-democracy. By contrast, Nehru never recovered personally from the shock of the defeat of 1962. Indians speculated about who was to replace him as Prime Minister. Lal Bahadur Shastri, became the new Prime Minister after Nehru's death in May 1964.

India's political system was subjected to a number of stresses and strains after 1962. The government had to divert expenditures to military uses and it had to raise additional resources for this. At the same time, the Congress Party declined in electoral appeal and organizational strength. The erosion of Congress's dominance that had begun in the 1962 general election continued after 1962. In his first year of office, Shastri, the new Prime Minister, faced several domestic and foreign problems. In January and February 1965, Tamils rioted in Madras against the central government's proposals to promote Hindi as an official language. Later in the same year, a disastrous harvest created food shortages, inflation, and a need to import foodgrains from abroad, threatening India's stability. Added to these domestic crises was steadily increasing tension with Pakistan.

For all these stresses and strains, India's political system showed resilience. The 1962 War strengthened national unity against the Chinese threat. The government's new economic measures may have been opposed by the those who bore the brunt of the new taxation, but the Indian elite and informed public opinion never questioned the need for increased military expenditures. The President of the Congress, Kamaraj, proposed that senior Congress leaders step down from their chief ministerships and parliamentary offices and devote themselves to organizational work. The *Kamaraj Plan* restored the status of the organizational wing of the party and gave it a say in the succession to Nehru.[13]

As Brecher notes, the Indian political elite showed several political skills in passing Nehru's mantle to Shastri.[14] These skills of forming and implementing a consensus were demonstrated by Shastri, who, despite being diminuitive in stature, showed firm leadership in creatively solving India's many domestic and foreign policy crises. Congress and opposition parties compromised over the role of Hindi and English as link languages between the states. In agriculture, the government began to improve the food distribution system and to make more agricultural inputs, such as high-yield seeds and fertilizers, available to farmers. In short, India's political system coped effectively with the mid-1960s crises.

The record of Pakistan's political system between 1963 and 1965 is an attempt by Ayub to institutionalize his concept of guided democracy. Pakistan's second constitution came into force on 8 June 1962, replacing martial law. A National Assembly and two Provincial Assemblies were then elected on a non-party basis by a small number of basic democrats who had themselves been nominated by Ayub. Ayub hoped that this presidential system would take root and that in time the basic democracies would expand political participation.

These hopes were unfulfilled. Ayub's system failed to take root partly because of Ayub's own political actions. He modified the constitution many times between 1962 and 1965. As a result, many Pakistanis saw it as a "plastic document" serving Ayub's personal interests.[15] Party politics reappeared in Pakistan when the National Assembly and two provincial assemblies were elected in 1962. No single federal party, however, emerged to overcome Pakistan's ethnic linguistic, and cultural cleavages.

Ayub's presidential system was especially unpopular with East Pakistanis, who saw it as an instrument of West Pakistani domination. Opposition parties in both wings demanded a parliamentary form of government with genuine federalism to safeguard the interests of Pakistan's provinces. To achieve these aims, the opposition made several attempts to unite against Ayub. The attempts failed. Some key opposition leaders, such the former Prime Minister, H. S. Suhrawardy, died. The opposition also failed to overcome its internal ideological and programmatic divisions.[16]

Ayub easily won the presidential election of 2 January 1965. He ran on the ticket of a revived (but nonetheless divided) Muslim League, hoping to use the name of the League to legitimize his candidacy. The Combined Opposition Parties' candidate was Miss Fatima Jinnah, the sister of the Quaid-i-Azam. Ayub won 63.3 percent of the valid votes in the election. He won a majority of votes in each province but did relatively better in West Pakistan. Still, the election returns showed strong opposition to Ayub from Pakistan's urban areas, particularly big cities like Karachi, Dacca, and Chittagong. By 1965 Ayub's constituency remained basically what it had been in 1963--the military, the rural middle classes, and the rural elite. A divided Muslim League was a poor instrument to broaden this constituency and it failed to mobilize support for Ayub amongst most of Pakistan's population.

In summary, the Indian and Pakistani political systems faced several challenges. The Indian system remained legitimate. It successfully managed political leadership, economic, and social crises. Evidently, Nehru's achievements (a working constitution, democratization, economic planning, and social reform) outlasted the author. In Pakistan, Ayub's apparent success in establishing guided democracy hid several underlying weaknesses. Party politics reappeared, and with it discontent with Ayub's government. Pakistan's political system had yet to acquire broad support from the population.

How did these changes in political capabilities affect Indo-Pakistani relations? It might seem that the Indian government was too absorbed with its many domestic problems to be responsive to Pakistan. But there is no evidence for this. The Indian government was able to manage its problems and to listen to Pakistani demands. The only problem was that the Indian government disliked what it heard: Pakistan was still insisting on self-determination for Kashmiris.

Another effect of India's political changes may have been to place in office a new Prime Minister inexperienced in foreign policy in general and in relations with Pakistan in particular. Yet once again, there is no evidence to show that Shastri's inexperience reduced the effectiveness of India's foreign policy. He took an active part in foreign policy and competently led Indian delegations to the Non-Aligned Summit Conference in Cairo in October 1964 and to the Commonwealth Prime Minister's Conference in London in July 1965. To be sure, gone was was Nehru's long experience of conducting relations with Pakistan, but Shastri closely followed Nehru's policies.(He offered Pakistan a No-War Pact in 1965.) Shastri more than compensated for his inexperience by firm leadership and by seeking expert advice in the security and foreign policymaking establishments. Under Shastri, India had its first External Affairs Minister, Swaran Singh. This was the first time that the offices of Prime Minister and Minister of External Affairs were held by different persons.

If India's political instability was more apparent than real, this was not the way that the instability was perceived in Pakistan. The Pakistani government saw India as weak. One official publication, for instance, noted that Pakistan could have taken advantage of India's domestic and foreign troubles to settle the outstanding disputes with India--the implication being that Pakistan would exploit these troubles if the Kashmir dispute was not solved to Pakistan's satisfaction.[17]

One final point about the impact of political changes in Pakistan on Indo-Pakistani relations: the martial law period (1958-62) increased the responsiveness of Pakistan's government, particularly its ability to negotiate with India on functional issues such as the Indus Waters. This responsiveness declined when party politics reemerged in Pakistan after the lifting of martial law in June 1962. The opposition was still aware that Ayub retained ultimate political power, but more open political activity allowed them to criticize his policies. When his policies towards India were attacked during the presidential campaign of 1965, Ayub defended them by presenting himself as the defender of Pakistan against an aggressive India. But this was merely election rhetoric, for in private Ayub sought improved relations with India.[18]

In summary, the major consequence of the political changes in India and Pakistan for their relations was that Ayub underestimated the strength of India's political institutions. India's apparent political instability only confirmed Ayub's other estimates of India's national power, particularly India's perceived military weaknesses.

MILITARY CAPABILITIES, POWER, AND INFLUENCE

After the 1962 Sino-Indian War, Indian defense planners saw two major security threats to India--China and Pakistan, either separately or in combination. Consequently, they expanded the armed forces to meet these increased threat perceptions.

There were two separate phases in this expansion. In the short-run, defense planners boosted India's defense capabilities. They increased the number of mountain divisions, and improved their equipment, communications, supply lines and training. The planners also rapidly expanded the officer corps. Once the planners were confident that some of the most obvious military weaknesses of 1962 had been remedied, they announced a long-run policy of expansion in early 1964 in India's First Five-Year Defense Plan. The total outlay of Rs. 5,000 crores ($10.4 billion) was to be spent on:

1. Creating a 825,000-man Army and modernizing its weapons and equipment.
2. Stabilizing the IAF at forty-five squadrons (a pre-1962 objective), reequiping it with modern aircraft, and providing ancillary facilities.
3. Keeping the Navy at approximately its present strength and replacing obsolete vessels with new foreign or Indian ships.
4. Building defense production plants to reduce dependence on foreign supplies.
5. Constructing and improving communications in the border areas to create an operational infrastructure.
6. Expanding research and development.[19]

By mid-1965 significant changes had taken place in the growth of military assets in India and Pakistan. The modernization program increased India's military expenditures, manpower, weapons and equipment, types of army units, and defense production. The program laid the potential for greater military assets, and added eleven Indian mountain divisions. The balance between India and Pakistan changed slowly, in infantry and armored divisions (appendix 3). India successfully equipped its army with small arms, artillery, ammunition, and other relatively simple stores. But the type and level of defense production between 1963 and 1965 was insufficient to meet the Indian government's strategy of preparing for a possible two-front war against Pakistan and China. For example, the new defense production program failed to meet India's military needs in the September 1965 Indo-Pakistan War. The licensed-produced lightweight fighter Gnats performed well in the war but not a single MiG-21 fighter or Vijayanta medium-tank had been produced. The production of aircraft under Soviet, British, and French licenses was disappointing from the viewpoint of quantity, aircraft performance, and the transfer of technology to India's aircraft industry. Of the six planned ordnance factories, only two were actually built by 1965.[20]

For its part, Pakistan's government perceived that the military balance was turning against Pakistan. It is now necessary to consider how the growth of military capabilities affected Indian and Pakistani military power and influence.

Some Pakistani government officials were undoubtedly satisfied by the defeat of India, their traditional enemy, at the hands of the Chinese. Wilcox writes, "The first reactions to Indian reverses in Pakistan were both sweet and sour. The sweet part, and it was savored, was the enjoyment one gets from seeing the neighborhood bully meeting a bigger bully. The sour part was in knowing that there was an even bigger bully in the neighborhood."[21]

Although the first part of the reaction is correct (leaving aside the question of whether India was a bully), Wilcox's view about the sour part is questionable. It is doubtful that the Pakistanis saw China as a threat, let alone a new neighborhood bully. The Pakistan government's interpretations of Chinese actions and capabilities after 1962 were limited. It saw nothing threatening about China's military presence in the Himalayas; indeed, on 2 March 1963, it signed a border agreement with China, in which it received a generous settlement of territory. If the Pakistani government ever feared the new "neighborhood bully," it was probably before 1959, when Ayub had offered India a joint defense of the subcontinent, which Nehru rejected. In all likelihood, the sour part about the 1962 War for Pakistan was the Indian government's consequent decision to build up its military strength.

Islamabad soon felt threatened by the largest and most rapid military build-up in independent India's history. From the statements made by Pakistani leaders at the time,[22] Pakistan's views of the military build-up may be summarized as follows. First, China's military attack in 1962 was punitive and limited and had resulted from Indian provocations. Secondly, India was unlikely to go to war with China after 1962. The Chinese had the military advantage in the Himalayas, and India was limited in the number of divisions that it could deploy against China. Thirdly, in the absence of a genuine threat, and given India's unwillingness to suffer the same fate as in 1962, the post-1962 Indian military build-up could only be directed against the smaller states of the subcontinent. The Indian bully would vent its frustrations on these smaller states, just as it had done in 1961, when an inability to make progress on the border dispute led India to invade, of all places, Portuguese Goa. Fourthly, the Chinese "bogey" was useful to India since it allowed her to extract economic sacrifices from its population and to receive arms assistance from the West under false pretences. Finally, India's increased strength--from both domestic and foreign sources--would only make the Indian government more intransigent on the Kashmir dispute.

In truth, the immediate effect of the 1962 War was to make the Indian government more receptive to negotiations with Pakistan over Kashmir. The United States and Britain, who were providing emergency military assistance to India, persuaded New Delhi to begin bilateral talks for resolving the Kashmir dispute. The talks began in Rawalpindi in late December and ended in May 1963 without any agreement on Kashmir.

Pakistan's government claimed that the talks failed because the Indian side had entered them in bad faith and because the Western powers had made insufficient use of their military and diplomatic leverage with India to press the Indian government to settle the Kashmir dispute.

The Indian government also charged Pakistan with lack of seriousness in negotiating. The Indian government argued that India had entered these talks because the British and American governments had suggested that a Kashmir settlement would strengthen India and Pakistan against the danger from China. The underlying assumption of these talks therefore was that Pakistan had the same perceptions of the Chinese threat that India did. This was incorrect because the Chinese and Pakistani governments were negotiating with each other over their common borders. After it had arrived in Rawalpindi on 26 December 1962 for the first round of talks, the Indian delegation was very surprised to learn that the Chinese and Pakistani governments had concluded an agreement in principle to demarcate their borders. India's delegation took this to be Pakistani pressure on India, but the delegation nonetheless continued with the talks in order to find a mutually acceptable solution to Kashmir.[23]

The Indian delegation soon discovered that Pakistan's position on Kashmir had remained unchanged. Even though India offered to eliminate the cease-fire line in Kashmir and convert it into an international boundary, Pakistan's only offer was that India could have part of Kathua district in Jammu province. For India, this showed that Pakistan was not serious in the negotiations.[24]

Pakistan failed to realize that Nehru, after the defeat by China, had suffered a severe blow--both at home and abroad--and that this made unilateral concessions to Pakistan less likely. India's bargaining power may have been weak, but it could not be coerced by Pakistan into accepting its inflexible demands in Kashmir.

The Pakistan government also gave little value to India's real concern for increasing its security in the wake of the 1962 War. Pakistan objected to the all-round increase in Indian military capabilities, and, specifically, to the raising of ten mountain divisions. As Ayub argued in his memoirs, "The fact of the matter is any [Indian] army meant for China would by the nature of things be so positioned as to be able to wheel round swiftly to attack East Pakistan. Thus both the Indian armies pose a grave threat to Pakistan."[25] Ayub's arguments seem convincing. The new Indian mountain divisions would also be a threat to what was, after all, the mountainous state of Kashmir. Nor could Pakistan's government have been reassured by the the fact that the Indian Army's High Altitude Warfare School was located at Gulmarg, only a few miles from the cease-fire line in Kashmir.

Pakistan's fears about the mountain divisions were real, but unfounded. Pakistan continued to enjoy the military advantage in Kashmir. Not all of the Indian mountain divisions were deployed in the state, and those that were had to defend both the border with China in Ladakh and the cease-fire line with Pakistan. Despite Ayub's claims, the mountain divisions were unsuitable for immediate operations in East Pakistan's flat, deltaic terrain. To use these divisions against East Pakistan, three conditions were necessary: India had to reach a border agreement with China, or China had to be deterred from attacking India, and the divisions had to be reorganized for fighting in the plains. After 1962 neither of the first two conditions were present for India to use the mountain divisions against Pakistan, even assuming that the Indian government wanted to do so. Finally, the major threat to Pakistan's security came not so much from these divisions but from the more general increase in Indian capabilities: in indigenous defense production, number of infantry divisions, firepower, and Indian air and naval capabilities.

Indian and Pakistani governments had fundamentally different threat perceptions. Pakistan saw the Indian build-up as being directed principally against it, while India saw it as meeting possible threats from Pakistan and China.

Adding to New Delhi's security problems after 1962 was China's detonation of a nuclear bomb in October 1964 and a further nuclear test in May 1965. This led Shastri's government to search for nuclear guarantees for the western powers against a country that had only recently fought against India. Shastri's policy was to renounce a similar Indian nuclear weapons program, even though some observers estimated that India had the capability to produce nuclear bombs in this period.[26]

With India's attention focused on China's conventional and nuclear capabilities, there was an asymmetry of attention at work in Indo-Pakistani relations. One Indian defense expert argues that Indian strategic planning in this period was poor and failed to anticipate the possible consequences of the Indian build-up on Pakistan.

> The Indian army has always conducted tactical war-gaming exercises--if we attack here with one corps the enemy will react thus, and so on. Strategic gaming is a much more sophisticated procedure--if we add 10 divisions how will Pakistan react in the next 5, 10, 20 years? The need for strategic gaming is obvious. Had it been conducted from 1963 onwards, it is possible that India could have anticipated that Pakistan, lacking the

resources to match the Indian build-up, would try to grab Kashmir.[27]

India did not ignore Pakistan. Rather its unresponsiveness arose from calculations of the opportunity costs of settling the dispute on Pakistan's terms. The Pakistan government insisted on a settlement that would give it most of Kashmir's territory. In return, India's ability to defend itself against China would not be increased but might even be reduced, more so because Sino-Pakistani relations were improving. Under these circumstances, the best that India could do was to repeat its offers of a No-War Pact and concentrate on developing its material and military assets. For Pakistan's government, this meant that the Kashmir dispute would be even more difficult to resolve once India had completed its military build-up. Pakistan feared the potential increase in the strength of the Indian armed forces. As long as the military balance had not turned against Pakistan, the Pakistan government believed that the Indian military could still be defeated in any test with Pakistan's armed forces.

Pakistan miscalculated the strength of India's social and political systems and the effectiveness of India's military. It also miscalculated India's hold on Kashmir's Muslims. This series of miscalculations led to war between the two countries in September 1965. To see why, it is necessary to examine, above all, the identitive relations between the two countries.

IDENTITIVE CAPABILITIES, POWER, AND INFLUENCE

Identitive relations between India and Pakistan deteriorated after 1962. Communal riots between Hindus and Muslims flared up in East Pakistan and the adjoining Indian states. Refugee movements from and to East Pakistan, which had declined between 1957 and 1962, now increased to pre-1957 magnitudes.[28] This communal conflict increased the distrust between Indian and Pakistani leaders and was one cause of the outbreak of the war between the two countries in September 1965.

Two major factors were responsible for the increase in communal conflict. First, from 1960 onwards the Indian government began evicting Muslims from West Bengal, Tripura, and Assam, arguing that they were illegal immigrants from Pakistan. The evictions increased after mid-1962, and by May 1964 the number of evictions totalled 164,746.[29] Pakistan's government protested that 95 percent of these Muslims were in fact Indians and that they were being evicted as part of a systematic Indian campaign to reduce East Pakistan's economic, social, and political viability.[30] The evictions did little to calm Pakistani fears that India ultimately intended to destroy Pakistan as an independent state.

Second, it was events in Kashmir in late 1963 that touched off the most serious outbreak of communal conflict. On 26 December 1963, someone stole a religious relic, a sacred hair of the Prophet Mohammed, from a mosque in Hazratbal in Kashmir. This led to rioting among Kashmiri Muslims and communal conflict in the Khulna district of East Pakistan. Communal conflict soon spread to Calcutta and back to East Pakistan. Hindu refugees coming into West Bengal, Madhya Pradesh, and Bihar brought tales of atrocities, which further inflamed communal relations in those states. On 26 March 1964, in one of his last broadcasts to the nation before his death in May 1964, Nehru appealed for communal calm in India and suggested to Ayub that Indian and Pakistani Home Ministers meet to curb the conflict.[31] The meeting took place in New Delhi from in April 1964 but broke down over the legal machinery for resolving the problem of the alleged illegal immigrants in India.

As always, Kashmir figured as the chief stumbling block to improved relations between India and Pakistan. The Pakistan government saw the integration of Kashmir into India as a challenge to Pakistan's national identity in South Asia. Indian policymakers, however, thought that Pakistan was using the Kashmir integration issue as a propaganda device to reinforce it cultural, religious, and hence political distinctiveness from India. Although the basic conflict between Indian secularism and Pakistani sectarianism was nothing new, identitive relations from 1963 to 1965 had two noticeable effects on overall bilateral relations: they led to an increase in tensions and the Pakistani government concluded that a Pakistani military intervention (either direct or covert) in Kashmir would receive popular support from Kashmiri Muslims.

THE SEPTEMBER 1965 WAR

Pakistani leaders went to war against India in 1965 for several reasons. First, direct negotiations with India failed in 1963, and so the Pakistanis saw little likelihood of diplomacy resolving the Kashmir dispute. Secondly, Pakistan's alliance with the United States and membership in CENTO and SEATO had failed to settle the dispute. Instead, the alliances only stiffened the Indian government's diplomatic and political resistance to Pakistani demands and earned the hostility of the USSR, which vetoed a Security Council resolution on Kashmir in 1962. It was thus up to Pakistan itself to take the military or diplomatic initiative to bring the dispute to world attention again. Thirdly, the war was a rational decision by Pakistan to resolve the Kashmir dispute by force before the military balance swung further in India's favor, especially in firepower, which the Pakistanis traditionally saw as their guarantee against Indian numerical superiority in manpower. Finally, Pakistan's government believed that the progressive integration of Kashmir into the Indian Union would make it more difficult to solve the dispute; India could present this integration as an accomplished fact. The 1964 religious rioting in Kashmir led some Pakistani decisionmakers to believe that Kashmiri Muslims would overwhelmingly support an armed Pakistani infiltration of Indian-held Kashmir. Such a strategy, if successful, would be less costly in Pakistani military losses and Indian retaliation than a direct Pakistani military invasion of Indian Kashmir. This strategy, which was mainly drawn up by Foreign Minister Bhutto, assumed that clashes between Indian and Pakistani military forces would be confined to the state of Jammu and Kashmir.

Armed clashes steadily increased between the two countries during 1964 and 1965. In April 1965, a limited conflict took place in the western border area known as the Rann of Kutch. The Indian and Pakistani governments had never demarcated the borders of this marshy area, which lay between Sind, Rajasthan, and Gujarat. When fighting broke out there in April 1965, the results were out of all proportion to the strategic value of the territory. Pakistan claimed military success, and this increased the confidence of its military and government leaders. After the conflict both sides mobilized their armed forces and became psychologically prepared for further conflict.

The most important military moves of the 1965 Indo-Pakistani War were Pakistan's infiltration of guerillas into Indian-held Kashmir in the first week of August, Pakistan's military attack in the Chaamb sector of the state on 1 September, and India's counterattack across the international boundary into West Pakistan on 6 September. All three military moves are surrounded by controversy.

In the first, the Pakistani authorities claimed that the guerillas--or "freedom fighters" as they called them--were armed Kashmiris. India immediately rejected this claim, arguing that the Pakistani government had planned the attack.

In the second, some military experts doubt that Pakistan's forces attacked in the Chaamb sector in order to cut off Indian forces in Kashmir. They note that the forces deployed in this Operation Grand-Slam were too small for that purpose.[32] Whether or not this was Pakistan's intention, the operation did escalate the conflict.

Shastri's government interpreted it as a military threat to Kashmir and responded by attacking across the international border, the third major move of the war. Here it is unclear if the Indian government intended to capture the major city of Lahore or to relieve Pakistan's military pressure on Kashmir. One school of thought in the Indian government did call for the occupation of a major Pakistani city to demonstrate Indian will. But if the aim was to capture Lahore for that purpose, then India failed. Pakistani armed forces strongly resisted at the Ichogil canal, which served as a defensive line for the city. By contrast, if the aim was more modestly to relieve pressure on Kashmir, then India succeeded.

Both sides suffered heavy losses in intense fighting in the air and on the ground.[33] Pakistan's armed forces rapidly ran out of ammunition, and India increasingly contained the Pakistani armed forces. Both sides agreed to accept a UN cease-fire resolution on 23 September 1965.

The war resulted in a military stalemate, but both sides could claim military, political, and diplomatic gains. India's political leadership "derived satisfaction from a number of sources: the infiltrators had not been able to rouse Kashmir to revolt; India's home-made weapons compared well with Pakistan's expensive imports; Pakistan's advantages from initiative had been destroyed; the armed forces shook off the memory of the Chinese mauling; communal incidents were completely absent; and democratic lay leaders could mobilize and organize as well as military presidents."[34] Similarly, Pakistani leaders could gain satisfaction from the superior performance of the the PAF and from the widespead international support that Pakistan received, particularly from Muslim nations.[35] Still, Pakistan's government failed militarily to capture Kashmir. As the status quo party in the dispute, India succeeded in maintaining its hold on the state.

CONCLUSION

Within three years of the Sino-Indian War of 1962, India was fighting its second war, this time against Pakistan. The causes of the 1965 War can be traced directly to the earlier conflict; the 1962 War resulted in India's program of military expansion and Pakistan's perceptions that India was militarily weak. These factors, plus the Pakistani government's view that India was socially, economically, and politically weak as well, were all responsible for Pakistan launching the September 1965 War. Pakistan's aim was to revise the political and territorial status of Kashmir. Despite the War's military stalemate, there were several important consequences for Indo-Pakistani relations, among them the balance of military power, which now shifted in India's favor following the September 1965 western arms embargo to India and Pakistan.

Notes

1. Edward S. Mason, *Economic Development in India and Pakistan* (Cambridge: Harvard Center for International Affairs, 1966), pp. 62-64.
2. Indian Planning Commission, *Third Five Year Plan* (New Delhi: Manager of Publications, 1961), pp. 55-56.
3. Mason, *Economic Development*, pp. 6-7
4. Pakistan, Planning Commission, *The Second Five Year Plan, 1960-65* (Karachi: Manager of Publications, 1961), pp. 7-8, 221-23.

5. India, Planning Commission, *Fourth Five Year Plan 1969-74* (New Delhi: Manager of Publications, 1970), p. 116.

6. Mellor defines net foreign resource transfer as a country's imports less exports. *The New Economics of Growth.* Pakistan received $5.16 net foreign resources per person; compared to $2.53 for India. International Monetary Fund, *International Financial Statistics*, vol. 23, December 1970 (Washington, D.C.: IMF, 1970), pp. 168-71, 254-57.

7. For an analysis of the commodity composition of Indo-Pakistan trade, see T. K. Jayaraman, "Intra-regional Trade in the Indian Subcontinent: 1962-70," *Foreign Trade Review* 11 (April-June 1976): 80-107.

8. Mellor, *New Economics*, pp. 210-11.

9. Pakistan, Central Statistical Office, *25 Years of Pakistan in Statistics 1947-1972* (Karachi: Manager of Publications, 1972), pp. 428-31.

10. Philip M. Phibbs, "India's Economic Aid Programs," *Current History* 54, 320 (April 1968), p. 237.

11. Pakistan, Planning Commission, *Third Plan*, p. 301.

12. Ibid.

13. Rajni Kothari, *Politics in India* (New Delhi: Orient Longman, 1970), p. 179.

14. Michael Brecher, Nehru's Mantle: *The Politics of Succession in India* (New York: Praeger, 1966), pp. 240-41.

15. Herbert Feldman, *From Crisis to Crisis: Pakistan 1962-1969* (London: Oxford University Press, 1972), pp. 32-33.

16. Ibid., pp. 68-79.

17. *Asian Recorder* 10 (2-8 September 1964), p. 6019.

18. Feldman, *From Crisis*, p. 75.

19. Details of the First Five Year Defense Plan are contained in Lorne J. Kavic, *India's Quest for Security: Defense Policies 1947-1965* (Berkeley and Los Angeles: University of California Press, 1967), pp. 192-93.

20. Raju G. C. Thomas, *The Defense of India: A Budgetary Perspective of Strategy and Politics* (Delhi: Macmillan Co. of India, 1978), p. 163.

21. Wayne A. Wilcox, *India, Pakistan, and the Rise of China* (New York: Walker & Co., 1964), p. 75.

22. These statements are contained in Zulfikar Ali Bhutto, *Foreign Policy of Pakistan: A Compendium of Speeches made in the National Assembly of Pakistan 1962-64* (Karachi: Pakistan Institute of International Affairs, 1964); and Mohammed Ayub Khan, *Pakistan Perspective* (Washington, D. C.: Embassy of Pakistan, n.d.)

23. Interview with Swaran Singh, San Francisco, California, 4 September 1983.

24. Ibid.

25. Khan, *Friends Not Masters*, p. 136.

26. Leonard Beaton, "Capabilities of Non-Nuclear Powers," in *A World of Nuclear Powers?* ed. Alistair Buchan (Engelwood Cliffs, N. J.: Prentice -Hall, 1966), p. 18.

27. Ravi Rikhye, "Nine Examples from recent Indian Experience, 1962-1980," in *Estimating Foreign Military Power*, ed. Philip Towle (New York: Holmes & Meier, 1982), p. 205.

28. Indian Commission of Jurists, *Recurrent Exodus of Minorities from East Pakistan and Disturbances in India* (New Delhi: Indian Commission of Jurists, 1965), p. 15.

29. G. W. Choudhury, *Pakistan's Relations with India 1947-1966* (New York: Praeger, 1968), p. 179.

30. Ayub Khan, First of the month broadcast, 1 May 1964, in *Ayub Soldier and Statesman: Speeches and Statements (1958-1965) of Field Marshal Mohammad Ayub Khan, President of Pakistan* ed. Rais Ahmed Jafri (Lahore: Mohammed Ali Academy, 1966), p. 229.

31. For texts of the Nehru-Ayub correspondence, see *Asian Recorder* 10 (15-21 April 1964), pp. 5774-75.

32. Edgar O'Ballance, "The India-Pakistan Campaign, 1965," *The Journal of the Royal United Services Institution* 111, 644 (November 1966), p. 332.

33. O'Ballance writes: "Published casualty figures are..also extremely conflicting...Pakistan admits to losing 1,030 killed, 2,171 wounded, and 630 missing (all during the period 1st to 23rd September) but claims that India suffered 9,500 killed, 11,000 wounded, and 1,700 missing. In November (1965) India admitted losing 2,212 killed, 7,636 wounded, and 1,500 missing; but refrained from commenting upon Pakistan's casualty claims." Ibid., p. 335.

34. W. H. Morris-Jones, "India: The Trial of Leadership," *Asian Survey* 6 (February 1966), p. 74.

35. Khalid Bin Sayeed, "1965--an epoch-making year in Pakistan--general elections and war with India," *Asian Survey* 6 (February 1966): 76-85.

CHAPTER SIX

INDIA EMERGES AS A CORE AREA: 1965-71

The 1965 War had caught India at the beginning of its long-term military modernization program. Pakistan had launched the war for this very reason: to settle the Kashmir dispute before India's military power turned irreversibly against Pakistan. The war ended in a military stalemate, but it was nonetheless a political defeat for Pakistan, the revisionist power. After 1965 the material and military balance of power turned even futher against Pakistan, culminating six years later in India's decisive defeat of Pakistan in the Bangladesh War. India succeeded in 1971 because it effectively mobilized its material and military resources between 1965 and 1971.

THE TASHKENT DECLARATION

On several occasions during the 1965 War, the Soviet Union offered to mediate the Indo-Pakistani dispute. The Soviet Union suggested that all three countries meet at Tashkent in Soviet Central Asia or any other Soviet city. Shastri accepted the offers on 23 November for three main reasons: to formalize the cease-fire and to prevent further outbreaks of fighting with Pakistan; to encourage a political solution to the Kashmir dispute without sacrificing India's legal, diplomatic, and political position on Kashmir; and, finally, to soften Western criticism that India was the belligerent in the 1965 War. For his part, Ayub accepted the Soviet offers for two reasons: to strengthen his domestic position, which had been weakened by the indecisive outcome of the war; and to gain diplomatic leverage against India in order to offset Pakistan's military failures and the Western arms embargo.

Soviet, Indian, and Pakistani leaders met at Tashkent on 4 January 1966. The Indian delegation pressed for a No-War Declaration between India and Pakistan, and most of the discussions that took place revolved around this issue. Both sides held to the positions originally staked out by Nehru and Liaquat Ali Khan in the No-War discussions of 1950-51. The Indian side wanted a declaration renouncing force as a method of resolving bilateral disputes. The Pakistani side resisted this. At the opening session of the conference, Ayub insisted that he would sign such a declaration only if the Kashmir dispute was settled first, saying, "A No War agreement between nations can work only if it is adopted after taking concrete steps for resolving the disputes which divide them. And disputes can be resolved only in a spirit of conciliation."[1] With deadlock on Kashmir, the No-War Declaration talks collapsed. In the end, both sides only reaffirmed their adherence to the UN Charter in abjuring force. The Tashkent Declaration mentioned Kashmir but only to state that both sides had set forth their respective positions on it.

In the Tashkent Declaration of 10 January 1966, the Indian and Pakistani sides resolved "to restore normal and peaceful relations between their countries and to promote understanding and friendly relations between their peoples," in the interests of the "welfare of the 600 million people of India and Pakistan."[2] Under the general provisions of the document, both sides agreed to "consider measures towards the restoration of economic and trade relations, communications as well as cultural relations between India and Pakistan, and to take measures to implement the existing agreements between India and Pakistan." (Article VI.) Other provisions called for discussion of outstanding disputes (refugees, illegal immigration, the return of assets seized during the 1965 War and so forth) and the creation of joint Indo-Pakistani bodies for consultation and cooperation.

The Declaration also had a number of specific provisions. First, by 25 February 1966 both countries were to withdraw all armed personnel to the positions that they held before 5 August 1965 (Article II). Secondly, both sides were to discourage hostile propaganda against the other and instead to promote favorable views of the other (Article IV). Thirdly, diplomatic relations were to be resumed

(Article V). Finally, they were to repatriate prisoners of war (Article VIII).

Both sides made progress in implementing the specific provisions of Tashkent. The top military officers of both countries met and agreed on several measures, including the release of prisoners of war, the number of troops to be left by both sides in Jammu and Kashmir, and the resumption of overflights of military aircraft on Indian and Pakistani territory. Both governments also lifted the ban on civilian overflights and took further measures to implement the Tashkent Declaration. Within two years they had resumed diplomatic relations, reopened telephone, postal, and telecommunication links, and returned shipping seized in the 1965 War.[3] Military expenditures declined in current and real terms in these two years.[4]

These measures merely restored relations between the two countries to their pre-1965 level. The Indian government found it much more difficult to restore the level of trade and to implement those articles of the Tashkent Declaration that called for wider regional economic cooperation. In March 1966, the Indian Foreign Minister, Swaran Singh, led a high-powered delegation to Islamabad to discuss regional cooperation. Whereas the Indian side was interested in buying natural gas, cement, and cotton from Pakistan in return for iron and steel, the Pakistani side, led by Bhutto, opened the talks by immediately raising the issue of Kashmir. Bhutto saw little purpose in cooperation without a resolution of the Kashmir dispute.[5] India came away empty-handed. On 26 May 1966, the Indian cabinet unilaterally lifted the ban on trade with Pakistan. Indian officials admitted that this decision would have no effect on bilateral trade unless Pakistan reciprocated by lifting its ban on exports to India.[6] The ministerial talks collapsed in May 1966. Indo-Pakistani relations continued to be deadlocked by the unbridgeable positions on Kashmir. Yet significant changes were taking place in the national capabilities of India and Pakistan that were to alter the balance of power between them.

MATERIAL CAPABILITIES, POWER, AND INFLUENCE

Economic

The immediate post-Tashkent period coincided with a severe Indian economic crisis. A disastrous drought in 1965-66, estimated to be India's worst in this century, reduced foodgrain production by 17 million tons, a decrease of 19 percent.[7] The monsoon of 1966-67 was also deficient, and although foodgrain production increased by 2.6 percent in 1966-67, this was still insufficient to restore per capita availability of foodgrains to their pre-1965 levels.[8]

The economic crisis reduced India's ability to act as a core area. The drop in foodgrain production made it dependent on food imports, which reached post-independence record levels: 7.5 million metric tons in 1965, 10.4 million in 1966, and 8.7 million in 1967.[9] The decline of India's jute and cotton production placed India in a much weaker position towards Pakistan. The Indian economy needed Pakistani raw jute and cotton to make up for domestic shortages. Pakistan, on the other hand, was self-sufficient in raw jute and cotton production and their manufactures. Moreover, Pakistan's government was unwilling to increase trade with India and resisted all appeals to do so, even after the Indian government lifted trade restrictions on 26 May 1966. As noted earlier, the Pakistani government was unwilling politically to restore trade relations as long as the Kashmir dispute was unresolved. The Pakistani government found that the trade cut-off had no significant effect on Pakistan's balance of payments and, indeed, that the balance of payments actually improved during the cut-off.[10]

The post-1965 trade decline was the steepest since the 1949-50 devaluation controversy. There were, however, two major differences between 1949 and 1965. First, the value of bilateral trade in 1965 was smaller, and thus the suspension of trade had a smaller effect on the two economies. Second, unlike 1949, when trade had been resumed within six months, albeit at a lower level, the period from 1965 to 1971 saw the longest continuous cut-off of trade between the two countries. Indo-Pakistani relations sank to their lowest level since independence.

India's economy recovered from the crisis of 1965-66. The Indian government gave greater priority to agriculture in the development process. This was necessary in order to achieve domestic economic growth, political stability, and national self-reliance. The government adopted some of the same policies that had been so successful in Pakistan's Second Five-Year Plan (1960-65): greater emphasis on incentives to producers (such as minimum floor prices and input subsidies) and making available more inputs of seeds, fertilizer, plant protection, and water.

Although Pakistan was certainly the innovator in these agricultural policies, both countries experienced their Green Revolutions at about the same time. These were made possible not only by policy changes but also two other factors: the introduction of high-yield varieties of wheat and rice and an increase in irrigation brought about by the new Indus Waters projects. The benefits of the Indus Waters Treaty were paying off for both countries; their Green Revolutions would have been impossible without the earlier example of regional cooperation.[11]

India was more successful than Pakistan in sustaining its Green Revolution and rate of economic growth. In late 1969 and early 1970, the Pakistani economy began to recover from the industrial and civil unrest that accompanied the downfall of Ayub in 1968-69. Unfortunately, a number of man-made and natural events then battered the economy. A disastrous cyclone and flooding in East Pakistan in 1970 and drought in West Pakistan reduced agricultural production in both wings. The following year economic production fell sharply in the eastern wing as a result of political unrest.

As Pakistan's economy faltered, India steadily acquired some of the characteristics of a core area, particularly rising economic capabilities in agriculture and industry. Agricultural productivity increased. The absolute production increases, however, were insufficient to increase per capita food availability in the country. The Green Revolution was still young as shown by its uneven impact in different crops and regions of the country. In sum, India had made impressive agricultural gains from 1966 to 1971 but was still short of its potential.

India's heavy industrialization also seemed to be paying off. By the end of 1969, many of the industrial projects begun in the previous plans were completed. Industrial capacity increased in iron and steel, aluminum, machine tools, and petrochemicals.[12] The Indian Planning Commission, in its Fourth Five-Year Plan document (1969-74), noted India's uneven industrial progress between 1961 and 1969. But it added that "in a wide range of industries, it will be possible merely by the *fuller utilization of existing capacity* [italics added]--as distinguished from new investment--to achieve substantially higher levels of production in the initial years of the Fourth Plan."[13]

In contrast, by 1971, Pakistan had made little progress in building a heavy industrial infrastructure. Some plants were built but capacity and production increases were small. Pakistan lagged behind India mainly because, after the 1965 War, the Pakistani government postponed the industrialization strategy of the Third Plan. In retrospect, this was a mistake; Pakistan would have been much stronger industrially in 1971 if it had continued with its original plans to industrialize. But from the perspective of the Pakistani leaders it was more important to maximize short-term economic gains and foreign exchange in order to pay for immediately needed weapons imports and to make up for shortages in foreign exchange. This meant trading off some of the long-term gains in industrial production.

Nuclear Energy

In the period from 1965 to 1971, India maintained its nuclear lead over Pakistan. The nuclear program, however, met several difficulties. In 1966 Dr. Homi Bhabha, the nuclear czar, died in a plane crash in Switzerland. This deprived the Indian nuclear power lobby of its most powerful voice. The two reactors at Tarapur, ordered on a turn-key basis from General Electric of America, went into commercial operation in October 1969, but with some initial engineering and construction problems. As for the other nuclear power stations, the work on a 200 MWe CANDU reactor (RAPP-1) in Rajasthan was nearing completion, and India's government ordered three additional power reactors. By the end of 1971, India's installed capacity was 396 MWe (appendix 8).

Pakistan's nuclear power program, while more modest than India's, made steady progress. The swimming-pool-type research reactor at PINSTECH went critical in December 1965. A CANDU reactor (KANUPP-1) was built near Karachi and went critical in 1969. It was originally designed to go into commercial operation by the end of 1970 but only did so in 1972. The PAEC also planned a nuclear reactor in East Pakistan. A Soviet study team, however, concluded that it would be uneconomic, and so funding for it fell through.

Political

The most immediate problem facing the Indian political elite after the Tashkent Conference was finding a successor to Shastri who died in the USSR on 11 January 1966, within hours of signing the Tashkent Declaration with Pakistan. The Congress Party now had to choose its second Prime Minister within two years. It chose Indira Gandhi, Nehru's daughter. The Party hoped that Mrs. Gandhi would give it greater electoral appeal in the next general elections because of the aura surrounding the Nehru name. In any case, the political bosses in the Congress--the "Syndicate"--were opposed to the candidacy of Morarji Desai. They believed that Mrs. Gandhi would be more pliable.

The problems facing Mrs. Gandhi were daunting. The most pressing problems were economic, specifically those of agriculture. As noted earlier, India's political leadership responded to the severe economic crisis of 1965-67 by changing agricultural policy. The new policy emphasized increased agricultural production, with the government providing more inputs and greater incentives to farmers. In broader economic policy, the government devalued the rupee on 6 June 1966 to make India's exports more competitive. Because the economic crisis upset planning assumptions and targets, the government had to postpone the start of India's Fourth Five-Year Plan, which was supposed to go into operation on 1 April 1966. This "plan holiday", as it was called, was the first break since 1951 in the series of Five Year plans.

India's general elections, though, could not be postponed. These were held on schedule in February 1967. The Indian electorate was dissatisfied with Congress's nonperformance in the economy and social reform. It gave the Congress Party its worst electoral setback since independence. Congress remained the majority party at the national level but lost 78 seats in the Lok Sabha and found its majority reduced from 219 to 23.[14] In the state assembly elections held at the same time, the Congress lost its majorities in eight states--Bihar, Kerala, Madras, Orissa, Punjab, Rajasthan, Uttar Pradesh, and West Bengal.

How did these political developments--succession, the economic policy changes, and the 1967 general elections--affect the Indian government's policies toward Pakistan? First, Shastri's death at Tashkent seemed to legitimize the policy of normalization of relations with Pakistan to the Indian public. According to Leo Rose, even those sections of the Indian administration opposed to concessions in the Declaration were forced to subdue their criticisms.[15] Secondly, the new Prime Minister, Mrs. Gandhi, was in a weak domestic political position and unable to carry out new initiatives regarding Kashmir, particularly concessions to Pakistan. As one Indian observer writes, "Indira Gandhi, when she stepped into Shastri's shoes, was in a much weaker position than even Shastri would have been. After having been elected over the opposition of Morarji Desai, who represented the hard-liners in the Congress Party, she could not dare to take risks by adopting a bold policy vis-à-vis Pakistan."[16]

Thirdly, domestic opposition to the devaluation of the rupee was intense. The opposition parties, both left and right, accused Mrs. Gandhi of bowing to American pressure in devaluing the rupee. Concessions to Pakistan were therefore unlikely, as Mrs. Gandhi could hardly afford to lay herself open again to the charge of sacrificing India's national interests. Finally, the 1967 general election weakened the government and made it less able to undertake new initiatives in foreign policy. Ayoob points out that the government was not in "a position to adopt a more flexible attitude toward Pakistan, Kashmir or Sheikh Abdullah, after the elections. In fact, on 10 May, 1967, in her first major statement on Indo-Pakistan relations after the elections, Indira Gandhi stated that India was prepared to talk with Pakistan on any subject, but 'there is nothing to negotiate on Kashmir.'"[17]

In Pakistan, meanwhile, the 1965 War increased domestic political instability. During the war, the Pakistani public had been led to believe by their government's propaganda that Pakistan was winning the war. When the government accepted a cease-fire on 22 September 1965, many Pakistanis were completely surprised. They could not understand why a cease-fire was necessary if the war was going their way and a military solution to the Kashmir dispute was at hand. Not only was Ayub blamed for failing to bring the war to a successful conclusion; Pakistani public opinion was also unprepared for the Tashkent Declaration's failure to win concessions from India over the Kashmir dispute. As a result, the 1965 War and Tashkent both weakened Ayub's political position. Severe rioting against the Declaration took place in January 1966 in West Pakistani cities. This further weakened Ayub's bargaining position.

East Pakistanis, too, lost confidence in the military government after the 1965 War. The military government had left only one division to defend East Pakistan. Even though most of the fighting took place on the India-West Pakistan borders, East Pakistanis felt that they had been left completely defenseless. This only added to their other grievances of economic, cultural, and political subordination to West Pakistan. On 23 March 1966, Sheikh Mujib, leader of the East Pakistan Awami League, presented his party's list of six demands for greater provincial autonomy. Each of the "Six Point" demands highlighted the particular grievances of the Awami League and the broad measures to be taken to rectify them.

The first point demanded a federal, parliamentary constitutional system based on direct elections and universal adult suffrage. The second demand was that federal powers should be limited to defense and foreign affairs; all other powers should reside in the states. Third, in order to prevent the flight of capital from East to West Pakistan, the Awami League demanded two separate but convertible currencies for each wing. Fourth, the states should have taxation and revenue collection powers. Fifth, the states should control their foreign exchange earnings, foreign trade, and commercial relations. Finally, the Awami League demanded that East Pakistan should have its own militia or paramilitary force.[18]

Ayub responded to the Six Points in four ways. First, he increased government expenditures in the eastern wing, hoping to meet some of the East Pakistani economic grievances. Secondly, he attempted to increase the cultural integration of the two wings, which meant reducing the identitive ties between East Pakistan and India. Thirdly, he attempted to rebuild the Muslim League as a mass organization and politically unifying party. Finally, he intensified coercion against Eastern opposition leaders.[19] On 23 April 1966, the government arrested Mujib and then tried him for sedition. Later it accused him of plotting with India to destroy Pakistan. It claimed to have evidence of a conspiracy between the jailed Mujib, his aides, and Indian agents operating in East Pakistan and the Indian border town of Agartala. (This came to be known as the "Agartala Conspiracy.") Ayub's contradictory combination of carrots and sticks failed to end the underlying regional discontent. If anything, the repression and charges of the Agartala Conspiracy only strengthened the East Pakistani movement for greater regional autonomy.

After 1967 a distinct change took place in the political assets of India and Pakistan. India, under Mrs. Gandhi, acquired a stronger government; Pakistan's political system disintegrated.

Although the 1967 general election reduced the Congress Party's dominance at the center and in the states, it also increased Mrs. Gandhi's personal political position in one respect: many of the members of the so-called Syndicate were defeated, including Kamaraj, S. K. Patil, and Atulya Ghosh. As noted earlier, the Syndicate had chosen Mrs. Gandhi as Prime Minister in 1966 because it believed that it could manipulate and control her. Mrs. Gandhi proved otherwise. In the three years after the 1967 general election, she consolidated her power by outmaneuvering her rivals, above all the conservative Finance Minister, Morarji Desai. To strengthen her power in the Congress and in the county, Mrs. Gandhi formulated a populist strategy, which included an appeal to India's socially disadvantaged (the untouchables, Muslims, the poor, and so forth), bank nationalization, and abolition of the princely privy purses. These leftist policies and personal differences in the Congress leadership over the election of the next President of India caused the Congress Party to split in 1969. But through a coalition at the center of loyal

Congressmen (the Congress (R)), the Communist Party of India (CPI), and the Tamil Regional Party (DMK), Mrs. Gandhi kept a working majority in the Lok Sabha.

In the fifth general election, held in March 1971, the opposition parties could do little more than agree on the slogan of *Indira hatao* (stop Indira). Mrs. Gandhi changed this to the campaign slogan of *garibi hatao* (stop poverty), thereby setting the terms of the electoral debate and at the same time shrewdly gauging the priorities and mood of the electorate.

The "Indira Wave" in the 1971 general election overwhelmed the opposition. The noncommunist opposition lost heavily, while the two communist parties--the CPI and the CPM--kept their electoral strength and actually gained seats. The Congress (R) won 67.9 percent of Lok Sabha seats on a popular vote of 43.6 percent.[20] This gave it a majority of 69 seats and an absolute majority for the first time since the Congress split of 1969.

In contrast to the strengthening of the political center in India, Pakistan's political center weakened. If Ayub's regime faced threats from East Pakistan on the issue of interregional equity, the regime ultimately fell on the issue of social equity within the western wing. The origins of the unrest can be traced to Pakistani economic planning. Ever since independence, Pakistani governments had followed an economic development strategy stressing the physical output of goods and services rather than social infrastructure, such as education, health, and housing.[21] This strategy did produce rapid economic growth but at the cost of increased class tensions and social unrest.

Civil unrest began at the start of the officially-sponsored celebrations for the "Development Decade" (1958-68). Thereafter, political agitations against the regime increased. Student demonstrations began in Rawalpindi in November 1968 and soon developed into a full-fledged political movement against Ayub's regime. The opposition parties formed the Pakistan Democratic Movement (PDM) and the Democratic Action Committee (DAC), with the main aim of restoring democracy in Pakistan. Several months of widespread civil unrest forced Ayub in March 1969 to agree to restore a democratic, federal, and parliamentary system, But these concessions were too late to save his regime. Faced with loss of support from the armed forces and a breakdown of administration, Ayub stepped down as President on 25 March 1969 and handed over power to General Yahya Khan, Commander-in-chief of the Army.

Ayub's political system collapsed with his downfall. The new Martial Law regime immediately abrogated the 1962 Constitution, banned political activity, and dismissed national and provincial assemblies and cabinets. Still, the new regime differed from the first martial law regime (1958-62) on the question of restoring democracy. The new regime clearly saw itself as temporary until a civilian government could be democratically elected. The agitations against Ayub convinced the military that a return to civilian rule was inevitable. In a sense, the military was merely carrying out Ayub's March 1969 concessions to the opposition. The military knew that these concessions would be difficult to reverse. Thus on 28 November 1969, Yahya announced that the ban on political activity would be lifted from 1 January 1970 and that elections would be held in October 1970. But the new regime went further than Ayub: it dissolved the One Unit Scheme and conceded representation in the new National Assembly on the basis of population rather than on parity between the wings. This gave East Pakistani members a majority of seats in the National Assembly.

The military's conditions for the transfer of power were set forth in greater detail, although not necessarily in greater clarity, in the Legal Framework Order (LFO) of 31 March 1970. This document outlined the distribution of seats in the national and provinical assemblies, the principle of their election, their rules of procedure, the time limit for framing the Constitution, and measures for the final authentication of the Constitution by the President. The LFO also set the general principles of the Constitution, which had to ensure Pakistan's independence and integrity, preserve Islamic values, adhere to democracy, ensure a balance between federal and provincial powers, and promote social, and particularly, regional equality.[22]

Pakistan held its first direct national election in December 1970, nineteen years after India's first general election and twenty-three years after Pakistan's independence. The election results showed that the country was divided regionally and politically. In the West,

Bhutto's Pakistan People's Party (PPP) ran on the platform of Islamic socialism at home and unremitting hostility to India. It captured 37.6 percent of the western vote and 88 of the 144 western seats. In the east, Mujib's Awami League ran on the platform of the Six Points for greater provincial autonomy. It captured 74.9 percent of the eastern vote and an astounding 167 of the 169 eastern seats. Because East Pakistan had a majority of National Assembly seats (53.99 percent), the Awami League's victory in the east also translated itself into a national majority.[23] Mujib expected to become the next Prime Minister of Pakistan.

The ensuing negotiations for a new government and Constitution involved three major actors: the Awami League, the PPP, and the military government. The Awami League interpreted its victory as a mandate for greater provincial autonomy, perhaps even confederation. The PPP also drew attention to the magnitude of its electoral victory. By emerging as the largest single party in the west, it demanded a voice in the formation of the new government and Constitution. In other words, the Awami League would have to bargain with it. Finally, the military had a direct stake in the triangular negotiations. As it made clear in the LFO, the military was sworn to defend Pakistan's territorial integrity and unity. It also sought to preserve its corporate interests,[24] and thus could not be neutral in the negotiations. In addition, a faction of the military leadership had misgivings over the democratic development of Pakistan since March 1969 and could not adjust itself to the prospect of a reduced influence for West Pakistan, particularly the Punjab, in Pakistan's political system.

Negotiations among the three parties took place in early 1971 but without any agreement on the composition of the new government. Bhutto failed to persuade Mujib to modify his Six Points or to share power at the center. Bhutto's role was that of a spoiler. He feared that the Awami League would make a coalition at the center with the smaller West Pakistani political parties and that this would erode the PPP's power base in the Punjab and Sind.[25] On 15 February 1971, knowing that he had political support within the military leadership, Bhutto announced a boycott of the National Assembly until the Awami League granted his demands for power-sharing. At this point, Yahya allowed Bhutto to place a virtual veto on the meeting of the National Assembly. On 6 March 1971, the military government postponed the National Assembly, and this renewed fears in East Pakistan that the military government would overturn the democratic election results by force. Widespread agitation erupted in East Pakistan, leading to the breakdown of civil administration and the passing of de facto political authority to the popular Awami League. The military government continued to negotiate with the Awami League, but at the same time it sent troop reinforcements to the East. Whether or not Yahya negotiated in good faith, the fact remains that the negotations came to an end on 23 March. Two days later, Yahya left for West Pakistan, having given orders for a military solution to the political crisis.

The 25 March military crackdown and the large loss of life accompanying the brutal way in which it was carried out, put an end to the political discussions and led to the start of a Bengali guerilla resistance against the military authorities. Henceforth, the guerillas and those members of the Awami League who had escaped imprisonment demanded national independence rather than autonomy for East Pakistan. The events from the military crackdown to the Indian invasion of East Pakistan in December 1971 will be discussed later in this chapter. But before doing so, it is necessary to conclude this section on political factors and then look at military and identitive factors leading up to the Bangladesh War.

How did the contrasting political development of India and Pakistan between 1967 and 1971 affect their mutual responsiveness? To begin with, it could be argued that both governments were too absorbed with domestic problems to pay attention to each other. Certainly, the problems were large for both of them. India had a weak central government and unstable state governments, and it was only from 1970 onwards that Mrs. Gandhi's political strength increased. Meanwhile, Pakistani governments faced mounting problems of East Pakistani regionalism and social discontent in West Pakistan.

The problems may have been large, but both countries continued to pay attention to each other. On Independence Day in 1968, Mrs. Gandhi reiterated her offer of a No-War Pact, claiming that "it would enable both countries to concentrate on the solution of internal problems and the strengthening of their economies."[26] Ayub replied that such a Pact had to be supplemented by specific measures to solve Indo-Pakistani disputes, and particularly that eternal obstacle--Kashmir. Ayub also made it clear that he still saw India as Pakistan's major security threat.[27]

If there was little progress in Indo-Pakistani relations, it was because progress involved domestic costs for both governments. Mrs. Gandhi did seek to normalize relations, but was in weak position to offer any concessions. As one Indian writer notes, "Things became worse when the Congress was divided into two organizations towards the end of 1969. Under such conditions, it was not possible for Indira Gandhi to any longer go out of her way to mend forces (sic) with Pakistan more so when Pakistan was in no mood to show any flexibility towards India."[28]

This suggests that it was the Pakistani rather than the Indian government that was the major obstacle to integration. Pakistani governments increasingly blamed India for their internal political problems, as shown by the Agartala Conspiracy. Moreover, some sections of the military were still strongly anti-Indian and felt cheated of the fruits of the 1965 War. The rise of Bhutto in opposition to Ayub in this period also affected Indo-Pakistani relations, for Bhutto took advantage of discontent against Ayub's foreign policy, particularly Ayub's policies towards India. And after Ayub's downfall in 1969, Bhutto continued his anti-Indian stance. During the general election of 1970 he and other West Pakistani politicians attempted to take the credit for starting the 1965 War. The general political atmosphere in West Pakistan, then, was one of continuing hostility towards India. Not surprisingly, Pakistani governments rebuffed repeated Indian offers of regional integration.

In summary, from 1965 to 1971 the Indian and Pakistani political systems were buffeted by similar sets of problems--political succession; maintaining social order, political stability and national integration; and resolving interregional and interclass disputes. But if the problems were similar, the way in which the political elites coped with them was different. Indeed, the directions taken by the two political systems were completely opposite. Whereas Pakistan began this period with a seemingly stable quasi-constitutional political system, it ended the period in political instability, the return of direct military rule, and national fragmentation. India, on the other hand, began this period with an untested Prime Minister and ended it with the same Prime Minister but one whose political power had increased after 1970. This pattern of political development accounts for the lack of responsiveness between the two countries. Although India repeatedly offered regional integration, Pakistani governments rebuffed these offers, seeing them as harmful to Pakistan's interests and to their own political interests.

MILITARY CAPABILITIES, POWER AND INFLUENCE

In this period a marked change took place in the balance of military power between India and Pakistan. India's defense efforts bore fruit in qualitative and quantitative improvements in its armed forces. By contrast, Pakistan's military capabilities declined sharply.

By 1971 the Indian army had reached and surpassed the force expansion targets set in 1964. It improved its capability of fighting a two-front war against Pakistan and China. Not only was the army larger and better-equipped, it was also better organized, trained, and more diversified in its skills. Such improvements, plus the government's long-term commitment to army modernization, all increased the Indian army's skill and effectiveness.

Pakistan doubled the number of its army divisions (appendix 3), but the Indian army could devote all of its time and attention to training, planning, and organization; Pakistan's army had to govern an increasingly unstable political system. It fell behind the Indian army in weapons and equipment, particularly in firepower. The Western arms embargo taxed the army's inventories of spare parts and this impaired its operational readiness and training. The Pakistan army changed from a largely American-equipped army to one relying on other foreign sources--French, Chinese, and Soviet. This increased number of sources reduced the army's standardization of arms and equipment.

The shift in balance of power was even more marked in air and naval forces. The size of the Indian Air Force almost tripled from 28,000 men before the 1965 War to 80,000 in mid-1971. This increase resulted from the stepped-up training programs after 1962 and the large increase in the size of the IAF's aircraft inventory (appendix 5). The number of the Pakistan Air Force's first- and second-line aircraft actually increased over 1965. But at every level of aircraft--fighters, bombers, transports, helicopters, and trainers--India's acquisitions were quantitatively and qualitatively greater than Pakistan's. With more diverse types of aircraft, the PAF came to have some of the same types of problems faced by India since independence, particularly in standardizing equipment and maintenance, spare parts, and inventories. But whereas India's diversification policy was deliberate (in order to safeguard its policy of nonalignment), Pakistan's diversification was more or less forced on it by the Western arms embargo and restrictive arms transfer policies.

Of all three services, the clearest shift in power took place between the Indian and Pakistani navies. India's navy increased in size from 16,000 men in 1965 to 40,000 in mid-1971, paralleling a large accretion in naval inventories This was the largest increase in the Indian Navy's history, and its effect was to increase its superiority over the Pakistani Navy on paper from six-to-one to at least ten-to-one.[29] As one Pakistani military authority writes, "...the *increase* [italics added] in the Indian Navy during the five years after the 1965 War was more than the total strength of the Pakistan Navy quantitatively and many more times qualitatively."[30]

Defense Production

An indication of the weakness of India's defense production capabilities at the beginning of this period came from the then-Defense Secretary, who in 1968 stated, "We sent a report to the Planning Commission in October 1965 pointing out the deficiencies from which we suffer, such as lack of special steel and alloys, explosives, and the quality of wool required for uniforms; we also pointed out that special stress must be laid on aeronautics and electronics, on instrumentation and on ship-building, and accessories for ships."[31]

By 1971 India was self-sufficient in small arms, light artillery and ammunition. It also made progress in building the Vijayanta tank, armored personnel carriers, and naval craft such as frigates, patrol boats, and minesweepers. But in other areas of defense production India's program of self-sufficiency had hardly got off the ground. Aircraft production was small and generally fell behind the original production schedules because of problems in design and development and production facilities. For instance, the first Indian model of the MiG-19 was introduced only in 1970.

The Western arms embargo gave Pakistan's government an incentive to increase defense production. For a short time after the war the government did stress indigenous production within Pakistan's limited financial, technical, and scientific resources. These efforts, however, were set back when the government postponed the planned heavy industrialization programs of the Third Five-Year Plan. The only significant developments in defense production were the establishment of an ordnance factory in East Pakistan in 1970 for producing small arms and ammunition, and the production of Cobra anti-tank missiles under license from West Germany.[32] Apart from clothing, minor aircraft items, small arms, some ammunition, and the Cobra missiles, Pakistan remained as dependent as ever upon foreign arms.

The foregoing analysis of the growth of military capabilities provides a background for examining the actual military policies of both countries.

Ayub's government was aware of the growing military strength of India and, at the same time, of Pakistan's weakened military position following the Western arms embargo of 1965. It had three choices: (1) recognizing India's superior military strength and adjusting to it by giving up any effective claims to Kashmir; (2) seeking a military solution to the dispute; or (3) sustaining large military expenditures in order to strengthen its bargaining power over Kashmir and to prevent the issue from lapsing.

The first choice was impracticable for the Pakistan government as long as the Kashmir issue was unresolved. As noted earlier, domestic opposition to the cease-fire with India on 23 September 1965 and to the Tashkent Declaration both weakened Ayub's political position. So accommodating India without settling the Kashmir dispute would have further weakened Ayub.

The second choice seemed to have been ruled out by the 1965 War, which showed Pakistan's government that the Indian military was stronger than once imagined. The War also weakened the myth that Pakistani soldiers, more specifically West Pakistanis, were somehow inherently superior to Indian soldiers in physique, skill, and courage.[33] Still, there were some members of the Pakistani military who believed that Pakistan had not lost the 1965 War and that with enough political determination the war could have been won. In short, although the confidence of the government and the military in winning a war against India was shaken, it was not destroyed.

This left the third choice: continuing the mobilization of military capabilities to keep the Kashmir issue alive. At first glance, this choice, too, seemed to have been foreclosed by the Western arms embargo. The embargo weakened Pakistan much more than India since the latter was less dependent upon Western arms and was more self-sufficient in arms production. Indeed, the embargo placed Pakistan in one of its most vulnerable military positions since independence.

Fortunately for Pakistan, the embargo was mitigated for several reasons. First, the government actively searched for vital spare parts from abroad and obtained them from private arms suppliers in western Europe. Soon after the 1965 War, the PAF quickly established a Procurements Division for this purpose. Secondly, Pakistan diversified its arms sources and found willing suppliers--China, France, Iran, Belgium and, after 1968, the Soviet Union, Jordan, Libya, and Saudi Arabia. Finally, the embargoes themselves were eased by Britain and the United States.

The Indian government's military policies after 1965 continued the policies of the First Defense Plan--that is, domestic self-sufficiency in arms production, an increase in manpower, and modernization--in order to fight a possible two-front war against Pakistan and China. The 1965 War only delayed this long-term modernization.[34] In the long run it made Indian policymakers even more determined to carry out these objectives. The 1965 War and the western arms embargo confirmed the wisdom of their post-1962 military policies.

As ever, the Indian government carefully noted Pakistan's continuing efforts to increase its military strength. The Indian Defense Minister, Swaran Singh, told the Lok Sabha on 14 February 1968 that Pakistan had virtually doubled its land forces since 1965, and that these now included two armored divisions. He also noted the strengthening of Pakistan's irregular forces, combat aircraft squadrons, and navy.[35] There is no doubt that this assessment was exaggerated; for example, although Pakistan's infantry divisions did double between 1965 and 1968, they lacked training and equipment. It is also hard to see how Pakistan could have had any long-range plans for naval expansion when resources were so scarce.[36] Singh's statements show, however, that the Indian government recognized that Pakistan's efforts to increase its military capabilities would not slacken.

New Delhi was much more concerned about outside military help to Pakistan, and it made energetic diplomatic efforts to halt all arms supplies to Pakistan, particularly from western Europe and the USSR. It reacted strongly to reports that West Germany had provided Pakistan with discarded F.86 aircraft. Eventually, it was able to get the aircraft removed from Pakistan. The Indian government also objected when the Soviets sold weapons to Pakistan. Although the transfer of T-54 and T-55 tanks did go through, the Soviets were made aware of the costs of their action on Indo-Soviet friendship.

New Delhi was concerned not only by arms transfers but also by military collusion between Pakistan and China. While the Indian government felt confident about containing a Pakistani military threat, it felt less so about a combined military attack by these two countries. This can be shown by India's perceptions of Pakistan's nuclear power program. The Indian government noted Pakistan's weak capabilities in nuclear weapons, but it was more concerned about possible nuclear collusion between Pakistan and China in nuclear weapons.[37]

To summarize, between 1965 and 1971, India's military capabilities increased at a faster rate than Pakistan's in all areas--quantity and quality of weapons and installations, the size and quality of its armed forces, and in skill, morale, and organization. The Pakistani government noted these relative military changes but mobilized outside support to offset India's military strength and the western arms embargo. Undaunted by these changes in the balance of military power, the Pakistani government continued its role as a counter-core to Indian dominance in South Asia. It saw that role as more important than ever for its continued existence as a sovereign state, particularly since identitive relations were also deteriorating between the two countries in this period.

IDENTITIVE CAPABILITIES, POWER AND INFLUENCE

Under Article VI of the Tashkent Agreement, India and Pakistan agreed to consider measures to restore cultural exchanges and to implement existing agreements. No progress was made in this area because the Pakistani government gave it low priority. Indeed, it followed a deliberate policy of reducing identitive ties with India.

Speaking on 18 November 1966 in London, Ayub Khan said that the conflict between India and Pakistan was based on conflicting ideologies--Islam and Hinduism. "They could live side by side," he argued, "but they could not owe alleigance to the same flag."[38] Besides the conflict between Indian secularism and Pakistan's two-nation theory, there were other factors at work in Pakistan reducing identitive ties with India. The East Pakistan autonomy movement threatened West Pakistani military and bureaucratic elites. As noted earlier, one of the ways in which the central government responded was by stressing the common Islamic character of East and West Pakistan and by deemphasizing East Pakistan's ethnic and cultural ties with India, particularly with West Bengal. The Governor of East Pakistan, Monem Khan, a loyal follower of Ayub, clamped down on the use of the Bengali language and took several measures to curb cultural influences from India, among them the banning of Tagore songs on radio and the prohibition of books from West Bengal. Monem Khan told an East Pakistan audience: "The Indian invasion of Pakistan has proved that we can no longer tolerate any infiltration of alien culture either in text books or in works of literature. If need be, we shall have to revise the syllabi of our universities to free ourselves from alien influence."[39]

Yet, rather than integrating East with West Pakistan, the central government's cultural policy had the opposite effect. East Pakistanis resented this policy and responded by increasing their efforts to preserve identitive ties with India. As one Indian author notes, East Pakistanis did not see these influences as alien but as an expression of their own culture.[40] The central government wrongly inferred that cultural influences from India would make East Pakistanis more subservient to India. It ignored the fact that cultural ties do not necessarily lead to political subservience. East Pakistani dissatisfaction with the central government's cultural policy was a major reasons for the post-1965 movement for autonomy and independence in East Pakistan.

The central government also sought to reduce identitive ties with India because it feared that those ties would increase harmful political influences from India, particularly the values of liberal-democracy and civilian rule. Here the central government's cultural policy was at least consistent with its economic policy, which also sought to reduce economic relations with India for some of the same reasons. The result, however, was that by 1971 India and Pakistan had fewer economic and identitive ties than they had at the end of 1965.

INDIA AS A CORE AREA IN THE 1971 CRISIS

By the end of the 1960s India had steadily increased its material and military capabilities compared to Pakistan. Pakistani governments suffered a severe loss of responsiveness due to social unrest, the downfall of Ayub, regional disputes over equity, and economic crises. These long-term changes between 1965 and 1971 are the underlying reason why India was able to defeat Pakistan in December 1971.

It would be wrong, though, to conclude that India's military victories were inevitable or that the Indian government was fully confident of its ability to act as a core area. The actual course of the East Pakistani crisis from the military crackdown of 25 March 1971 to the Pakistani military surrender at Dacca on 16 December 1971 shows that the Indian decision to intervene military was made reluctantly and only after all other means for a solution had been exhausted. It also shows that Indian policy was partly dictated by the *fear of a loss of responsiveness*--that the Bangladesh crisis would lead to social, economic and political unrest in India's already volatile northeastern states; that the leadership of the Bangladesh liberation movement would pass from the middle class Awami League into the hands of radical leftist elements, which would have a radicalizing effect in India's northeast; and, finally, that a diplomatic, political, or military setback to India over the crisis would dissipate the political effects of Mrs. Gandhi's hard-won electoral victory of March 1971.

The relationships between India's growing capabilities as a core area and the inevitability of conflict with Pakistan are thus far from simple, despite Pakistani arguments. Pakistani government officials and scholars claim that the Indian government was intent on war from the outset of the crisis in March 1971.[41] They argue, first, that Indian governments continued to cherish the historic dream of breaking up Pakistan, of cutting her down to size. Second, they argue that this opportunity was afforded by the East Pakistan crisis, a crisis that India itself had actively abetted. To support their arguments, Pakistanis cite K. Subrahmanyam, the director of India's Institute for Defense Studies and Analyses, who in 1971 stated: "What India must realize is the fact that the break-up of Pakistan is in our interest, an opportunity the like of which will never come again."[42] Pakistanis also support this claim by mentioning the hijacking of an Indian Airlines plane to Lahore, Pakistan, on 30 January 1971 by two persons whom the Pakistani military government orginally called Kashmiri freedom-fighters. The passengers were returned to India but the plane was blown up in full view of the authorities at Lahore. Later, a Pakistani Commission of Inquiry concluded that the hijacking was an Indian plot and a pretext for disrupting civilian and military communications between East and West Pakistan.

The evidence disproves Pakistani claims that India deliberately planned to break up Pakistan. First, Indian policy had always been to promote the Pakistan's territorial integrity, outside the Kashmir issue, in the belief that this support would further India's own security in the subcontinent. Indian government's recognized the interdependence of India and Pakistan in national integration; any attempt by India to encourage secessionist movements in Pakistan would only add to India's own integration problems, such as Nagaland and Mizoram.[43]

Secondly, the argument that the East Pakistan crisis was an historic opportunity for India is also incorrect. The Pakistani references to K. Subrahmanyam, the head of a semi-official think-tank, are unconvincing; Mrs. Gandhi's official statements of Indian policy stressed the need for preserving Pakistan's territorial integrity.[44] More convincing evidence of Indian policy comes from examining the benefits to India of the political changes in Pakistan before the military crackdown of March 1971. The Indian government expected the Pakistani election results of December 1970 to be fully implemented. It hoped that this would open a new, more cooperative chapter in Indo-Pakistani relations. The overwhelming Awami League victory in East Pakistan and its status as a majority party for all Pakistan, drew a favorable reaction from the Indian government for many reasons. Pakistan seemed to be moving closer to the Indian model of political development by holding its first democratic, direct general election. The outcome promised to be a new constitution and a return to civilian government.[45] Moreover, the Awami League, as the new majority party of Pakistan stood for some of the same political ideals as Congress--that is, democracy, socialism, and a nonaligned foreign policy.[46] Finally, the Awami League sought improved economic, political, and cultural ties with India and placed less emphasis on the Kashmir dispute in Pakistan's security and foreign policy.[47]

It would therefore have been in India's interests for the Awami League to become the governing party of Pakistan and for Sheikh Mujib to become the Prime Minister, all within the framework of a united Pakistan.

Internal developments in India also dictated a policy of peace for Mrs. Gandhi's government. In March 1971, there was a general feeling in the government, Parliament, and among public opinion that India had just turned the corner politically and economically. Politically, India's fifth general election returned a strong Congress Party at the center for the first time since 1967. The major domestic objectives of the new government were increased economic growth and social equity. Economically, the recent harvest had been good, industrial production was increasing and the Indian economy appeared set for a period of expansion.[48] What the Indian government needed, then, was international, regional, and domestic stability in order to increase economic growth and to fulfill promises of greater equity. What it did not need were political or economic shocks or regional adventures.

Finally, it remains to assess Pakistani charges that the Indian government was behind the hijacking affair of January-February 1971. The evidence for a plot is unclear. It is known that the Pakistan government and West Pakistani political leaders initially praised the hijacking; only later, after the military crackdown of March 1971, did they label it an Indian consipiracy. The Pakistani government correctly pointed out that the Indian government's response to the hijacking disrupted civilian and military communications between the two wings of Pakistan. On 2 February 1971, the Indian government banned overflights of Pakistani military aircraft. It followed this two days later by banning overflights of civilian aircraft. By forcing Pakistanis to take the longer sea and air route via Ceylon, the Indian government hampered the political negotiations that were going on at this time between the Pakistani military government and West and East Pakistani leaders.

The hampering of political negotiations in any case did not serve India's interests. It was an unintended consequence of India's actions and not the objective. The decision was coercive: to persuade the Pakistan government to pay compensation for the hijacked plane. At the same time, the ban on overflights had costs for India itself. Civilian and military flights over East Pakistan from India to the northeastern sector had to be rerouted, as did the international flight over West Pakistan.

The Pakistan government's military crackdown on 25 March 1971 forced New Delhi to reevaluate its policy towards the East Pakistan crisis. Initially, New Delhi supported the armed resistance to the Pakistani military and hoped that this resistance by itself would defeat the military.[49] Indian policy changed again when Bengali refugees streamed into India and when the Pakistani military appeared to be consolidating its military hold in East Pakistan by the end of May 1971.

The Indian government's perceptions of its own capabilities and the those of Pakistan significantly affected the development of the crisis. In the first place, the Congress government's political position after the March 1971 general election was strong, although Mrs.

Gandhi often stated that her room for maneuver in any negotiations with Pakistan was limited. She cited the resentement in India in 1966 over the troop withdrawals following the Tashkent Declaration.[50] Secondly, the Indian government realized that the Pakistani military crackdown had united India in sympathy for the Bengali people and against the Pakistani government. Mrs. Gandhi's main problem was to restrain domestic demands for immediately recognizing Bangladesh or for taking premature military action against Pakistan.[51] Withstanding these domestic pressures, the government delayed formally recognizing the state of Bangladesh. Instead, it provided military assistance to the armed resistance and facilities for the unofficial government-in-exile. Indian leaders also began to use the term "Bangladesh" instead of "East Pakistan."

Thirdly, the Indian government realized, at that early stage, that a formal recognition would escalate tensions with India at a time when India was militarily unprepared to fight a two-front war against Pakistan. It recognized that its material and military resources would have to be more fully mobilized if India was to take the offensive in the east and defend itself in the west.[52] The Indian government noted Pakistan's strategic advantages and military assets in both parts of Pakistan; at no time did the Indian government underestimate Pakistan's military capabilities. It also took into account the possibility of Chinese military intervention on the side of Pakistan. To invade East Pakistan, India would have to redeploy some of its mountain divisions facing China, and this meant neutralizing the Chinese threat diplomatically and militarily.

Finally, the Indian government recognized that it had limited financial resources to meet the refugee influx and to prepare for possible military action. No economic surpluses were available to divert to these uses, and so the expenditures would have to come at the sacrifice of India's economic development and military modernization programs. Mrs. Gandhi frequently called upon all sections of the Indian population to maintain essential economic production in the country.[53]

The Indian government's perceptions of Pakistan's material and military capabilities were important in the evolution of India's policy. First, the Indian government realized that the East Pakistani revolt against the Pakistani military was popular. The evidence came in the form of continuing guerilla resistance; defections from units of the East Bengal regiment, East Pakistan rifles, and the police; and from political exiles who established a government-in-exile in Calcutta. The Indian government may have overestimated the ability of the guerilla resistance in liberating East Pakistan, but it knew that any invasion of East Pakistan would be aided by the local population. Secondly, the Indian government believed Yahya's government to be unpopular in West Pakistan and that it was using India as a scapegoat for its own domestic weaknesses.[54] Finally, the Indian government argued that the Pakistani government was able to persist in this hostility to India because of international material and military support.[55]

The development of India's policy toward Pakistan flowed from these perceptions of Indian and Pakistani capabilities. The Indian government's policy was consistent and firm. First, India's security and territorial integrity had to be safeguarded. Secondly, any solution to the crisis had to take into account the political wishes of the East Bengalis. India could not negotiate with Pakistan for the East Bengalis, and thus the crisis could not be converted into a purely bilateral Indo-Pakistani dispute.[56] In line with this policy, the Indian government requested that Mujib be released from prison. Thirdly, the refugees had to go back to East Pakistan. India was unable and unwilling to absorb them as it had done after partition, in the early 1950s and from 1963 to 1965. Finally, the solution to the entire crisis was political, rather than economic. The economic burden of the refugees, although large and growing, could be borne by India, if necessary; but this was not the major issue for India. Only when the political conditions had been created in East Pakistan could the refugees return.[57]

When a political solution to the crisis failed to materialize, the Indian government gradually began to build up its ability to respond to the crisis militarily. India also attempted to isolate Pakistan internationally. Not only did India receive international sympathy for the refugee burden, it also signed a twenty-year Treaty of Peace, Friendship, and Cooperation with the Soviet Union on 9 August 1971. This stipulated that both countries would undertake "to refrain from giving any assistance to any third Party taking part in an armed conflict with the other Party."[58] Even more important, both countries agreed that in the event of an attack or threatened attack from any third party, they would "immediately start mutual consultations with a view to eliminating this threat and taking appropriate effective measures to ensure peace and security for their countries."[59]

The Treaty benefitted India in several ways. It assured Soviet diplomatic and political support against a Chinese military threat in the aid of Pakistan. Although Mrs. Gandhi pointed to its deterrent value against "any rash adventurism on the part of Islamabad," it is clear that the main deterrent value was against China.[60] The Treaty also calmed India's nightmare of coalitions regarding a possible Sino-American axis resulting from the evolving Sino-American detente of 1971.

Indo-Pakistani relations deteriorated in the summer and fall of 1971. The Indian military increased its support to the guerillas by providing training and supplies and by placing them under its operational command. The guerilla groups stepped up their offensives against the Pakistan military, which responded by shelling across the East Pakistan-India border. Border incursions from both sides took place, and in October and November, India and Pakistani regular troops frequently clashed at the East Pakistani border towns of Hilli, Boyra, and Kamalpur. On the strategic level, India and Pakistan mobilized their land, naval, and air forces for operations on both the eastern and western fronts. By the end of November, India had approximately eight divisions of 160,000 men, grouped into three army corps and a communication zone headquarters, deployed along the East Pakistan border. Supporting them were 180 tanks, 150 plus fighter aircraft, 12 bombers, and 100,000 *Mukti Bahini* irregulars. These faced four Pakistani divisions of 73,000 men and 60,000 irregulars, together with 100 tanks and 18 fighter planes. On the western front there was less of an imbalance between Indian and Pakistani land forces. Thirteen Indian divisions numbering 320,000 men, plus 1,270 tanks, 335 fighter aircraft and 40 bombers, faced 12 Pakistani divisions numbering 240,000 men, plus 700 tanks, 190 fighters and 25 bombers.[61]

On 3 December 1971, the PAF launched preemptive air-strikes *à la* Israel against IAF bases at Amritsar, Pathankot, Srinagar, and

Agra. These failed because the number of aircraft involved was too small in relation to the objective and because the IAF had taken defensive and precautionary measures against such an attack. India immediately retaliated by launching ground and air attacks on the western and eastern fronts. On the eastern front, Lt-General Jagjit Singh Aurora, used an indirect approach and by-passed fortified Pakistani positions, thereby cutting them off. Soviet diplomatic support in the UN enabled India to resist Chinese and American military pressure once the hostilities were underway. Indian forces, supported by the *Mukti Bahini* and the Bengali population, rapidly crossed East Bengal's numerous rivers and converged on Dacca, which surrendered on 16 December 1971. Taking only ten days, the Indian armed forces defeated Pakistan's armed forces in the east, capturing 90,000 prisoners, along with their weapons and equipment. This was undoubtedly the greatest victory of Indian arms since independence.

Perhaps India's victory was due not so much to its own military prowess as it was to a combination of a) Pakistani disadvantages, errors, and military incompetence; b) East Pakistani armed resistance to the Pakistani military; and c) Soviet military backing to India in the absence of comparable support to Pakistan. All of these factors detract from the view of India as a core area in the region.

No doubt each of these factors contributed to the final outcome. The Pakistanis committed several military errors. They defended the borders of East Pakistan without reference to strategic factors, they failed to coordinate operations among the three services, and they attempted a surprise attack on IAF bases without sufficient strength.[62] East Bengali resistance was important in the Indian victory for several reasons. First, resistance forces confined the Pakistanis to their cantonments. They also disrupted communications and industry and generally demoralized the Pakistani military forces before the December War. Secondly, defecting Bengali forces reduced the size of Pakistan's available military strength in the eastern wing and took with them to the Indian side valuable operational plans and intelligence. Finally, once the invasion began, resistance forces and the Bengali population provided valuable intelligence about troop dispositions, sizes, and the nature of the terrain. They also helped the

Indian military by ferrying supplies and equipment during the operations.[63] The Soviet Union contributed to the Indian victory in several ways. It deterred China from a military intervention, which allowed India to redeploy its mountain divisions to the East Pakistani front. It also guaranteed to replace the Indian army's stock of weapons transferred to the *Mukti Bahini*. Above all, the Soviet Union provided diplomatic cover in the United Nations.

The Pakistani, Bengali, and Soviet contributions only partly explain the outcome of the war. First, although Pakistani troops in East Pakistan were at a strategic disadvantage in being geographically cut off from West Pakistan by a 3,000 mile supply line. India also had some disadvantages. East Pakistan's river-crossed terrain favored the defender. Moreover, India had only a two-to-one advantage in regular troops instead of the three-to-one advantage normally required for an attacking force.[64] (Pakistani troops on both the eastern and western fronts strongly resisted the Indian attacks.[65]) Second, Bengali guerilla resistance by itself had failed to free East Pakistan by the end of 1971 and seemed unlikely to do so for a long time. Finally, no significant military aid was given to either India or Pakistan in 1971.[66] Soviet weapons, such as PT-76 amphibious tanks and missile boats, were important in the military operations, but it was the Indian military's use of them that made them so effective. Soviet support to India did not extend to a military blank check in the subcontinent. The USSR restrained India by attempting to limit India's political and military objectives to the liberation of East Pakistan.[67]

India's military achievements in the 1971 War were substantial, especially when viewed against the debacle of 1962 and the indecisive outcome of the 1965 Indo-Pakistan War. In the first place, India's ban on civilian and military overflights in February 1971, its naval blockade of East and West Pakistan during the War, and its air superiority all show its ability to act as a core area in determining the military and communication patterns between the noncontiguous parts of Pakistan in South Asia.[68] In the second place, India's political authorities gave the three services clear military objectives, which they carried out in a coordinated series of operations on two major fronts. And, in the third place, when hostilities began, the Pakistani troops in East Pakistan were thrown off balance by Aurora's indirect approach, particularly by an entirely unexpected attack from the Indian army's IV corps from Tripura.[69]

The 1971 War was decisive. Pakistan surrendered all ground, air, and naval forces in the eastern wing. In the western wing it lost 5,000 square miles of territory to Indian forces.[70] India's triumph threw West Pakistan into turmoil. Yahya Khan resigned as President and Chief Martial Law Administrator on 20 December 1971. He was succeeded by Zulfikar Ali Bhutto, the only politician of sufficient national stature in what remained of Pakistan.

CONCLUSION

India had several economic and political weaknesses in the mid-1960s. These included drought, disastrous harvests, and economic recession. There were also political succession problems, internal instability over language and regional issues, and an electoral setback for the Congress Party in the 1967 general elections. But towards the end of the 1960s, at the very time when Pakistan was beset by social turmoil over East Pakistani regionalism and disputes over equity, India acquired several capabilities as a core area. These were the fruits of earlier decisions to build up heavy industry under the Five-Year Plans, to begin agricultural reforms, and the modernize the military under the First and Second Five-Year Defense Plans. Politically, Mrs. Gandhi consolidated her hold on the Congress Party and led her Congress (R) faction to a sweeping victory in the 1971 general election. When civil war erupted in Pakistan in March 1971, India was in a stronger position relative to Pakistan. This position was further strengthened by the Indo-Soviet Treaty of Peace, Friendship, and Cooperation of August 1971, which India signed in order to neutralize Chinese aid to Pakistan. The 1971 War was a decisive defeat for Pakistan.

Notes

1. Speech by Mohammed Ayub Khan at the opening session of the Tashkent meeting, 4 January 1966, in R. K. Jain, *Soviet-South Asian Relations 1947-1978*, vol. 1 (Atlantic Highlands, N. J.: Humanities Press, 1979), pp. 168-74.
2. Ibid., p. 95.
3. Mohammed Ayoob, "India and Pakistan: relations since Tashkent," in *Foreign Policies in South Asia*, ed. S. P. Varma and K. P. Misra (New Delhi: Orient Longmans, 1969), pp. 220-21.
4. India's military expenditure declined in real terms from $1.55 billion in 1966 to $1.52 billion in 1967; Pakistan's declined from $398.62 million to $339.69 million. U.S. Department of State, Arms Control and Disarmament Agency, *World Military Expenditures and Arms Trade 1963-1973* (Washington, D.C.: U.S. Government Printing Office, 1975), pp. 37, 50.
5. Interview with Swaran Singh, San Francisco, California, 4 September 1983.
6. *Asian Recorder* 12 (18-24 June 1966), p. 7136.
7. John W. Mellor, *The New Economics of Growth* (Ithaca, N. Y.: Cornell University Press, 1976), p. 45.
8. Ibid.
9. Ibid., p. 299.
10. Ayoob, "India and Pakistan," pp. 221-22.
11. This is noted by N. D. Gulhati, the Chief Indian representative at the Indus Waters Treaty negotiations, in *Indus Waters Treaty: An Exercise in International Mediation* (Bombay: Allied Publishers, 1973), pp. 366-70.
12. India, Planning Commission, *Fourth Five Year Plan 1969-74* (Delhi: The Manager, Publications Branch, 1970), Table 1, pp. 299-300.
13. Ibid., pp. 297-98.
14. Robert L. Hardgrave, Jr., *India: Government and Politics in a Developing Nation*, 2d ed. (New York: Harcourt Brace Jovanovich, 1975), pp. 178-79.
15. Leo E. Rose, "The Foreign Policy of India," in *World Politics*, ed. James N. Rosenau et al. (New York: Free Press, 1976), p. 216, fn. 13.
16. Ayoob, "India and Pakistan," p. 227.
17. Ibid.
18. Sheikh Mujib Rahman, "Six Point Formula--Our Right to Live," in *Bangladesh Documents*, vol. 1 (New Delhi: Ministry of External Affairs, 1971), pp. 23-33.
19. Talukder Maniruzzaman, "National Integration and Political Development in Pakistan," *Asian Survey* 7 (December 1967), pp. 883-84.
20. Hardgrave, *India*, p. 179.
21. For comments on this strategy, see Joseph J. Stern and Walter P. Falcon, *Growth and Development in Pakistan 1955-1969* (Cambridge, Mass.: Harvard University Center for International Affairs, 1970), pp. 58-63. For a comparison with India, see Wayne Wilcox, "New Elites of India and Pakistan," *Trans-action* 4 (September 1967): 43-50.
22. "The Legal Framework Order, 1970," in Pakistan, Ministry of Information and Broadcasting, *White Paper on the Crisis in East Pakistan* (Islamabad: Manager, Printing Corporation of Pakistan Press, 1971), appendix B, p. 24.

23. Craig Baxter, "Pakistan Votes--1970," *Asian Survey* 11 (March 1971), p. 211.
24. David Dunbar [psued.], "Pakistan: The Failure of Political Negotiations," *Asian Survey* 12 (May 1972), p. 445.
25. This is the hypothesis of Rehman Sobhan, "Negotiating for Bangla Desh: A Participant's view," in *Bangladesh Documents*, vol. 2 (New Delhi: Ministry of External Affairs, 1972), p. 191.
26. *Asian Recorder* 14 (26 August--1 September 1968), p. 8493.
27. *Keesing's Contemporary Archives* (2-9 November 1968), p. 23003.
28. D. C. Jha, "Indo-Pakistani Relations since the Tashkent Declaration," *The Indian Journal of Political Science* 32 (October-December 1971), p. 517.
29. Ravi Kaul, "The Indo-Pakistani War and the Changing Balance of Power in the Indian Ocean," *United States Naval Institute Proceedings* 99 (May 1973), p. 186.
30. Fazal Muqeem Khan, *Pakistan's Crisis in Leadership* (Islamabad: National Book Foundation, 1973), p. 221.
31. H.C. Sarin, "Defense Production," in *Defense of India*, Press Institute of India (New Delhi: Vikas, 1969), p. 50.
32. SIPRI, *The Arms Trade with the Third World* (New York; Humanities, 1971), pp. 732-33.
33. M. Attiqur Rahman, *Our Defense Cause* (London: White Lion, 1976), pp. 37-38.
34. The 1965 War furthered India's military modernization in one respect: India lost generally obsolete equipment. Pakistan lost newer, more expensive equipment, which was replaced by inferior equipment. K. Subrahmanyam, "The Defense Effort," *Seminar* 110 (October 1968), p. 18.
35. *Asian Recorder* 14 (25-31 March 1968), p. 8240.
36. For instance, Fazal Muqeem Khan notes that after the 1965 War, the Pakistan Navy received the least money of the three services, and that this was insufficient to pay for the three French submarines, let alone maintain existing ships and facilities. *Pakistan's Crisis*, pp. 221-22.
37. *Asian Recorder* 12 (27 August-2 September 1966), p. 7254.
38. *Asian Recorder* 13 (8-14 January 1967), pp. 7489-90.
39. Quoted in M. V. Lakhi, "The Two Wings," *Seminar* 117 (May 1969), p. 19.
40. Ibid.
41. See, for example, Pakistan, Ministry of Information and National Affairs, *White Paper on the Crisis*, pp. 45-53; Choudhury, *Last Days*, pp. 210-14, and Khan, *Pakistan's Crisis*, pp. 132-46.
42. Quoted in Choudhury, *Last Days*, p. 211.
43. The interdependence of India and Pakistan in political integration was examined by H. V. Hodson in a perceptive article, "Can India and Pakistan Survive?" *Royal Central Asian Journal* 56 (October 1969): 259-71.
44. Indira Gandhi, *India and Bangladesh: Selected Speeches and Statements March to December 1971* (New Delhi: Orient Longman, 1972), p. 73.
45. Ibid., p. 9.
46. Ibid., pp. 11-12.
47. Ibid, pp. 91.

48. Ibid., p. 42.
49. D. K. Palit, *The Lightning Campaign: The Indo-Pakistan War 1971* (New Delhi: Thomson Press, 1972), p. 49.
50. Indira Gandhi, *India and Bangladesh*, p. 98.
51. Ibid., pp. 20-23.
52. For a discussion of the need for this mobilization, see Palit, *Lightning*, pp. 63-70.
53. Ibid., p. 19.
54. Ibid., pp. 40-41.
55. Ibid, p. 123.
56. Ibid., pp. 67-68.
57. Ibid., p. 30.
58. Jain, *Soviet-South Asian Relations*, vol. 1, p. 115.
59. Ibid., pp. 115-16.
60. Indira Gandhi, *India and Bangladesh*, p. 41.
61. The International Institute for Strategic Studies, *Strategic Survey 1971* (London: IISS, 1972), p. 52.
62. The lack of Pakistani military coordination is shown in two examples, both involving the navy. First, Yahya Khan did not consult with the Pakistan navy before he decided to use force on 25 March 1971. According to F. M. Khan, "The C-in-C had learnt about it only through a chance remark by the President on the midnight of March 25 at Karachi Airport, where the C-in-C had gone to receive the President on his return from Dacca." *Pakistan's Crisis*, pp. 223-24. Secondly, the Pakistan government later noted, "The fact is startling but authentic that the Chief of Staff of the Pakistan Navy was informed of the outbreak of hostilities in 1971 only by a radio news bulletin to which he happened to listen." White Paper on Higher Defense Organization, in *Defense Journal* 2 (July-August 1976), p. 17.
63. According to F. M. Khan, Bengali defections from the military after March 1971 reduced the army's total strength by 20 percent and the navy's by 38 percent. The PAF lost 35 pilots and 25 percent of its maintenance personnel. These defectors took with them to the Indian side operational secrets and plans and information about Pakistan's defense system. *Pakistan's Crisis*, pp. 149, 223, and 237.
64. Palit, *Lighting*, p. 100.
65. Ibid., pp. 16-17.
66. Robert Victor Jackson, *South Asian Crisis: India, Pakistan and Bangladesh* (New York: Praeger, 1975), p. 107.
67. Ibid., pp. 139-40 and 153.
68. The ability of countries situated between the noncontiguous parts of another country to influence the latter's communication patterns and military power is noted in Richard L. Merritt, "Noncontiguity and Political Integration," in *Linkage Politics*, ed. James N. Rosenau (New York: Free Press, 1969), pp. 268-72.
69. Maharaj K. Chopra, "Military Operations in Bangladesh," *Military Review* 52 (May 1972), p. 60. Other military accounts of the 1971 War include Onkar Marwah, "India's Military Intervention in East Pakistan, 1971-72," *Modern Asian Studies* 13 (October 1979): 549-80; Ravi Rikhye, "Why India Won: The 14-Day War." *Armed Forces Journal* 109 (April 1972): 38-41; Kaul, "The Indo-Pakistan

War,"; and Air Marshal M. S. Chaturvedi, *History of the Indian Air Force* (New Delhi: Vikas, 1978), chapter 13.

70. Pakistan's total casualties were 7,982 killed; 9,547 wounded and 84,000 POW and missing. Pakistan lost 220 tanks, 83 aircraft and 22 naval vessels. India's casualties were 3,037 killed, 7,300 wounded; and 1,561 POW and missing. India lost 83 tanks, 54 aircraft and 1 naval vessel. International Institute for Strategic Studies, *Strategic Survey 1971*, p. 52.

CHAPTER SEVEN

THE "NEW PAKISTAN": 1971-79

The 1971 War and the birth of Bangladesh decisively shifted the balance of material and military power in the subcontinent. The war was a military and political victory for India. It was also a psychological victory over Pakistan, its traditional adversary. The break-up of Pakistan seemed to reaffirm India's secular and democratic system and to discredit the two-nation theory. By turning "half its enemy into a friend,"[1] India became the dominant regional power. The most decisive shifts in assets and power were in population, GNP, and burdens of military expenditure. The only favorable result for Pakistan was an increase in per capita income, which resulted from the loss of the much larger and poorer population of East Pakistan.[2]

A number of short- and long-term factors, however, prevented India from capitalizing on its 1971 victory to build a new regional order. The long-term factors stem from India's and Pakistan's different growth rates of material and military assets after 1971. In the short-term, the Pakistani government held a number of assets, which it skillfully used in the postwar bargaining with India and Bangladesh. The assets held by each of the three sides determined the outcomes of the postwar settlement. These assets may be listed as follows:

India

1. 93,000 POWs from East Pakistan
2. 540 POWs from the western front
3. 5,139 square miles of captured West Pakistani territory

4. captured war material
5. use of Bangladesh as a third-party to increase India's room for maneuver

Pakistan

1. Mujib Rahman jailed in West Pakistan
2. a number of Bengali soldiers in custody in West Pakistan
3. Bengali population in West Pakistan
4. 616 Indian POWs
5. 100 square miles of captured Indian territory
6. the power of recognizing Bangladesh
7. In coordination with China, a veto of Bangladesh's membership in the UN
8. diplomatic support from the Middle East

Bangladesh

1. 600,000 non-Bengalis, mostly Biharis, in Bangladesh
2. joint custody of West Pakistani POWs with India
3. a say in the division of Pakistan's pre-1971 domestic and international assets and liabilities

Bhutto skillfully used Pakistan's assets in bargaining with India and Bangladesh. In setting out to consolidate his position both at home and abroad, Bhutto faced one clear task--the need to rebuild Pakistan's national institutions and international prestige. He immediately set out to do this by a number of interlinked domestic, regional, and international actions. First, he moved boldly on the domestic front by establishing his political authority. He removed several senior military officers, announced economic and social reforms, and reached an accord on 5 March 1972 with the opposition parties on a working political system, pending a more permanent constitution. Secondly, Bhutto sought to readjust Pakistan's foreign policy to the new subcontinental realities. Although well known for his anti-Indian foreign policy, he was enough of a realist to recognize that Pakistan was too weak to continue its confrontation with India. As he told

Pakistan's National Assembly in April 1972, "...when I assumed the responsibility of Government and viewed the debris, I resolved in my mind that the only sane course to follow was to seek an accommodation with India on the basis of an honorable and just settlement."[3] One of Bhutto's first moves was to release Mujib from prison in West Pakistan on 3 January 1972 and send him home to Bangladesh via London. Bhutto also responded favorably to Mrs. Gandhi's unconditional offer of peace talks. In late April 1972, senior Indian and Pakistani officials held preliminary meetings at Muree, Pakistan, to prepare for a summit meeting of Bhutto and Mrs. Gandhi. Finally, Bhutto conducted an active diplomatic campaign to reestablish Pakistan's international prestige and to strengthen his own bargaining position with India. This began with a visit to Afghanistan in January 1972 and was followed by visits to several Middle Eastern countries and to the Soviet Union and China, all before Bhutto's meeting with Mrs. Gandhi.

After this preliminary jockeying to improve bargaining positions, the summit began at Simla on 28 June 1972. The Indian side sought a comprehensive settlement of Indo-Pakistani disputes, including Kashmir, the release of POWs, the exchange of captured territories, and a No-War pact. The Pakistani side sought an incremental approach; it wanted to settle the 1971 War issues and leave Kashmir in the background.

Bhutto sought an incremental approach for several reasons. First, a No-War pact, by limiting the size of Pakistan's armed forces was unacceptable. Bhutto was a yet unsure of his support among the Pakistani military.[4] Secondly, Bhutto was also unsure of India's military and political intentions in the subcontinent. Like Pakistani leaders before him, he sought specific proof of Indian goodwill before agreeing to such a pact. Finally, Bhutto's approach recognized the new balance of power between India and Pakistan and the fact that a settlement was more likely to be reached on the 1971 issues than on the much more more intractable Kashmir dispute, where India was much in a much stronger military position. In his first months in office, Bhutto de-emphasized the Kashmir dispute and left it to the Kashmiris themselves to take the initiative in fighting for their self-determination.[5] The Kashmir issue was not forgotten; it was merely given a lower priority as Pakistan concentrated on the immediate issues of national reconstruction. In short, Bhutto's foreign policy cautiously related ends to means.

At Simla, India once again failed to persuade Pakistan to sign a No-War Pact and establish a security-community in South Asia. But the Simla Agreement went much further than previous Indo-Pakistani agreements. For the first time both sides formally subscribed to the principle of bilateralism in their relations--that is, to settle their differences by peaceful means through bilateral negotiations or by any other peaceful means mutually agreed upon between them. Their disputes would be settled, as far as possible, without the intervention of third parties. This was the most significant part of the agreement; Pakistan formally recognized one of India's most consistent post-independence foreign policy principles--to insulate the subcontinent from the influence of external powers.

Both governments agreed to withdraw their forces to their side of the international border. In Jammu and Kashmir, "the line of control resulting from the cease-fire of 17 December 1971 shall be respected by both sides without prejudice to the recognized position of either side. Neither side shall seek to alter it unilaterally, irrespective of mutual differences and legal interpretations. Both sides further undertake to refrain from the threat or use of force in violation of this line."[6] Other provisions of the Simla Agreement called for restoring communications; promoting trade, travel, and economic, scientific, and cultural cooperation; and for discouraging hostile propaganda against the other country.

Several problems of implementation remained after the Simla summit. Troop withdrawals were held up by differences in Indian and Pakistani legal, military, and diplomatic positions on the new line of control in Kashmir. The Indian government argued that its territorial gains in Kashmir in the 1971 War had made the old 1949 cease-fire line obsolete. Consequently, the UN no longer had any standing in the Kashmir dispute. The Pakistani government's position was the reverse: the 1949 cease-fire line was still valid, as was UN participation. After months of bargaining between military representatives, Pakistan reluctantly agreed to the Indian position, and both countries demarcated a new line of control on 17 December

1972. By the end of that month, both sides withdrew their troops and exchanged POWs captured on the western front.

The major problems in subcontinental diplomacy continued to be the release of Pakistani POWS from the eastern front and the recognition of Bangladesh by Pakistan--issues that were left unresolved at Simla. The impassse was eventually resolved because of changes in the bargaining assets held by each of the three sides. Bhutto rightly pointed out that the POWs were a "waning asset" for India.[7] Not only did India have to feed, clothe, and house them, it also faced international and domestic criticisms for their continued detention. The Indian government denied that it was holding human life as a bargaining counter; but in truth it was putting pressure on Bhutto to come to terms with India and Bangladesh. Bhutto could not ignore domestic opinion and forget the POWs. If the continued detention was part of India's policy of demilitarizing Pakistan, then it was a very inappropriate instrument with which to do so. India did hold the equivalent of four and a half Pakistani divisions, thereby reducing Pakistan's available military forces, but Bhutto began to raise two new divisions to replace them. The Indian and Bangladeshi bargaining positions were further weakened by China's veto of Bangladesh's application for UN membership on 25 August.

Pakistan's nonrecognition of Bangladesh was also a waning asset. Bangladesh's government slowly established its domestic viability and international identity. In the first half of 1972, several states, including the United States, the USSR, and Britain, recognized Bangladesh. Pakistan's nonrecognition became superfluous. The nonrecognition hurt Pakistan economically since it was still paying the debts from international obligations incurred before the 1971 War. Pakistan therefore had to come to come to terms with Bangladesh over the division of their pre-1971 assets and liabilities.[8] Bhutto also realized that nonrecognition virtually guaranteed continued Indian influence in Bangladesh. At least by recognizing Bangladesh, Pakistan would have a chance to reduce this Indian influence.

By early 1973 the Indian government concluded that India and Bangladesh would have to give concessions to Pakistan in order to break the impasse in normalizing relations. On 17 April 1973, India and Bangladesh offered to simultaneously exchange Pakistani POWs, civilian internees, and non-Bengalis for Bengalis stranded in West Pakistan. They hoped that this offer would solve the humanitarian problems arising from the 1971 War. Negotiations then followed between India and Pakistan over the next year. Pakistan's government bowed to the inevitable and recognized Bangladesh on 22 February 1974. This led the way to the first series of trilateral talks between India, Pakistan, and Bangladesh and to the resolution of the other two problems. In trilateral talks at New Delhi in April 1974, Pakistan's representative apologized on behalf of his government for any war crimes that might have been committed; in return the Bangladesh government dropped the war crimes issue in the interests of South Asian reconciliation.

The April 1974 Delhi Agreement significantly normalized relations in the subcontinent. It settled the major territorial, military, diplomatic, and humanitarian issues of the 1971 War. In the two years of postwar bargaining, India had scored some important diplomatic successes, particularly over the issue of bilateralism. Bangladesh had gained recognition of its national sovereignty. Pakistan regained its territory and POWs and avoided the humiliating trials of some of its POWS. But Bhutto knew that Pakistan's diplomatic gains had been largely from a position of weakness relative to India. Although his short-term objective was to settle the issues arising from the 1971 War, he knew that the long-term objective had to be one of mobilizing Pakistan's resources in order to redress the balance of power with India.

MATERIAL CAPABILITIES, POWER, AND INFLUENCE

Economic

After 1971 two important factors determined Indian and Pakistani economic growth rates: recovery from the 1971 War and adjustments to the effects of the 1973-74 quadrupling of international oil prices. For India the recovery from the war meant adjusting its developmental and military expenditures and providing aid to the new state of Bangladesh. For Pakistan the recovery meant rebuilding economic confidence at home and searching for new export markets to replace the internal market lost in Bangladesh. Just as both countries were carrying out their recoveries, they were hit by an inflationary international economic environment, particularly in oil, food, and fertilizers. The prospects for sustained economic growth were unfavorable in India and Pakistan.

Pakistan's GNP growth rate was greater than India's (47.4 percent against 27.4 percent).[9] Pakistan's agricultural growth was also stronger than India's, with Pakistan registering proportionately greater increases in wheat yields and production and rice production.[10]

The Indian record was better in industry, mainly because India started from a much more established resource and production base than Pakistan. India's industrial superiority showed in the larger absolute and proportional increases in all sectors, particularly mining, chemicals, and metal industries. As a result the gap between Indian and Pakistani industry widened. For example, while India's production of pig iron and steel ingots both increased by about 36 percent, Pakistan's iron and steel industry had yet to get off the ground. The production of mild steel products increased to 362,000 tons from 196,000 tons, but most of this increase came from scrap.[11]

India's international economic trading position was also stronger than Pakistan's. The growth rate of Indian exports was larger and the growth rate of imports was smaller than Pakistan's. Moreover, by 1979 India was stronger in international reserves and servicing its debts.[12]

There are many reasons for this overall economic performance. After 1971, the Indian economy suffered from successive droughts, poor harvests and then inflation, which was also fired by world-wide inflation in oil, food, and fertilizers. Agricultural production declined sharply between 1972 and 1975 and also contributed to the slowing down of the rate of growth of industrial production. With population increasing at an annual average rate of 2.1 percent, the agricultural and industrial declines in income resulted in a general decline in the living standards of the mass of the Indian population.

Although agriculture was not a factor in India's relative economic strength between 1972 and 1975, it was in the case of Pakistan. Food and cash crop production recovered from the effects of the 1970-71 crisis, and Pakistan had a surplus of cotton and rice for export. The Pakistani economy did remarkably well in recovering from the 1970-71 crisis, especially in light of the economic problems facing Pakistan. Pakistan had lost 53 percent of its population. It had also lost the major source of its central government revenues, foreign exchange earnings, and the market for the industrial products of the western wing. The choices facing Pakistan were to increase government revenues, reduce expenditures, and search for new export markets. Pakistan's government itself singled out three major sets of problems: (1) changes in the economy's production and trading patterns (2) problems of the war, such as diversion of resources for military uses, interruptions in the flow of foreign trade, and localized shortages due to the disruption of transport and distribution services, and (3) the necessity for increasing social justice.[13]

Some Pakistanis doubted that Pakistan could become economically viable given these problems. Fortunately, there were a number of favorable economic factors. First, although Pakistan lost 53 percent of its population, it lost only 14 percent of its territory. Secondly, per capita income rose statistically with the removal of East Pakistan's population from the national sample. Thirdly, except for the Pakistan oil refinery at Karachi and the loss of some industrial infrastructure in East Pakistan, most of Pakistan's industry remained intact. Fourthly, the loss of the food-deficit area of East Pakistan meant that Pakistan could become self-sufficient in food and a net food exporter. Finally, there was much room for improving economic efficiency. The effects of the Green Revolution were still to be felt in agriculture, and industrial efficiency could be improved by abolishing the multiple exchange rate system, which distorted price signals in the economy and created excess industrial capacity. But with the shock of the Bangladesh War occupying Pakistani attention, these advantages were only dimly perceived in the first few months after the war.

Pakistan's government set out to rebuild the economy. In changing production and trading patterns, its most significant measures were devaluation and export promotion. On 11 May 1972, it abolished the multiple exchange rate system and devalued the Pakistani rupee. The objectives of this devaluation were to make

Pakistani exports more competitive, to encourage the development of a capital goods industry in Pakistan, and to free the economy from governmental control.[14]

Other economic reforms aimed to increase social equity and national self-reliance. The government's labor policy established procedures for settling labor disputes, for improving social security schemes, and for increasing worker participation in management. A new educational policy, announced on 18 March 1972, aimed at universal free education, the nationalization of private schools and colleges, and an expansion of the number of universities.[15]

On 3 January 1972, the government nationalized (or rather gained control of the management of) twenty key firms in the economy. This measure was meant to reduce the economic, social, and political power of Pakistan's so- called "twenty-two" families and to redirect investments to economic sectors vital to national self-reliance.[16] Following this, the government began a number of projects to give Pakistan an infrastructure of heavy industry and communications. These "grand solutions," as one Pakistani political economist calls them, had several common features: all were initiated outside the planning framework, all were approved on noneconomic criteria, and all had high capital costs and long gestation periods.[17]

Bhutto's economic and social reforms and development strategy had several important consequences for the growth of Pakistan's economic assets and power. In the first place, private business confidence in his regime deteriorated and finally collapsed with the concessions to labor and the nationalization of industries. Capital fled abroad and private investment in manufacturing declined sharply. This largely accounts for the slowing down of the rate of increase of GDP between 1974-77.[18] Second, the "grand solutions," with their high capital costs and long gestation periods, contributed little to Pakistan's economic growth between 1971 and 1979. Indeed, Burki argues that the investment in these projects had high opportunity costs for other sectors of the economy, particularly agriculture and small and medium-sized industries where economic growth would have been faster if more resources had been devoted to them.[19]

After Bhutto's overthrow in July 1977, the new military government attempted to increase business confidence and to realign Pakistan's economic objectives with its resources. The government moved to attract foreign investment and to create a favorable domestic climate for business investment and growth. The government constitutionally guaranteed no further nationalization, strictly demarcated private and public sector economic activity, began procedures to return nationalized industries to their former owners, encouraged private sector investment in large-scale projects, and imposed stricter labor discipline. In addition, in 1978, the military government replaced Bhutto's annual economic plans with a reintroduced five-year planning mechanism. This ended the ad hoc economic decision-making of the Bhutto era and reimposed a measure of planning discipline.[20]

In concluding this survey of the growth of Indian and Pakistani economic assets, it is important to note that, although India's economic growth was slower than Pakistan's between 1971 and 1975, the Indian economy did relatively better after 1975. This was not only because of Pakistan's economic policy failures but also because of Indian economic policy successes and a series of good monsoons and harvests after 1975. Indian food production rose, bringing greater price stability and overall economic growth. The lower inflation made India's exports more competitive and boosted export volume. Between 1975 and 1979, food stocks increased to record levels, saving India scarce foreign exchange. An increase in workers' remittances further strengthened the Indian economy and offset India's oil bills. By 1979, India's international liquidity had increased to $7.7 billion from $1.2 billion in 1971 .[21]

How did the Indian and Pakistani relative economic growth rates affect their relations? Between 1971 and 1975 there was a gap between India's economic capabilities and its power and influence. Like the post-Tashkent period, 1966-67, the post-Simla period corresponded to a severe economic crisis in India. Food grain shortages led to increased imports at a time when food was both scarce and expensive on the international marketplace. Increased prices of oil, fertilizers, machinery, and equipment further strained India's balance of payments.

Pakistan, on the other hand, was able to recover economically relative to India. By reforming its exchange rate and promoting exports, it successfully redirected its trade and established its international economic viability. Noting the large increase in Pakistan's exports and the doubling of its foreign exchange reserves, Bhutto argued that "These facts, incidentally, are a conclusive rebuttal of the canard, spread during the ubiquitous propaganda campaign of 1971, that the economy of West Pakistan was sustained by the export earnings of East Pakistan and would collapse if denied that support."[22]

The oil price increases of 1973-74 also hit Pakistan's economy hard. Still, Pakistan managed to reduce the strain on its balance of payments. It increased its trade with the oil-rich states and received workers' remittances and foreign aid from the Middle East. The Pakistani economy became increasingly tied to the economies of the Middle East; Pakistani manpower and skills complemented Middle Eastern capital.

The oil price increases of 1973-74 had a twofold impact on India's position as an economic core in South Asia. On the one hand, the transfer of resources to OPEC weakened India in the short-term and took away economic resources that might have been available for use at home and in the region.[23] On the other hand, the oil-rich Middle East states provided economic resources to Pakistan and Bangladesh, competing with India's position as an economic core. For example, although India provided much-needed initial aid for rebuilding Bangladesh's economy, it was unable to sustain the level of aid. Eventually, other countries, including those from the Middle East, overtook India in aiding Bangladesh.[24]

India's power and influence may have been reduced but it still remained as responsive as ever to regional integration. The case of Bangladesh gives an inaccurate picture of India as a core area; India compensated for its scarce resources by increasing its responsiveness. After the Bangladesh War, India was prepared to sacrifice its own economic development to help the new nation recover. India's total costs of looking after the refugees, conducting the war, and reconstructing Bangladesh has been estimated at about $2 billion.[25] Further, India's reduced aid to Bangladesh was also the result of the assassination of Sheikh Mujib in August 1975 and his replacement by regimes who wanted to be more independent of India. In fact, total foreign aid under India's International Technical and Economic Cooperation Program (ITEC) actually increased sixfold from 1971 to 1978.[26]

Despite the increasingly important extraregional influence of the Middle East, several potential economic ties remained between India and Pakistan. India's agricultural crisis of 1972-75 left it in need of cotton, wheat and rice, which could have been imported from the suplus areas of Pakistan. Pakistan's plans to build the Karachi Steel Mill gave India an opportunity to export its competitively priced iron ore and coal to Pakistan. The balance of payments difficulties of both countries gave another incentive to bilateral trade. Increased trade in local curencies would conserve scarce foreign exchange reserves. This was one reason why, in 1974, both joined the Asian Clearing Union, a multilateral organization designed to provide clearing arrangements to save foreign exchange and to promote the use of domestic currencies in trade transactions among developing countries.

The evident economic advantages failed to promote Indo-Pakistani trade. The steps towards reopening bilateral trade relations were cautious. In principle, Pakistan's government had less objections to increased trade with India. Bhutto's incremental approach at Simla placed Kashmir in the background and thus removed this issue as a precondition for developing trade and other forms of economic cooperation. In practice, though, there were a number of political obstacles. The political-military issues from the last war had to be cleared, specifically, the return of territories and POWs and the recognition of Bangladesh. There were also differences over the trading framework between the two countries, such as the role of private versus public trading, the manner of currency payments, shipping services, and, finally, the degree of Pakistani dependence on Indian trade.[27]

Talks on the reopening of Indo-Pakistani trade began in November 1974 and resulted in the signing of a trade protocol on 30 November 1974. This allowed for the resumption of trade from 7 December 1974. It also paved the way for a more permanent and comprehensive agreement, which was signed on 23 January 1975.

The volume of bilateral trade expansion thereafter was very small compared to total Indian and Pakistani foreign trade, largely because the pace of reopening was determined by the noneconomic factors mentioned above. But given that there had been virtually no trade between the countries between 1965 and 1975, the most significant fact is not that the trade was small but that there was any trade at all.

Nuclear Energy

Indian policy continued to be one of developing nuclear science and technology for peaceful purposes, such as energy and production of isotopes for medicine, agriculture, and industry. But after 1971, the Indian government accelerated its nuclear (and space) programs.

India had several major nuclear achievements. First, it conducted a "peaceful nuclear explosion" (PNE) at Pokharan in the Rajasthan desert on 18 May 1974, making India the sixth nation to explode a nuclear device. Secondly, it commissioned the first unit of the Rajasthan nuclear power plant (RAPP-1) and was building five more reactors (appendix 8). Thirdly, in July 1978 India opened a heavy water plant at Tuticorin in Tamil Nadu. It developed two other plants (one at Talcher in Orissa and the other at Kota, Rajasthan). Fourthly, India worked on a fast breeder reactor at Kalpakkam, Tamil Nadu. Finally, India commissioned a Variable Energy Cyclotron at Calcutta.[28]

India's progress in nuclear energy seems impressive, but there are conflicting views about the actual progress. On the one hand, official Indian reports and the writings of some scholars suggest that by 1979 India had generally met its objectives of technical progress and self-sufficiency. Marwah argues that by 1977 in only one or two "isolated fields was Indian technical competence in the nuclear field not proceeding according to schedule. Assuming peaceful intent, the country had acquired the ability to fabricate all sensitive nuclear instrumentation, fueling assemblies, special alloys and materials, heavy water coolants, plutonium and thorium from its own separation plants, and--according to speculation--thermonulcear substances."[29]

Other evidence supports the view that India's nuclear energy programs suffered from technical difficulties, unrealistic and inadequate planning, inflated official claims, time and cost overruns, and lack of public scrutiny.[30] First, the original planned schedules for the commercial opening of the Rajasthan, Madras, and Narora power plants had to be postponed, while the Tarapur and RAPP-1 plants operated inefficiently.[31] Secondly, India failed to achieve self-sufficiency in heavy water production because of technical difficulties in developing an indigenous production process, labor unrest at the Kota plant, and an explosion at the Baroda plant on 3 December 1977, which caused an annual shortage of 67.2 tonnes of heavy water.[32] Finally, although other examples could be given, India had not moved from natural uranium to an indigenous thorium breeder technology as envisaged in the long-range plans drawn up by Dr. Homi Bhahba in the 1950s. By 1979 work was still underway in finishing a fast breeder reactor in collaboration with France.[33]

Slow domestic progress and increased foreign restrictions on the transfer of nuclear technology following the 1974 explosion all worked to reduce India's self-sufficiency. India's foreign dependence increased as suppliers demanded and received safeguards on India's nuclear technology. For instance, India was unable to make up from domestic sources the shortfall in heavy water supplies caused by Canada's decision in 1976 to halt all technology transfers to India. The Indian government then began negotiations with the Soviet Union for the supply of heavy water. It received the heavy water only when it agreed to Soviet demands for safeguards.

Pakistan's progress in nuclear energy was also very slow. The 1971 War was a special setback for its nuclear program because Pakistan lost several skilled Bengali scientists and technicians. Pakistan also lost the investments in nuclear energy that it had made in the eastern wing.[34] Immediately after the war, Bhutto began a determined program to achieve a nuclear weapons option for Pakistan. The government secretly pursued a two-track route to nuclear weapons--the enriched uranium and the plutonium routes. In March 1976, it signed an agreement with France to build a chemical reprocessing facility, which was hardly justified since Pakistan had only one commercial nuclear power plant producing plutonium. World suspicions were further heightened when the Pakistani authorities began secretly purchasing materials to build a centrifuge plant for enriching uranium.[35] The Carter administration reacted by strongly pressurizing France to back out of the chemical reprocessing deal, which France did in 1978. In February 1979, the Carter administration suspended military and economic assistance to Pakistan in accordance wth the Nuclear Non-Proliferation Act of 1978. No commercial nuclear energy plants came into operation during this period (appendix 8).

Political

After 1972, Mrs. Gandhi's domestic political strength steadily declined to the low point of the 1975-77 state of emergency and her defeat in the March 1977 general elections. Mrs. Gandhi and the Congress Party were thrown out of office by the Janata Party, a coalition of ideologically diverse political parties. In Pakistan, Bhutto rebuilt the political system but failed to institutionalize it. Like Mrs. Gandhi, he also called elections in March 1977, but his demise came about not through the elections, which he apparently won, but through a military coup in July 1977. Both Mrs. Gandhi and Bhutto were replaced by governments intent on making their predecessors accountable for their political actions. There were, however, different patterns of restoration in 1977: India went from a "constitutional dictatorship" to a democratic political system; Pakistan from a weak constitutional system to a military regime. The purpose of the following section is to describe these political changes and then to see how they affected Indo-Pakistani relations.

India. In the short-run, the 1971 victory over Pakistan strengthened Mrs. Gandhi and the Congress Party's at home. In the March 1972 state assembly elections, held in 16 states and 2 Union territories, the Congress (R) gained 48.0 percent of the vote, 70.2 percent of the total seats, and control of 15 states.[36] It appeared that Mrs. Gandhi and the Congress (R) were unbeatable and that India was set for a long period of economic and social reform.

By the beginning of 1973, the euphoric days of the Congress (R)'s election victories and India's defeat of Pakistan had been replaced by economic crisis and popular discontent against the government. Mrs. Gandhi's government--despite its large electoral majorities in the Lok Sabha and the states--found it difficult to fulfill its promises of economic and social reform. Aid to Bangladesh, droughts, poor harvests, and inflation all constrained the government's economic programs. As Rudolph points out, although the 1971 and 1972 elections certainly widened the parameters within which the government could act, political constraints remained. At the state and local level a coalition of urban and rural elites dominated the Congress Party and resisted Mrs. Gandhi's programs for restributing wealth and income.[37]

Before 1969, Congress and the opposition basically agreed about the rules of the constitutional and political system. But after the Congress split and the 1971-72 elections, parties such as the Congress (O), Swatantra, and the Jan Sangh found themselves weaker at the center and in the states. As a response to corruption in the political system and Mrs. Gandhi's populism, the non-communist parties came to rely increasingly on extra-parliamentary methods, particularly in corrupt Congress governments in Gujarat and Bihar.[38]

The opposition's aim of removing Mrs. Gandhi from power appeared to have been achieved on 12 June 1975 when the Allahabad High Court found Mrs. Gandhi guilty of electoral malpractices in her 1971 general election constituency campaign. The Court barred her from holding elective office for six years and ordered her to vacate her Lok Sabha seat. It also delayed execution of her sentence in order to allow the Prime Minister to appeal to the Supreme Court. The opposition clamored for Mrs. Gandhi's immediate resignation. Mrs. Gandhi, fearing the loss of the support within her own party and opposition appeals to the loyalty of the army and police, imposed a state of emergency on 26 June 1975. The government arrested opposition leaders, imposed press censorship, banned extreme left- and right-wing organizations, and curtailed civil liberties. This was all done under Article 352 of the Constitution, which allowed for a state of emergency for reasons of domestic instability.

Mrs. Gandhi then attempted to consolidate her power. On 1 July she announced a "Twenty-Point Program" of economic and social reforms. Other measures enlarged the powers of the executive and curtailed civil liberties. In a longer perspective, the Prime Minister began to revise the Indian Constitution. The 42nd amendment, which the rump Parliament approved on 2 November

1976, strengthened the powers of the Prime Minister, the executive in general, and the center in relation to the states.

The following year, Mrs. Gandhi called for new general elections for March 1977. India's economy had improved since 1975, the opposition appeared fragmented, and Mrs. Gandhi hoped that a victory in the new elections would legitimize the emergency and the constitutional and political changes made under it. Instead of legitimizing the emergency, the elections discredited it. Mrs. Gandhi and the Congress were turned out of office by the Janata party, a coalition of the Congress (O), the Jan Sangh, the Bharatiya Lok Dal (BLD), the Socialist Party, and defectors from the Congress under the Congress for Democracy. The Janata captured 298 seats to the Congress's 153. This gave it a majority of 57 seats in the Lok Sabha.[39]

Led by Morarji Desai as Prime Minister, the Janata government set out to undo the emergency. It released all political prisoners, restored civil liberties, repealed censorship, discontinued the Maintenance of Internal Security Act (MISA), and passed the 43rd and 44th amendments, which overturned the amendments passed during the emergency.[40]

Despite its achievements in restoring democracy, the Janata government could not overcome its internal ideological and personal divisions. As a result, the Janata coalition broke up, paralyzing the government and administration. Mrs. Gandhi took advantage of these internal divisions to make a political recovery. Her new party, the Congress (I) (I for Indira), won two state by-elections in south India in February 1978. Mrs. Gandhi herself returned to national politics when she was elected to the Lok Sabha in November 1978. On 15 July 1979, Morarji Desai resigned as Prime Minister following parliamentary defections from the Janata Party. He was succeeded by Charan Singh of the BLD, who also failed to muster a parliamentary majority. Singh resigned on 20 August but stayed on as caretaker Prime Minister. Thus by the end of 1979, India had the weakest central government in its thirty-two year history.

Pakistan. The crucial challenges facing Bhutto in December 1971 were how to consolidate his own political power and rebuild Pakistan's political system. It is likely that Bhutto saw both challenges as linked: as Bhutto rose so did Pakistan and vice versa.

Bhutto had a number of political assets when he became President of Pakistan on 21 December 1971. He was, first of all, the only major politician of any national following in what remained of Pakistan. His knowledge and experience in foreign policy complemented his domestic political skills. His political party, the PPP, had won a majority of seats in the western wing in the December 1970 general election and was therefore clothed with some political legitimacy. Moreover, the general election and the exit of East Pakistan seemed to reduce the salience of religion and regionalism in Pakistani politics.[41] The military was discredited by the debacle of 1971, was internally divided, and was in no immediate position to challenge Bhutto.

These assets, though, were not as clear-cut as they seemed. First, although Bhutto was the dominant national figure, he was also vulnerable to the question of his personal responsibility for the break-up of Pakistan.[42] Secondly, the PPP drew its greatest political support from the Punjab and Sind, the wealthiest and most populous provinces of Pakistan. It was much weaker in the peripheral provinces of Baluchistan and the NWFP. Here the opposition parties, the National Awami Party (NAP) and the Jamiat-ulama-i-Islam (JUI), drew their major support. The peripheral provinces, and to some extent the Sind, were suspicious of the Punjab, which dominated the new Pakistan more than ever in population, share of GNP, and political power.[43] Regionalism still remained in Pakistan. Finally, although the military was temporarily eclipsed, it still remained a factor in Pakistani politics as long as Bhutto was unsure of his domestic political support and as long as the external security environment remained hostile and uncertain.

Bhutto strengthened his political position with a series of constitutional and political compromises with the opposition. On 5 March 1972, the PPP, the NAP, and other opposition parties agreed on the ground rules for an interim political system and for constitution-making. On 11 April 1973, members of the National Assembly adopted a final Constitution, which provided for a parliamentary, federal system with strong powers for the Prime Minister and a limited role for the armed forces. As in West Germany's political system, the Prime Minister could only be removed by a vote of no-confidence if that vote also named his successor. Under the Constitution, members of the armed forces had to take an oath to uphold the constitution and to remain apolitical.

This promising return to parliamentary, federal, democratic, and civilian rule was vitiated by several political developments that ultimately led to Bhutto's downfall. First, Bhutto's political methods were far from democratic. The armed forces put down a tribal rebellion in Baluchistan by force. The government frequently charged the opposition parties with antinational activities. In 1973 Bhutto dismissed opposition ministries in Baluchistan and the NWFP. In 1975 the NAP was banned and its leader, Wali Khan, arrested. In general, Bhutto's methods of political integration failed to contain regionalism and in fact exacerbated it. Secondly, the PPP failed to develop as a national party. It declined organizationally as Bhutto sought to remove any challenges to his authority from the party.

Finally, the balance of power between the civilian government and the military changed. The military's confidence increased as its budgets increased and as it took part in nation-building activities between 1972 and 1977, such as flood relief operations during August 1973.[44] Nor was the military insulated from national politics. It was called out to aid the civil power on several occasions. It put down language riots in Sind in 1972, labor unrest in Karachi in 1972, and tribal insurgencies in Baluchistan between 1973 and 1977. The turning point came when the military was called out to contain the prolonged riots that followed the March 1977 general election. Eventually, on 5 July 1977, the armed forces realized that there was little prospect of the government and opposition reaching a political compromise. It therefore overthrew Bhutto and declared martial law.

The new military government, under the Chief of the Army Staff, General Muhammad Zia-ul-Haq, immediately set out to reduce the social divisions resulting from Bhutto's rule and to dismantle Bhutto's political structures and legacies. It banned political activity, gave amnesty to Baluch insurgents, released regional leaders, and offered political negotiations to integrate Baluchistan and the NWFP more fully into Pakistan's economic, social, and political systems. The government dismantled Bhutto's political structure by dissolving the PPP and the paramilitary Federal Security Force (FSF), which the military had seen as a threat to its corporate interests. On 3 September 1977, the government arrested Bhutto for the 1974 murder of the father of one of his political opponents. It found Bhutto guilty of these murder charges and hanged him on 4 April 1979.

Despite an official policy of returning Pakistan to civilian rule once conditions had returned to normal, the military gradually began to institutionalize its rule. It began a policy of "Islamization" in order to legitimize military rule and increase Pakistan's political integration. The economic, social, and political systems were all to be transformed so that they could be consistent with Islamic principles. Such a policy increased the government's support, particularly among the religious parties, but, by the end of 1979, Pakistan still faced some of the old problems inherent in Islamization, particularly in applying broad religious principles to the political and economic systems and in reaching a consensus between secularists and modernists.

The political changes in India and Pakistan significantly affected their relations. Between 1971 and 1972, the Indian government was sufficiently strong to be responsive to Pakistan's various difficulties. For all their animosities, Mrs. Gandhi was determined to work with Bhutto. She was aware, for example, of Bhutto's political difficulties in coming to Simla and she praised his realism and courage in doing so.[45] According to Swaran Singh, India's External Affairs Minister, the Indian side realized that Bhutto was in a weak domestic position to accept a formal No-War Pact and to settle the Kashmir issue.[46]

The demands placed upon Pakistan at Simla were also limited by India's interests in a stable political system in Pakistan. The Indian government realized that a punitive settlement of the 1971 War would destablize Pakistan, possibly leading to its further fragmentation and the return of military rule. Mrs. Gandhi preferred a democratic regime because she saw it as more accommodating to India than a military one.[47]

The impact of the emergency (1975-77) on India's responsiveness to Pakistan is harder to trace. On the one hand, it could be argued that the emergency was significant for Indo-Pakistani relations. It was an attempt to control India's intenal political behavior, and as such it allowed the Indian government to be more responsive to Pakistan. Mrs. Gandhi, according to this line of thinking, had greater room for maneuver now that parliamentary opinion could be ignored in formulating foreign policy. Also a number of anti-Pakistani politicians were in jail, and this allowed her to be more responsive to Pakistan. Bhutto noted that the jailing of these politicians was one positive aspect of the emergency declaration in India. He reacted cautiously, however, to the the emergency, preferring to call it an internal matter for India. Still, he was uneasy about how the emergency would affect India's relations with Pakistan. As he remarked, "We have to be watchful lest Mrs. Gandhi, bedevilled and bewildered by the present crisis, seeks to extricate herself from this mess by embarking upon an adventuristic course against Pakistan.[48]

On the other hand, there is the view that the emergency had little impact on India's foreign policy in general and India's policy toward Pakistan in particular.[49] If Mrs. Gandhi had wanted to follow a particular policy toward Pakistan, then nothing prevented her domestically before 1975 from doing so. Parliament and anti-Pakistani politicians had little effect on India's policy before 1975. Nor were Indian policymakers so preoccupied with internal problems that they ignored relations with Pakistan. In any case the emergency did not lead to any dramatic improvement or deterioration in Indo-Pakistani relations. Both countries restored ambassadorial representation in 1976, but this was a logical step from the preceding Simla Agreement of 1972.[50]

Perhaps more important for Indo-Pakistani relations was one internal Indian development before the emergency: the political rehabilitation of Sheikh Abdullah as Chief Minister of Kashmir in February 1975. The Indian government had imprisoned the charismatic Kashmiri leader for most of the period between 1953 and 1975 for insisting on a plebiscite and national self-determination for the Kashmiri people. Under the terms of the February 1975 agreement with Mrs. Gandhi, the Sheikh agreed to drop these demands in return for political power in Kashmir and guarantees of Kashmir's continued autonomy under the Indian Constitution. Not only did the agreement strengthen the Indian government's domestic political position (for Kashmir had always been symbolic of Indian political integration[51]), it also strengthened its position relative to Pakistan, which now saw the Kashmiris being integrated more fully into India's political system under a popular local leader.

The rapid political changes in both countries in 1977 placed Indo-Pakistani relations in a state of flux and even threatened to set back the process of normalization. India's general election, Mrs. Gandhi's defeat, and the Janata victory had a direct impact on the Pakistani political system, which was conducting a general election campaign at about the same time. According to an American political scientist who covered both campaigns, "The results of the Indian elections seemed to impress the Pakistanis in many ways, apparently leading many to wonder why India could hold free and peaceful elections while they could not, and to consider 'the Indian example' of ousting a seemingly strongly entrenched authoritarian regime through the electoral process as a possible way out of the confusion, violence, and threats to the integrity and stability of the country that characterized the postelection scene in their country."[52]

The new Janata government offered a No-War Pact to Pakistan in April 1977. Bhutto rejected it, probably because he wanted more time to assess the strength of the new government. As it turned out, it was Bhutto who had very little time in office. The return of military government in Pakistan was greeted with some suspicion by the new Janata government, but these initial suspicions were eventually eased. This is partly due to the Janata government's foreign policy, which stressed two clear themes: *genuine nonalignment* toward the superpowers and *beneficial bilateralism* in India's relations with its South Asian neighbors. Underlying the latter theme was the assumption that India as the dominant power in South Asia (or core area, although it was never couched in such academic language) had to reassure its smaller neighbors and take the initiative in resolving bilateral disputes. This policy then clearly shows the Indian government's responsiveness to the smaller South Asian states.

The differences in foreign policy between the Congress and the Janata can be exaggerated, but beneficial bilateralism did represent a departure in India's relations with its neighbors.[53] These differences in substance, nuance, and style, can be traced to domestic roots: the new Janata government sought not only to restore democracy in India and to hold Mrs. Gandhi accountable, it also sought to project a more restrained image of Indian power abroad, particularly in the subcontinent. The Janata government saw the disciplining of executive power at home and the disciplining of Indian power abroad as two sides of the same coin--the removal of Mrs. Gandhi's legacies.[54]

For Pakistan, the positive fruits of the Janata's policy were a successful visit by External Affairs Minister Vajpayee to Islamabad in February 1978 (the first visit by an Indian cabinet minister in twelve years) and the signing of the Salal Dam Agreement in April 1978. India adjusted the technical design of the Indian project and compensated Pakistan for some of its environmental effects in neighboring Pakistani areas.[55]

Such regional initiatives were conducted quite early in the life of the Janata government. They could not be sustained after 1979 because of internal divisions within the Janata government. In the 1980 general election campaign, Mrs. Gandhi accused the Janata of neglecting India's regional interests by being too accommodating to the wishes of the smaller states.

In summary, despite severe domestic problems, Indian governments remained responsive to Pakistan. Immediately after the Bangladesh War, Mrs. Gandhi's government recognized that Bhutto was politically weak at home and could not accept any peace treaty that even remotely smacked of a dictated peace. Later, when Mrs. Gandhi imposed the state of emergency in June 1975, there was no noticeable change in Indo-Pakistani relations. After Mrs. Gandhi's defeat in the 1977 general election, the new Janata government sought improved regional relations. Its policy of beneficial bilateralism assumed that India had the capabilities to be a core area in South Asia and that India had to be responsive to smaller states like Pakistan.

MILITARY CAPABILITIES, POWER AND INFLUENCE

As 1972 began, a central objective of India's military policy was to consolidate India's status as the dominant military power in South Asia, a status confirmed by the military victory over Pakistan in December 1971. Yet India's military policy was only partly focused on Pakistan and the region. The Indian government had to take note of growing superpower presence in the Indian Ocean and the state of the superpower nuclear balance. Also worrisome were increased arms transfers to the Middle East, instability in Iran, and growing Soviet intervention in Afghanistan. Unlike India's policy of consolidation, Pakistan's military policy after 1971 could only be one of reconstructing its armed forces and redefining its security. Pakistan's government realized that the balance of power had turned overwhelmingly in India's favor in GNP, population, territory, and defense burdens. It nevertheless continued to spend heavily on the armed forces in order to narrow the relative military gap between India and Pakistan and to safeguard Pakistan's sovereignty.

Armies

The Indian army's numerical strength steadily increased (appendices 2 and 3). It modernized its weapons and equipment by reducing the number of aging Centurions, AMX-13, and PT-76 tanks, doubling the number of T-54/55 tanks, and by tripling the number of Vijayantas. Added to these was an expanded and diverse production of small arms, ammunition, field guns, and anti-tank missiles. Overall, these changes represented an accretion of the army's weapons inventories.

The Pakistan army's total size increased from 340,000 in mid-1971 to 400,000 in mid-1979, which represented a net increase of three infantry divisions and three independent infantry brigades. Arms transfers from abroad were small and were probably enough to replace the army's existing arms inventories. This meant that the expanded army was underequipped by the end of the 1970s.

Air Forces

The Indian Air Force steadily expanded its manpower, weapons, and equipment (appendices 2, 5, and 7). It modernized its aircraft inventories by increasing the number of MiG-21 squadrons, reducing the number of Gnats, Su-7, and Hunter F.6 front-line squadrons, and by phasing out of its Mystere fighter squadrons. The IAF came to rely on its MiGs as the backbone of its front-line aircraft. Most of the arms transfers of aircraft and missiles to the IAF came in the form of licensed production, except for 50 Mielec TS-22 trainers from Poland and 7 Il-38 May reconnaissance planes from the USSR.

Overall, from indigenous and foreign sources, aircraft inventories increased, although for particular categories, such as transport aircraft, it is likely that some inventories decreased.

The Pakistan Air Force, by contrast, found it difficult to recover from the 1971 War.[56] Its major aircraft imports came from China, Iran, and France, and were enough to replace aircraft inventories. The PAF would have preferred more advanced aircraft than the Chinese-built MiGs, but the United States refused to supply A-17 aircraft, and Pakistan could not afford to buy more French aircraft. The PAF's manpower remained static between 1972 and 1979 (appendix 2).

Navies

Although still the smallest of the three services, the Indian Navy had the fastest rate of growth of manpower and budgetary allocations after 1971.[57] This relative growth reflected the government's awareness of the potential threats to India's security from the sea. In particular, the government took into account: first, the strategic lessons from the 1971 War, when the Nixon administration dispatched a naval task force to the Bay of Bengal; second, the increase in the strength of superpower naval forces in the Indian Ocean; third, the arms build-up in the Middle East; and, finally, the need to protect India's expanding shipping and off-shore oil industries.[58]

The Indian Navy's modernization between 1972 and 1979 made it increasingly capable of operating two fleets independently on both sides of the Indian peninsula. Improved naval bases, communications, organization, and weapons and equipment, all made this possible. But, of the three services, the navy was the most dependent upon off-the-shelf purchases of foreign weapons, most of which came from one source, the Soviet Union. A number of craft were discarded from the navy's inventories through scrapping, transfer to the new Coast Guard (a paramilitary organization established in 1978), or through arms transfers to Bangladesh. Overall, the navy's inventories increased.

A number of factors determined the growth of the Pakistan Navy after 1971: it had to make up for the losses in the 1971 War; it had to readjust to its new geographical status in the subcontinent; and, as a capital-intensive service, it had to compete with the other two services for scarce resources. Two defense experts noted in 1978 that "Pakistan's surface fleet appears to be moving away from larger capital ships and toward fast frigates and patrol aircraft which are highly maneuverable and also carry a sizeable and effective weapons arsenal. This trend reflects perhaps Pakistani reaction to its inability to break India's 1971 naval blockade."[59] Major acquisitions included one destroyer, one submarine and six midget submarines. Pakistan maintained its position in light forces, receiving several Chinese fast-attack craft and patrol boats. As a whole, the arms transfers replaced the navy's inventories, although the number of frigates decreased. The navy's manpower increased from 10,000 to 12,000.

Defense Production

Indian policymakers concluded from the 1971 War that more effort was needed to reach the military self-sufficiency. The Second Five-Year Defense Plan (1969-74) was interrupted by the 1971 War, but the plan's objectives were more valid than ever. By the end of 1979, the specific project objectives of the Second and Third Defense Plans were generally achieved. In the 1970s, the government began several new projects to furnish the armed forces with a new generation of weapons.[60] Indian defense production outstripped Pakistan's in quantity and value of production, diversity of items, and sophistication.

Compared to India, Pakistan's industrial base grew very little to support a self-sufficient defense industry.[61] Even so, Bhutto was determined to increase Pakistan's self-sufficiency as much as possible. In the military field, this meant expanding domestic defense production. The most important development was the establishment of a Pakistan Aeronautical Complex (PAC) at Kamra with Chinese assistance. Like India in the period from 1947-53, Pakistan's fledgling aircraft industry began with the assembly of light aircraft under license and with plans for the licensed production of more advanced aircraft. In 1976 the PAC assembled its first Saab Safari/Supporter, and in the same year concluded a license production agreement with the United States for T-41D Mescalero trainers. Pakistan also began negotiating with France to produce Mirage III aircraft. The only progress that Pakistan made in this period was in improving its ability to upgrade its tanks and service its existing aircraft.

How did this continuous modernization of India's military assets affect India's policies of regional integration with Pakistan? The Indian government was much more concerned about military aid to Pakistan from China, the Middle East, and the United States than it was about Pakistan's own military capabilities, which it saw, anyway, as being limited. India's policy was to promote Pakistan's viability because a strong Pakistan on India's northwestern border was much more preferable than several small, weak independent states that might invite foreign intervention into South Asia. India's interest in a strong Pakistan, however, was subject to the qualification that this strength would not be with external military assistance or at the expense of India's regional dominance.

The 1971 War was a severe blow to the prestige of Pakistan's military, which had always prided itself on a supposed military and moral superiority over its Indian counterpart. But the war also eased the military's task of defending what remained of Pakistan. True, Pakistan still lacked defensive depth against India and could no longer by itself distract India along two fronts. But the loss of the eastern wing simplified Pakistan's military problems. Pakistan was now geographically compact, which meant that the military could concentrate its forces in one theater. Consequently, the military's organizational, logistical, and communication problems were simpler. Of course, India could also concentrate its forces against Pakistan in one theater, but the Indian military had to take into account a possible two-front war against Pakistan and China.

Another favorable result of the 1971 War was that the Pakistani military was more, rather than less, representative of civilian society in its ethnic composition. Even though Punjabis and Pathans still dominated the armed forces, the debilitating conflicts about representation of East and West Pakistanis in the armed forces were reduced. This freed the military and political authorities to make more decisions on military factors alone rather than having to take into account factors such as ethnic balance and regional distribution of military expenditure.

Finally, the military's defeat in 1971 and the return of civilian government gave the military an opportunity to resume its primary role: the defense of the country, not its governance. Pakistanis partly blamed the 1971 defeat on the military's intervention in Pakistan's politics and administration to the neglect of its professional effectiveness. They increasingly recognized that changes were needed in higher defense organization (particularly in the coordination between the three services), training, research, and strategic thinking. The 1971 War administered a shock to Pakistan's military in much the same way that the 1962 Sino-Indian War did to the Indian military.

The military's determination to renew itself is one reason why Pakistan's post-1971 military expenditures remained high. But there were other reasons too. First, in the two years or so following the 1971 War, Pakistan's security relations with India remained highly uncertain. India held four and a half Pakistani army divisions as prisoners of war. India also held 5,139 square miles of Pakistani territory, and its military position in Kashmir was stronger. The Delhi Agreement of April 1974 settled most of the issues of the 1971 War, but this was followed in the next month by India's nuclear explosion. Given these developments, an increase in military expenditures was meant to demonstrate the military's deterrent value and Pakistan's resolve in safeguarding its sovereignty.

Secondly, the high military expenditures reflected Pakistani domestic politics. Bhutto sought to consolidate his influence in the armed forces by continuing the high expenditures. These expenditures were also needed to quell tribal insurgencies in the border province of Baluchistan.

Finally, Pakistan's relations with Afghanistan deteriorated after July 1973 when Prince Daoud overthrew his cousin King Zahir Shah. As Prime Minister between 1953-63, Daoud had been well known for strongly supporting Pakhtoonistan. Relations between Pakistan and Afghanistan did improve in the mid-1970s, largely through the mediation efforts of the Shah of Iran, but a new era of uncertainty arose when Daoud was overthrown in April 1978 by the Khalq faction of the Marxist People's Democratic Party of Afghanistan (PDPA). These domestic Afghan developments, coupled with growing Soviet military and political involvement after 1978 and Pakistan's continuing problems in Baluchistan and the NWFP, made the Pakistan government increasingly aware of security threats from Afghanistan.

This is not to say that Pakistan's security prospects were uniformly bleak between 1972 and 1979. An increasingly powerful Iran emerged as a strong and explicit backer of Pakistan's territorial integrity, at least until the downfall of the Shah in 1979. The Shah saw Pakistan as a buffer against India and as a brake against Baluchi nationalism within Iran. The Chinese showed their support for Pakistan by economic and military aid, diplomatic support, and by completing in 1978 the Karakoram Highway linking Xinjiang province with Islamabad via Pakistani-occupied Kashmir. Iranian and Chinese support for Pakistan's national sovereignty strengthened Pakistan's security, but the military assistance provided by these countries fell short of Pakistan's needs for sophisticated and diverse weapons. Here Pakistan's resource environment seemed to brighten when the United States government lifted its arms embargo to the subcontinent in 1975. American arms transfers to Pakistan, however, were small. The Carter administration sought to block Pakistan's nuclear proliferation; in any case, it placed more emphasis on India as the "new influential" in the region.

As noted earlier, Indian defense planning was no longer made entirely with reference to Pakistan. But India's asymmetry of attention affected Pakistan's security. Within a week of the Indian nuclear explosion of 18 May 1974, Mrs. Gandhi sent a letter to Prime Minister Bhutto to reassure him and the Pakistani people that the Indian test was for peaceful purposes. She argued that the PNE had no political or military implications, that it was needed to develop alternative sources of energy in an era of world energy crisis, and that all effort had been made to safeguard the health and population of neighboring countries after the explosion.[62]

Bhutto's position was that the nuclear test had significantly changed Pakistan's security environment. His reply to Mrs. Gandhi distinguished between India's capabilities and intentions; whatever India may say about the purposes of the test, Pakistan could not ignore India's newly demonstrated capabilities. Most significantly, Bhutto placed the Indian nuclear test in the context of India's other emerging capabilities in space research.[63]

How valid were these Indian and Pakistani positions on the nuclear test? The Indian argument that the test was for peaceful purposes seems plausible, as does the Indian claim that safety measures were taken to reduce the environmental impact of the test on neighboring countries.[64] But the claim that the test had no political or military implications is dubious. Although the actual time and location of the test had no particular implications for Pakistan and the world,[65] the test was meant to demonstrate India's opposition to the discriminatory aspects of the current nuclear nonproliferation regime--that the NPT created two categories of states, the nuclear "haves" and the "have-nots," that it gave insufficient security guarantees to nonnuclear states, that its provisions were weak, and that it made no distinction between peaceful and nonpeaceful nuclear explosions.

The decision to explode India's nuclear device was not a mere technical decision. The Indian government anticipated the reactions of other countries, particularly Pakistan. Indian officials perceived that some countries would be hostile but that Pakistan would be put in a proper frame of mind by the Indian test regarding India's technological capabilities.

In short, the test had political and military implications. The Indian government's denial of those implications was therefore meant to increase the ambiguity about India's nuclear intentions and thereby increase India's options--that is, demonstrate a capability of producing nuclear weapons but foreswear actual nuclearization.[66] India demonstrated its opposition to the NPT and the ineffectiveness of that treaty for nuclear nonproliferation. The formation of the London Suppliers Group to increase safeguards on the transfer of nuclear technology was the direct result of India's 1974 explosion.

Whatever the Indian government might say about the political and military implications, Bhutto's government did draw inferences from the test. Pakistan's position that the test had changed its security environment was correct. In the government's words, the test gave a "rude jolt" to the Pakistani people.[67] It had undoubtedly changed Pakistan's security environment. Two points may be noted about Pakistan's immediate response to the test. First, as noted earlier, the government linked the test to India's capabilities in space research.

This shows that it was at least aware of India's space programs, even if India was still far away from a nuclear delivery system and command and control systems.[68] Second, Pakistan's government indicated its own weaknesses in developing nuclear energy and weapons. Specifically, Bhutto noted that it would be several years before Pakistan's nuclear programs could get off the ground.[69]

In the long-term, Pakistan's government responded to the Indian test in several ways. At the rhetorical level, it attempted to denigrate India's capabilities. Bhutto called India a "phoney nuclear power," meaning that India lacked the necessary scientific, technological, and industrial infrastructure to compete with other nuclear powers.[70] But if Bhutto really believed that India was a phoney nuclear power, then why did he exaggerate the significance of India's nuclear explosion? One explanation is that Bhutto was aware of India's greater nuclear energy development compared with Pakistan but that he also knew that India was having difficulties in developing its nuclear energy.

At the diplomatic level, the Pakistan government stressed the seriousness of the new development to several foreign governments. Bhutto asked India to reaffirm the Simla principles--that is, refrain from the threat or use of force against each other's territorial integrity or political independence. He also repeated his proposal for a nuclear-weapons-free zone in South Asia. The immediate effect of the nuclear explosion on Indo-Pakistani regional integration was that Pakistan postponed scheduled talks on restoring communication links and travel facilities between the two countries. These talks were resumed in September 1974 after Pakistan was satisfied that the Indian government had publicly restated its adherence to the Simla principles.[71]

Pakistan also responded to the test by increasing military expenditures and by attempting to modernize its conventional forces. Bhutto used the perceived nuclear threats from India as a lever to extract military resources from the United States. Finally, Pakistan responded to India's test by developing its own nuclear program, although we have seen that Pakistan's program was too ambitious and that this response was the least credible of all Pakistani responses. There was, and still is, much speculation whether Pakistan intended to make nuclear weapons. Evidence for the view that it did comes from the Pakistani search for a chemical separation plant from France and the secret purchase of materials for a centrifuge enrichment plant. But it is likely that both Bhutto's and Zia's governments followed a nuclear weapons strategy similar to India's--that is increase capabilities to produce nuclear weapons while publicly affirming their adherence to nonproliferation. Besides the economic, scientific and military constraints on a nuclear weapons program, the government also took into account other constraints, such as the effct a weapons program would have on an arms race with India and on international aid to Pakistan.

To sum up: this discussion of military assets, power, and influence indicates that after 1971, and particularly after the Indian nuclear test of May 1974, nuclear issues became more important in Indo-Pakistani relations, much more so than the earlier periods when India's nuclear weapons capabilities were undemonstrated. Bhutto's government responded to the 1974 test by seeking nuclear guarantees, accelerating Pakistan's own nuclear weapons option, and attempting to increase Pakistan's conventional military strength. In the 1972-79 period as a whole, Pakistani governments actively sought to mobilize military strength in order to maintain Pakistan's national sovereignty, integrity and Islamic values. The following section examines these national values and other identitive relations with India in greater detail. Military factors are not understandable without reference to the severe identitiy crisis Pakistan faced after 1971 and the search to define its values.

IDENTITIVE CAPABILITIES, POWER AND INFLUENCE

The traumatic civil war of 1971 and Pakistan's dismemberment raised fundamental questions about Pakistan's national identity.[72] The secession of East Pakistan had been accompanied by brutal conflict among Muslims and seemed to prove Indian claims that religion was a weak basis for nationality in South Asia. Pakistan was no longer the major homeland for the Muslims in the subcontinent. Indeed, Pakistan's Muslim population of 67 million was closely followed by India's (64 million) and Bangladesh (61 million).[73] Thus about two-thirds of South Asian Muslims fell under secular government.

Pakistan's government sought several ways to resolve this identity crisis and to counter Indian claims of the superiority of secularism over sectarianism. First, Bhutto reaffirmed the validity of the two-nation theory by asking rhetorically: How can one speak of the end of that theory when there are now three major nations in South Asia? He saw the existence of two Muslim states to be consistent with the Lahore Resolution of 23 March 1940, which called for independent states in the Muslim-majority areas of the subcontinent.[74] This appears to be a consolation of history since Bhutto had fought so hard for a united Pakistan during the 1970-71 East Pakistan crisis.

Secondly, Pakistan established its new Muslim identity in a practical way by emphasizing its religious, cultural, and political links with the rest of the Muslim world, particularly with the Middle East. This had been made easier by East Pakistan's secession; Pakistanis could now direct their attention away from the subcontinent and towards their Middle Eastern brethren. Besides their military, economic and strategic support, identitive support from the Middle Eastern countries enabled Pakistani governments to resist what they saw as identitive power from India.[75] Increasing economic trends and patterns of migration drew Pakistan further into the Muslim fold. This was symbolized by Pakistan's hosting of the 1974 Islamic Conference.

Other than the Pakistan government's desire to keep Pakistan culturally separate from India, it is difficult to generalize about the effect of the changes in identitive assets between India and Pakistan. Regarding political complementarity, Indian governments preferred a civilian democratic government in Pakistan to a military one. But Mrs. Gandhi's state of emergency in 1975-77 reduced India's influence over the types of regimes in South Asia. It tarnished India's image and hence influence. Pakistan's government passed up this opportunity to show the gap between India's democratic ideals and practices, probably because Bhutto himself in this period was moving toward authoritarian rule in Pakistan.[76] The 1977 changes in governments in both countries seemed to restore the previous antagonisms between Indian democracy and Pakistani military government. But as noted earlier, both governments were pragmatic in their bilateral relations, which improved between 1977 and 1979.

Bhutto's withdrawal of Pakistan from the Commonwealth in 1972 and Zia's Islamization policies reduced the identitive ties between India and Pakistan. These actions had very little effect on their relations and were offset by Pakistan's decisions in 1979 to leave CENTO and to join (with Indian support) the Non-Aligned Movement. On certain international issues, like the NIEO and its associated demands--debt relief, and so forth, Indian and Pakistani positions were similar.

In summary, the realignment of national power in the subcontinent in 1971 challenged Pakistan's national identity. Pakistani elites and publics met this challenge by increasing their identification with the Middle Eastern and Islamic countries. Maintaining Pakistan's separate identity was a common objective of both Bhutto's and Zia's governments.

CONCLUSION

The most important event in the development of a security-community in the subcontinent was the Simla Agreement of 1972. This was a diplomatic victory for India for two reasons: it served as the functional equivalent of a No-War Treaty, and Pakistan for the first time accepted the principle of bilateralism in its relations with India. India thus furthered its aims of insulating the subcontinent from the external intervention of powers, such as China and the United States.

Simla was, though, a limited diplomatic victory for India. India conceded Pakistan's position about the need for third party mediation, allowing for such mediation when both parties agreed upon it. Bhutto used this part of the Simla Agreement to justify the presentation of Pakistan's disputes with India before the UN and the International Court of Justice. Nor did Bhutto's formal acceptance of bilateralism prevent him from mobilizing external support, whether from China, the Middle East, or the United States. This suggests that Bhutto's acceptance of bilateralism was qualified and that it was a tactical acceptance made while Pakistan was materially and militarily weak. Bhutto's long-term objectives were to increase Pakistan's national capabilities in order to reduce or eliminate perceived threats to Pakistan's sovereignty. He made it clear that Pakistan would never accept Indian "hegemony" in the subcontinent, meaning by hegemony India's control of national decision-making in the subcontinent.[77]

Yet it would be wrong to conclude that Pakistan accepted bilateralism for expedient reasons. Although this principle may have been accepted reluctantly, given India's material and military preponderence over Pakistan, Pakistan realized that there were no alternatives to seeking an accommodation with India. Even after India's nuclear test of May 1974, which the Pakistan government saw as the most serious development in Pakistan's security since independence, the Pakistan government did not repudiate Simla. Instead, it pressed India to reiterate the Simla principles, particularly those relating to the peaceful settlement of disputes and abjuring of the threat or use of force. In short, both India and Pakistan had their own reasons for institutionalizing the Simla Agreement. Pakistan's interests in peaceful relations with India increased towards the end of the 1970s, following political instability in neighboring Iran and Afghanistan. The Soviet invasion of Afghanistan on 26 December 1979 significantly changed regional relations in South Asia. The invasion ensured that the 1980s would be a new era for Indo-Pakistani relations.

Notes

1. The phrase is from Maurice Zinkin, "The Political Aftermath of the Indo-Pakistan War," *Survival* 14 (March-April 1972), p. 55. On 19 March 1972, India and Bangladesh signed a Treaty of Friendship, Cooperation and Peace. In retrospect this friendship was short; relations became strained after the assassination of Sheikh Mujib on 15 August 1975 by a group of anti-Indian junior army officers.

2. From 1971 to 1972, the ratio of Indian to Pakistani population increased from 4.3:1 to 9.3:1; territory from 3.1:1 to 3.6:1; and GNP from 5.3:1 to 8.3:1. India's military expenditure as a percent of GNP remained relatively constant, while Pakistan's increased from 4.8 to 8.7 percent. Pakistan's per capita GNP increased from $81 to $109. These data have been derived from United States, Arms Control and Disarmament Agency, *World Military Expenditures and Arms Trade 1963-1973* (Washington, D. C.: U.S. Government Printing Office, 1975), pp. 52, 62; and United Nations, *Statistical Yearbooks 1971 & 1972*.

3. Speech to National Assembly of Pakistan, 14 April 1972, reprinted in *Pakistan Horizon* 25 (Second Quarter 1972), p. 116.

4. Lawrence Ziring, "Bhutto's Foreign Policy, 1972-73," in *Contemporary Problems of Pakistan*, ed. J. Henry Korson (Leiden: E. J. Brill, 1974), p. 69.

5. Interview with Richard Lindley, ITN, 25 April 1972, reprinted in *Pakistan Horizon* 25 (Second Quarter 1972), p. 124.

6. The text of the Simla Treaty is reprinted in *Survival* 14 (September-October 1972), p. 242.

7. Interview with Arnaud de Borchgrave, Newsweek, 3 April 1972, reprinted in *Pakistan Horizon* 25 (Second Quarter 1972), p. 114.

8. Mohammed Ayoob, *India, Pakistan & Bangladesh* (New Delhi: Indian Council for World Affairs, 1975), p. 109.

9. U. S., Arms Control and Disarmament Agency, *World Military Expenditures and Arms Trade 1963-73*, pp. 52, 62.

10. United Nations, Food and Agriculture Organization, *Production Yearbooks, 1972 and 1979.*

11. Between 1970-71 and 1978-79, India's production of pig iron increased from 6.99 to 9.49 million tonnes and steel ingots from 6.4 to 8.35 million tonnes. India, Ministry of Finance, *Economic Survey 1980-81* (Delhi: Controller of Publications, 1981), p. 84. The figures for Pakistan's production of mild steel products are from Pakistan, Ministry of Finance, *Economic Survey 1979-80* Statistical Annexure (Islamabad: Finance Division, 1980), p. 51.

12. World Bank, *World Development Report 1981* (New York: Oxford University Press, 1981), p. 80.

13. Pakistan, Ministry of Finance, *Economic Survey 1971-72* (Karachi: Manager of Publications, 1972), xi.

14. Gilbert T. Brown, "Pakistan's Economic Development After 1971," in *Pakistan: The Long View*, ed. Lawrence Ziring, Ralph Braibanti, and W. Howard Wriggins (Durham, N. C.: Duke University Press, 1977), p. 200.

15. Bhutto's educational policies are assessed in J. Henry Korson, "Bhutto's Educational Reform," in Korson, *Contemporary Problems*, pp. 119-46.

16. These industries included iron and steel, basic metal industries, heavy engineering, heavy electrical machinery, assembly and manufacture of motor vehicles, tractor plants, heavy and basic chemicals, petrochemicals, cement, and public industries. But as W. Eric Gustafson notes, "Pakistan's capacity in almost all of these areas was slim indeed, and not very much at all was being nationalized." "Economic Reforms under the Bhutto Regime," in Korson, *Contemporary Problems*, p. 82. Nationalization did not touch Pakistan's largest industry, textiles.

17. Shahid Javed Burki, *Pakistan Under Bhutto, 1971-1977* (New York: St. Martin's Press, 1980), pp. 148-54.

18. Ibid., p. 163.

19. Ibid., p. 154.

20. For details of the military government's new economic policies, see William L. Richter, "Persistent Praetorianism: Pakistan's Third Military Regime," *Pacific Affairs* 51 (Fall 1978), p. 420; and in *Pakistan Year Book 1980-81* (Karachi: East and West Publishing Company, 1980), pp. 373-78.

21. International Monetary Fund, *International Financial Statistics* October 1974, pp. 178-79, November 1980, pp. 190-191. (Washington, D.C.: International Monetary Fund, 1975 and 1976).

22. Zulfikar Ali Bhutto, "Pakistan Builds Anew," *Foreign Affairs* 51 (April 1973), p. 543.

23. India's weaknesses as a core area are discussed in Bhabani Sen Gupta, "Waiting for India: India's Role As a Regional Power," *Journal of International Affairs* 29 (Fall 1975): 171-84.

24. Up to March 1978, Bangladesh received the following foreign aid (in US $ million): United States $1,045.1; International Development Association and World Bank $945.3; Japan $528.3; West Germany $417.3; Canada $358.8; OPEC $324.7; and India $311 million. Iftekhar A. Chowdhury, "Strategy of a Small Power in a Subsystem: Bangladesh's External Relations," *Australian Outlook* 34 (April 1980), pp. 95-96.

25. Onkar Marwah, "India's Military Intervention in East Pakistan, 1971-72," *Modern Asian Studies* 13 (October 1979), p. 577.

26. Dewan C. Vohra, *India's Aid Diplomacy in the Third World* (New Delhi: Vikas, 1980), p. 143.

27. For details of these differences, see Surendra Chopra, "Prospects of Indo-Pakistan Trade," *The Indian Journal of Political Science* 38 (October-December 1977): 476-93.

28. Details of the progress made in the last four areas are contained in India, Department of Atomic Energy, *Annual Report 1978-79* (Bombay: Publications Officer, DAE, 1979).

29. Onkar Marwah, "India's Nuclear and Space Programs: Intent and Policy," *International Security* 2 (Fall 1977), p. 99.

30. Critical analyses of India's nuclear program include Ashok Kapur, *International Nuclear Proliferation*, particularly pp. 191-95; Ravindra Tomar, "The Indian Nuclear Power Program: Myths and Mirages," *Asian Survey* 20 (May 1980): 517-31; and R. R. Subramaniam, "India's Nuclear Situation: Where to?" *IDSA Journal* 10 (April-June 1978): 304-21.

31. Details of the delays and inefficient operation of the nuclear power plants are contained in Tomar, "Indian Nuclear Power Program."

32. Subramaniam, "India's Nuclear Situation," p. 315.

33. By 1979 the civil works for the reactor building and the buildings to house other units, such as the turbine and steam generator, had been completed. Department of Atomic Energy, *Annual Report 1978-79*, pp. 43-44.

34. P. B. Sinha and R. R. Subramaniam, *Nuclear Pakistan: Atomic Threat to South Asia* (New Delhi: Vision Books, 1980), pp. 36-37.

35. Ibid., pp. 107-27.

36. Marcus F. Franda, "India's 1972 State Elections," *American Universities Field Staff Reports, South Asia Series*, 16, 1 (April 1972).

37. Susanne Hoeber Rudolph, "The Writ from Delhi: The Indian Government's Capabilities after the 1971 Election," *Asian Survey* 11 (October 1971): 958-69.

38. For analyses of these disturbances, see Dawn E. Jones and Rodney W. Jones, "Urban Upheaval in India: The 1974 Nav Nirman Riots in Gujarat," *Asian Survey* 16 (November 1976): 1012-33; and John R. Wood, "Extra-Parliamentary

Opposition in India: An Analysis of Populist Agitations in Gujarat and Bihar," *Pacific Affairs* 49 (Fall 1975): 313-34.

39. Myron Weiner, *India at the Polls: The Parliamentary Elections of 1977* (Washington, D. C.: American Enterprise Institute for Public Policy Research, 1978), p. 71.

40. Michael Henderson, "Setting India's Democratic House in Order: Constitutional Amendments," *Asian Survey* 19 (October 1979): 945-56.

41. Burki, *Pakistan*, p. 92.

42. Ibid.

43. In 1972, the Punjab had 58 percent of Pakistan's population, 61.1 percent of the GDP, 67.2 percent of foodgrain output, and 65.5 percent of the value of industrial output. Ibid, p. 94.

44. Hasan Askari Rizvi, *The Military and Politics in Pakistan* (Lahore: Progressive Publishers, 1974), p. 264.

45. Gandhi, "India and the World," p. 72.

46. Interview with Swaran Singh, San Francisco, California, 3 September 1983.

47. Gandhi, "India and the World," p. 71.

48. *Pakistan Horizon* 28 (Third Quarter 1975), p. 155. See also his interview with George Hutchinson of the *Spectator* in Zulfikar Ali Bhutto, *The Third World: New Directions* (London: Quartet Books, 1977), pp. 101-2; and Leo E. Rose, "The Emergency and India's External Relations," in *Indian Democracy in Crisis* (Northridge, CA: California State University Foundation, Northridge, 1976), pp. 100-103.

49. Mohammed Ayoob, "India and Pakistan: Prospects for Detente," *Pacific Community* 8 (October 1976), p. 157.

50. Ibid., p. 157.

51. David E. Lockwood, "Kashmir: Sheikh Abdullah's Reinstatement," *The World Today* 31 (June 1975), pp. 254-55.

52. Norman D. Palmer, "The Two Elections: A Comparative Analysis," *Asian Survey* 17 (July 1977), p. 658

53. The success of this policy is analyzed in S. D. Muni, "India's "Beneficial Bilateralism" in South Asia," *India Quarterly* 35 (October-December 1979): 417-33.

54. Atal Behari Vajpayee, "Continuity and Change in India's Foreign Policy," in Vajpayee, *New Dimensions of India's Foreign Policy* (New Delhi: Vision Books, 1979), p. 62.

55. Muni, "India's "Beneficial"," p.420.

56. Frank Bray and Alvin J. Cottrell, "The Armed Forces of India, Iran and Pakistan: A Comparative Assessment," in *R.U.S.I. and Brassey's Defense Yearbook 1977/78*, ed. Royal Services Institute for Defence Studies (Boulder, Colo.: Westview Press, 1977), p. 26.

57. Raju Thomas, "The Armed Services and the Indian Defense Budget," *Asian Survey* 20 (March 1980), p. 284.

58. The various reasons for a naval buildup are examined by Raju Thomas in "The Politics of Indian Naval Re-armament, 1962-1974," *Pacific Community* 6 (April 1975):452-74; and "The Indian Navy in the Seventies," *Pacific Affairs* 48 (Winter 1975-76): 500-18.

59. Bray and Cottrell, "Armed Forces," p. 31.

60. The Indian government was negotiating with West Germany for the licensed production of submarines. A "Godavari" class frigate was being constructed at Magazon Docks. The government began several other projects to provide the armed forces with a new generation of weapons. Among these were: the successor to the Gnat fighter, a military version of the HS-748 light transport plane, the Jaguar deep penetration fighter-bomber, a STOL plane, a light basic trainer, an armed light helicopter, an armored personnel carrier, and the licensed production of the T-72 main battle tank from the USSR.

61. An analysis of Pakistan's defense capabilities is contained in Samuel Baid and Sreedhar, "Pakistan's Defense Potential," *Foreign Affairs Reports* 25 (April 1976):53-66.

62. Letter from the Indian Prime Minister to Prime Minister Bhutto, 22 May 1974, reprinted in *Pakistan Horizon* 27 (Third Quarter 1974), pp. 197-98.

63. The Prime Minister of Pakistan's reply, 5 June 1974, ibid., pp. 198-200. The Indian government set up a Space Commission and a Department of Space in June 1972. These bodies began work on rockets, launch vehicles and satellite building.

64. Marwah writes, "...the possiblity exists that special safety features were built into the device, that it was a "clean" explosion. Thus, there was no radiation and heat venting after the nuclear test. Health technicians were able to enter the area within thirty minutes of the blast." "India's Nuclear Program: Decisions, Intent, and Policy, 1950-1976," in *Asia's Nuclear Future*, ed. William H. Overholt (Boulder, Colo.: Westview Press, 1977), p. 174.

65. The test was made before the meeting in Paris of the Aid-India Consortium. The Indian government conducted the test in Rajasthan because it is India's foremost desert state, and not because the state borders on Pakistan. An example of the latter error can be found in Shirin Tahir-Kheli, "The Foreign Policy of "New" Pakistan," *Orbis* 20 (Fall 1976), p. 753.

66. The concept of *nuclear options diplomacy* is examined in Ashok Kapur, *International Nuclear Proliferation: Multilateral Diplomacy and Regional Aspects* (New York: Praeger, 1979).

67. Letter from Mr. Aziz Ahmed, Pakistan's Foreign Minister of State for Defense and Foreign Affairs, to Swaran Singh, India's External Affairs Minister, 9 July 1974, reprinted in *Pakistan Horizon* 27 (Third Quarter 1974), p. 203.

68. India's delivery and command and control systems capabilities are discussed in Subrahmanyam, "India's Nuclear Policy," in *Nuclear Proliferation and the Near-Nuclear Countries*, ed. Onkar Marwah and Ann Schulz (Cambridge: Ballinger Publishing Co., 1975), p. 138.

69. Statement of the Prime Minister of Pakistan regarding the Indian nuclear explosion, 19 May 1974, reprinted in *Pakistan Horizon* 27 (Second Quarter 1974), pp. 131-34.

70. Interview with David Frost, *Pakistan Horizon* 28 (Third Quarter 1975), p. 145.

71. Letter from Mr. Aziz Ahmed to Swaran Singh, 10 August 1974, reprinted in *Pakistan Horizon* 27 (Third Quarter 1974), p. 205.

72. See, for example, Hafeez Malik, "Nationalism and the Quest for Ideology," in Ziring, Braibanti, and Wriggins, eds., *Pakistan: The Long View*, pp. 271-300;

and Saleem M. Qureshi, "Pakistani Nationalism Reconsidered," *Pacific Affairs* 45 (Winter 1972-73): 556-72.

73. Clarence Maloney, *Peoples of South Asia* (New York: Holt, Rinehart & Winston, 1974), pp. 156-57.

74. Bhutto, "Pakistan Builds Anew," p. 545.

75. The differences in Indian and Pakistani identitive attitudes shows clearly in Bhutto's and Mrs. Gandhi's interviews with Oriana Fallaci, *Interview with History* (New York: Liveright, 1976), pp. 119 and 162-64.

76. Rose, "Emergency," p. 101.

77. Bhutto, "Pakistan Builds Anew," p. 546.

CHAPTER EIGHT

INDO-PAKISTANI RELATIONS IN THE EIGHTIES

The Soviet invasion of Afghanistan in December 1979 profoundly transformed the strategic assumptions of Indian and Pakistani foreign policies. India and Pakistan also had to take into account the overthrow of the Shah of Iran by Islamic fundamentalists, the oil price shock of 1979, America's strategic response to the Soviet intervention in Afghanistan and the instability in the Middle East, and, finally, the Iran-Iraq War. All these events altered the way in which India and Pakistan calculated the costs and benefits of their conflict and cooperation. With the Middle East in turmoil and with the Soviet Union physically occupying a neighboring country, the opportunity costs of continued Indo-Pakistan conflict increased.

The major external powers--the United States, China, and the Soviet Union--all increased their aid levels to an increasingly important South Asia. American and Chinese aid bolstered Pakistan.[1] India became more important to the Soviet Union, which was determined to win international support for its adventure in Afghanistan and to maintain diplomatic and military pressure against Pakistan and China.

Foreign aid to the subcontinent billowed to such an extent that the new balance of material and military power between India and Pakistan was conducted at higher quantitative (and perhaps qualitative) levels. Quite simply, unprecedented amounts of foreign aid flowed to both countries. In November 1980, the International Monetary Fund (IMF) approved an extended fund facility (EFF) loan of $1.7 billion to help Pakistan cover its balance of payments deficits.

At that time this was the largest IMF loan ever to a developing country. Yet exactly a year later, India received an EFF loan of $5.4 billion to adjust its balance of payments. Not only was this a new IMF record, it was also India's largest single foreign loan since independence.

Similar records were set in military aid. In May 1980, the Indian and Soviet governments signed a $1.63 billion arms deal, at that time the the largest single military aid deal in India's history and estimated by some sources to have been worth more in real terms than the nominal $1.63 billion.[2] As if this was not striking enough, in April 1982 India signed a $2.6 billion agreement with France to buy and produce under licence 150 high performance Mirage 2000 aircraft. The Indian government later cancelled the licensed production part of the package, but the purchase still set Indian records. Pakistan's military and economic aid packages from the United States totalled $3.2 billion for 1981-86 and and $4.02 billion for 1987-93. This is the largest amount of aid since the Mutual Defense Assistance Program of 1954-65.

Against this background of altered strategic and resource environments, this chapter probes the growth of Indian and Pakistani material, military, and identitive assets and their impact on the two countries' conflict and cooperation.

MATERIAL CAPABILITIES, POWER AND INFLUENCE

Economic

Both economies have done well in the 1980s, with Pakistan's economy doing slightly better than India's. Between 1980-84, Pakistan's real GNP increased by 6.3 percent compared to India's 5.3 percent increase.[3]

The reasons behind Pakistan's performance were strong industrial and agricultural growth and continued private remittances from abroad, despite a dip in these remittances in 1985-86. The World Bank noted that although Fifth Plan growth rates were below target, they were substantially above rates achieved during 1970-78 and very respectable compared to the performance of other LDCs over the same period.[4]

In order to maintain this strong economic growth, the strategy of Pakistan's Sixth Plan (1983-88) is to increase agricultural production and exports, invest heavily in energy and irrigation, and to improve social services and living standards for the poor, one of the traditional areas of neglect in Pakistani planning.

The Indian economy has been robust in the 1980s. The bright spots include strong performances in oil production and agriculture. Oil production more than doubled from 11.7 million tonnes in 1979-80 to 28.9 million in 1984-85, thereby easing India's balance of payments.[5] Agricultural production reached record levels in 1983-84 and 1986-87, keeping ahead of India's 2.3 percent population growth rate.

India's Sixth Plan emphasized the development of energy resources in order to break the infrastructural bottlenecks and to reduce dependence upon foreign oil and oil products. Outlays on oil exploration increased in the Sixth Plan and in subsequent annual revisions. The Plan also targetted new capacity in thermal and nuclear power stations and in steel and fertilizer plants. While there were additions to capacity in these areas, inefficient management resulted in lower utilization of capacity.[6] The new industrial capacities of the Sixth Plan will come increasingly on line during the rest of the 1980s.

The Indian Planning Commission targetted a 5 percent growth rate for the Seventh Plan (1986-91). The new plan emphasized food production, employment, increased investment in energy, and improved productivity. It gave priority to increasing the efficiency of existing infrastructural projects rather than to laying new capacities.

To tackle the deep-rooted problems of low productivity, Rajiv's government increased fiscal incentives, reduced government regulations (such as licensing, monopolies, practices), and promoted newer, more technologically advanced industries in India. The government identified a number of strategic industries capable of increasing productivity throughout the Indian economy. These were telecommunications, data processing, electronics, and transportation. The aim, as Rajiv noted, is to take India into the twenty-first century.

How has their comparative economic growth affected Indo-Pakistan economic relations? First, as in previous periods, India's economic growth has been broad-based in agriculture and industry;

Pakistan's has been in agriculture with very little industrial capacity laid. (Pakistan's Steel Mill Project was inauguarated in January 1985.) In the long run this balanced Indian growth will widen the potential power gaps between the two countries in industry, military strength, and technology.

Secondly, this modernization and development program leaves India capital-poor instead of capital-rich and thus limited in its ability to offer capital to Pakistan. What it can offer though is technical expertise in the form of joint ventures. Finally, both economies are still complementary. The building of Pakistan's Steel Mill has not reduced the complementarity of the two economies in the short-run. Pakistan has exported its surplus pig iron to India, and India signed a long-term contract for the sale of iron ore to Pakistan. This suggests that the trade relations between the two countries may not necessarily be that of India's export of manufactured goods in return for Pakistan's primary goods.

The major barriers to increased bilateral trade have been political rather than economic. Pakistani government officials and businessmen feared being swamped by Indian industry if completely free trade were allowed. Pakistan's policies of national self-reliance in economic development limit India's position as an economic core. India's comparative advantages in steel, electronics, and chemicals have not been allowed to operate in the Pakistani market because the Pakistani government insisted that trade be mutually beneficial and not hurt Pakistan's infant industry in these sectors.[7]

Food is another example of lost trade opportunities for both countries. India had a record wheat harvest in 1984-85, which led to problems of storage, distribution, and disposal. The Indian government proposed to dispose this surplus abroad. It offered two million tons of wheat to Pakistan in May 1985 in return for fertilizer under a barter arrangement. Pakistan's wheat crop in that same period fell short by over two million tonnes. The Pakistani authorities agreed to consider the Indian proposal, but were never enthusiastic about it. Pakistan claimed that it had already made agreements with the United States and Australia to purchase wheat.

Progress on trade has been slow but significant nonetheless. In bilateral bargaining it has been India that has pushed for an expansion of trade, acceptance of the principle of non-discrimination, more joint ventures, and greater contact between the businessmen of both countries. Pakistan has been more cautious. On 11 March 1986, it lifted the ten year old ban on private trade with India. Pakistani businessmen can now import forty-two items from India, including tea, timber, spices, technical books, refrigerators, air conditioners, and compressors. Pakistan also accepted in principle the idea of non-discrimination in trade relations with India and the formation of contacts between the chambers of commerce of both countries. Much depends on how these agreements are implemented, but it is likely that trade relations will improve because both countries realize that progress can be made in the area of trade, unlike the more contentious military and political issues.

Nuclear Energy

India opened its first indigenously designed and built nuclear power plant at Kalpakkam in Tamil Nadu (MAPP-1) in July 1983. This brought India's total installed nuclear power production capacity to 1095 MW. Four more reactors are under construction--two at Narora in Uttar Pradesh and two at Kakrapar in Gujarat.

The Department of Atomic Energy continued its attempts to move India to the next stages of its atomic power program. In 1984 the *Purnima II* research reactor went critical. The following year India's largest research reactor, the *Dhruva*, went critical on August 8, 1985. The reactor was entirely built by Indians and therefore not subject to international inspections. On 18 October 1985, India began operating its Fast Breeder Test Reactor (FBTR)--the first in the developing world, confirming its leading postion in nuclear power in the developing countries.

As in previous periods, India's nuclear power program still suffers from inefficencies, delays, and dependence on foreign sources for supplies such as heavy water. India is still far from achieving the first stage of the Bhabha profile (natural uranium reactors) let alone the next two stages (plutonium and thorium fast breeders).

Pakistan also made progress in achieving self-sufficiency in the nuclear fuel cycle. On 31 August 1980, it completed a nuclear fuel fabrication facility, which will use Pakistan's domestic uranium reserves. In April 1985 Pakistan's Ambassador to India told a meeting of South Asian journalists that Pakistan could enrich uranium to five percent.[8] Work also continued on an experimental plutonium reprocessing laboratory at PINSTECH. The aim of Pakistan's program is to build light water nuclear power plants with enriched uranium fuel. This has caused concern abroad over the peaceful intent of Pakistan's nuclear program. Pakistan is enriching uranium before it has the capacity to use it.

Progress in Pakistan's civilian nuclear power program has been slow. Like some of India's power reactors, such as Tarapur units 1 and 2, the Karachi Nuclear Power Plant (KANNUP) has operated below its installed capacity. This is the only reactor in commercial operation. The government is interested in building a second nuclear power reactor at Chashma in the Punjab, but nuclear supplier countries have agreed not to bid on it until Pakistan increases its safeguards.[9] In contrast to India, Pakistan is presently incapable of designing and constructing its own nuclear power plants.

Political

In the 1980s, Mrs. Gandhi returned to power, was assassinated in 1984, and was succeeded by her son, Rajiv. In neighboring Pakistan, Zia continued his attempts to legitimize his regime, but died in an airplane crash in August 1988. Parliamentary elections in November resulted in the election of a coalition government led by Benazir Bhutto of the PPP.

India. Mrs. Gandhi won the 1980 general election because the electorate was dissatisfied with the Janata's economic, social, and political performance, particularly with its failure to maintain law and order. Mrs. Gandhi naturally saw her victory as a mandate to establish strong central authority in India. Yet regional challenges to Mrs. Gandhi were the biggest problem for the Prime Minister and cost her her life in October 1984.

The Akali Dal, a regional party in the Punjab, demanded greater state autonomy. A minority of Sikhs, some of them violent, even demanded a separate nation called "Khalistan." In Assam, another strategic Indian state, a student-led native movement demanded that the central government halt illegal immigration from Bangladesh and expel immigrants who had come to Assam after 1951.

Of these two, Mrs. Gandhi's most serious challenge was instability in the Punjab. When a number of militants led by Jarnail Singh Bhindranwale occupied the Golden Temple in Amritsar and threatened to expand their activities, Mrs. Gandhi sent in the Indian Army on 12 June 1984 to root them out. Operation Bluestar, as it was called, succeeded in its military aim. In the longer term, it created anger amongst Sikhs. Ultimately, it cost Mrs. Gandhi her life. On 31 October 1984, two of her Sikh bodyguards assassinated Mrs. Gandhi at her residence in New Delhi.

The President of India chose Rajiv Gandhi to succeed his mother in October 1984. In the general election in December 1984 the Congress gained its most impressive election victory since independence. It won 78 percent of the seats in the Lok Sabha and routed the opposition. So roundly was the opposition beaten that the major opposition party to the Congress was now the Telegu Desam, a regional party from Andhra Pradesh, but hardly a national opposition party.

Rajiv's style of leadership was as important as the size of the election victory. His youthfulness and a number of rapid economic liberalization policy decisions made soon after taking power all projected the image of a young, dynamic, and fresh leader. With an unchallenged parliamentary majority, Rajiv has been responsive to the demands of the opposition.

The Congress has been weakened by electoral losses in West Bengal and Haryana, scandals over defense contracts, and expulsions of dissident Congressmen such as Arun Nehru and the former Finance and Defense Minister V. P. Singh. The greatest challenge to Rajiv has come from V. P. Singh. In 1988, Singh formed the Janata Dal party with opposition parties and accused Rajiv of being personally involved in corruption. So far, though, Rajiv has managed to retain the support of his Congress MPs in the Lok Sabha.

Rajiv is closer to Nehru's model of center-state relations than to Indira's model. He has been willing to devolve political power to the states for the benefit of political stability in the states. In August 1985 Rajiv Gandhi's government reached agreements with opposition leaders in the Punjab and Assam. Rajiv was conciliatory and conceded some of the demands of the regional parties. After the accords in Punjab and Assam, both the Akali Dal and the Assamese party swept into power in the state elections. Rajiv followed these successes the next year by reaching an agreement to restore peace to the Union territory of Mizoram. Under the terms of the 30 June 1986 agreement, the leader of the secessionist Mizo National Front (MNF), Mr. Laldenga, agreed to work within the constitutional framework of a united India. In return, the central government agreed to make Mizoram a state, to rehabilitate the former terrorists, and to hold democratic elections in Mizoram.

Instability still exists in states such as Kashmir, West Bengal (where a Nepalese political party is seeking a separate state of Gurkhaland in the Darjeeling district), and Goa and Tripura. The Punjab accord floundered with the assassination of the Akali Dal leader, Harchand Singh Longowal, disagreement between Punjab and neighboring Harayana state on transferring the joint capital of Chandigarh to Punjab, and continued terrorism. Terrorist acts are still prevalent, forcing Rajiv to impose central rule on the Punjab in May 1987. Despite flexibility, Rajiv faces severe tests in implementing his policies of political integration and of creating buffers between state instability and threats to national integration.

Pakistan. Zia's strategy of legitimization was to use the Islamic religion to integrate Pakistani society regionally, ethnically, ideologically, and by social class. This, plus Zia's strong personal belief in Islam, won him support among the "Islam-pasand" ("Islam loving") parties--the JI, JUI and JUP. Zia used a referendum in December 1984 on the issue of Islamization to justify his continued rule until 1990. Zia demonstrated his political skills in a number of ways. First, he co-opted politicians and middle-class professionals into his military government. Secondly, he carefully cultivated his power base--the army--and crushed any signs of revolt from the armed forces. He amended the 1973 Constitution to ensure that the armed forces would not be held accountable for the actions taken during the martial law period. Finally, Zia gauged the mood of the Pakistani public in, for example, the extent of its support for United States military and economic aid and use of Pakistani bases.

Despite these attempts at strengthening his political power, Zia faced internal opposition. Several opposition parties combined in February 1981 to form the Movement for the Restoration of Democracy. The MRD demanded an immediate end to martial law, revival of the unamended 1973 Constitution, removal of the ban on political parties, and immediate democratic elections. The MRD was unimpressed by Zia's 1984 referendum and charged that the partyless elections of February 1985 and the civilianization of government were a sham.

The severest challenge to Zia came in mid-1986 when Benazir Bhutto, daughter of former Prime Minister Ali Bhutto, returned to Pakistan and showed that the PPP retained extensive popular support. The opposition, though, faced several hurdles, including internal rivalries and strains within the PPP and rivalries amongst the members of the MRD.[10] The first round of agitations by Benazir failed to topple the Zia regime or to force it to concede fresh and fair elections. Zia's regime weathered this challenge.

Zia's rule ended in August 1988, when the plane that he was travelling on exploded in mysterious circumstances. In Pakistan's first free elections since 1977, Benazir Bhutto's PPP emerged as the largest party in the National Assembly. Benazir Bhutto became Prime Minister when the PPP formed a coalition government with smaller parties.

Benazir Bhutto inherited a divided Pakistan. Zia's government had failed to integrate Pakistan. At best it militarily contained regional discontent, such as the outbreak in Sind province in 1983. Regional differences, particularly resentment of continued Punjabi domination of Pakistani society, remain below the surface. An ominous development for Pakistani unity is the 1986 formation of the Sind-Baluch-Pushtun Front (SBPF), which demanded a decentralized confederal form of government. Zia's government responded to this Front by arresting and trying its leaders, including Mumtaz Bhutto and Hafiz Pirzada. It remains for Benazir Bhutto to resolve Pakistan's formidable problems of national integration.

In summary, both Indian and Pakistani governments were battered by acute problems of political succession, domestic political instability, political integration, and lack of economic, social, and political performance.

The internal political changes in India and Pakistan have strongly affected their bilateral relations. Pakistan's government greeted the restoration of strong central leadership under Mrs. Gandhi in 1980 with apprehension. In the general election campaign of 1980, Gandhi charged that the Janata's policy of beneficial bilateralism was overly accommodating to the smaller South Asian states. Once in power, though, Mrs. Gandhi saw the value of cooperating with Pakistan in reducing tensions. During her period of office both countries agreed to form a bilateral Indo-Pakistan Joint Commission and participate in a multilateral forum for South Asian cooperation.

The change in leadership in India from Mrs. Gandhi to her son also brought little or no change in domestic responsiveness. Rajiv continued traditional Indian foreign policies of nonalignment and of preeminence in the subcontinent. His large election victory in 1984 also gave him a strong position in negotiating with Pakistan; the domestic opposition was decimated and less of a restraint on Rajiv's foreign policy. Zia himself took pains not to take advantage of the assassination crisis in India. At New Delhi for Mrs. Gandhi's funeral, he pledged to search for peace with the new Prime Minister.

Rajiv's leadership weakened in 1986-88. Election losses, regional instability, scandals, and internal party splits reduced his flexibility in handling Indo-Pakistan relations. At the same time, as if to compensate for internal weakness, Rajiv, like his mother before him, spoke ominously of foreign forces that were seeking to destabilize India.

Zia also faced domestic constraints in his policy towards India. Two major constraints were the opinions of the military and domestic opposition. Of these two, domestic opposition was the least significant. Benazir Bhutto argued that the Simla Accord was sufficient and preferrable to a No-War Pact or even a comprehensive Treaty of Peace, Friendship and Cooperation. But her emphasis on a piecemeal approach to relations with India fitted Zia's policy anyway. Instead, Zia had to be more concerned about the Pakistan armed forces' attitude toward normalization with India. Zia knew that any concessions to India that would adversely affect Pakistan's sovereignty or the corporate interests of the military (such as limitations on size and deployments and sources of arms supplies) would be resisted by the military.

Regime-type differences have become less salient in Indo-Pakistan relations since the deaths of Mrs. Gandhi and Zia. Mrs. Gandhi had placed Zia's regime on the defensive by charging that his regime was unrepresentative. In August 1983 she went further by supporting the MRD and calling for the release of Wali Khan. Zia accused Mrs. Gandhi's of interfering in Pakistan's internal affairs. For him, these were examples of the inconsistency between India's formal policy of noninterference and its actual practice.[11]

Rajiv played down regime differences and concentrated on negotiating with Zia, even though the Indian Prime Minister was aware that the MRD did not want him to negotiate with Zia's government. The Indian government carefully avoided comment on the lifting of martial law, but it did note that effective power still remained in the hands of the military. In December 1988, Rajiv welcomed the election of Benazir Bhutto. For the first time since 1977, both India and Pakistan have democratically-elected governments.

Where the countries have differed is in the question of political integration. As in the past, both governments have been able to promote or hinder political integration in the other country. But between 1980 and 1983 they carefully discussed these problems in a very low key. The situation changed after 1983. Pakistan accused India of fomenting the Sind rebellion. India charged that Pakistan was encouraging Sikh secessionists in the Punjab. Relations ruptured in June 1984 following the Indian army's action in the Golden Temple. The Indian government accused Pakistan of sheltering and training Sikh terrorists. To signal its displeasure it broke off the scheduled talks of the Indo-Pakistan Joint Commission. There was talk of "war clouds."

Has Pakistan helped Sikh terrorists? India claims that Pakistan certainly has. The proof includes evidence from interrogating terrorists captured as they crossed the border into India. On several occasions the Indian government confronted Pakistan with this evidence. Pakistan publicly denied helping Sikh secessionists and refused to accept India's information. Such claims and counterclaims may be placed in perspective by noting several points. First, no doubt certain Indian and Pakistan officials have taken satisfaction at the troubles in the other country. But there are limits to how far each government is prepared to go in taking advantage of these troubles. Pakistan knows that Khalistan would take some of its own territory. Benazir Bhutto warned that any Pakistani policy of fomenting the Sikh problem could backfire on Pakistan.[12] Khalistan for historical reasons would include Lahore, which was the seat of government of the eighteenth century Sikh warrior Ranjit Singh. India could also counter Pakistani help to Sikh secessionists by balkanizing Pakistan.

Secondly, any India encouragement of secessionism in Pakistan, and particularly of the Sind, would lead to the break up of Pakistan. Indian officials know that this is against India's interests and could backfire on India, which has its own problems of integration. Thirdly, the Sikh troubles originate from within Punjab, and not from Pakistan or even for that matter from Britain, Canada or the United States. Finally, both India and Pakistan eventually surmounted the mutual charges of domestic interference. In January 1985, Rajiv made the trial of the Sikh hijackers in Pakistan a precondition for resuming Indo-Pakistan talks. He was satisfied when Zia promptly speeded up the trial of Sikh hijackers.

MILITARY CAPABILIITIES, POWER AND INFLUENCE

The present military buildup in the subcontinent is only partly the result of the new strategic environment following the Soviet intervention in Afghanistan. India's military modernization program predates the Soviet intervention. Its May 1980 arms agreement with the Soviet Union was under negotiation during the Janata period and then concluded by Mrs. Gandhi's government. During the 1980s, the Pakistani military consistently sought to upgrade its military strength, even if the resource environment seemed bleak.

Pakistan's external resource environment for arms brightened after 1979 for the first time since the MDAP period of 1954-65. The Carter administration's new policy towards Pakistan deemphasized global order issues such as nuclear proliferation and human rights.

What mattered was bolstering Pakistani power against Soviet expansionist threats. Zia rejected Carter's offer of $400 million--half in economic and half in military aid--as "peanuts." He felt that the opportunity costs of this United States package were too high. It would not add much to Pakistan's security, though the size of the package would be high enough to increase Soviet and Indian hostility towards Pakistan. Zia also realized that he was in a strong negotiating position with a United States increasingly concerned about the Soviet intervention in Afghanistan. His gamble paid off. He eventually received a much higher level of aid in November 1981 when the United States Congress approved the Reagan administration's $3.2 billion aid package to Pakistan.

Armies

In relative terms the Indian army's manpower increased in size by 15.7 percent between 1979 and 1987, compared with Pakistan's 12.5 percent increase (appendix 2). India added four infantry divisions and two independent armored brigades. Pakistan added one infantry division and one independent armored brigade (appendix 3).

In equipment the Indian army added 350 Vijayanta tanks and 350 of the newer Soviet T-72 tanks. It discarded its obsolete Centurions and upgraded its tank inventory by modifying its T-72 for night vision and its PT-176 light tanks by adding antiaircraft weapons. Pakistan added 400 Chinese-built T-59 tanks and 120 American M-48 tanks. It has kept its relative parity in tanks with India, but India's stock of tanks remained superior. The Pakistan army boosted its capabilites by receiving American Cobra anti-tank helicopters, TOW antitank missiles, and the Firefinder radar system AN/TPQ 37.

Air Forces

The Indian air force maintained its military edge over Pakistan, despite the latter's acquisition of two squadrons of F-16s. The IAF added Jaguars, Mirage-2000s (which are as good if not better than the F-16s), and the advanced Soviet MiG-29s. It also began modernizing its reconnaissance and transport squadrons and ground defense equipment.

The PAF began the 1980s by discarding its obsolete F.86 Sabres and by acquiring Chinese MiG-19s and American F-16s. The PAF also refitted its Mirage jets and MiG-19s with new navigation attack and weapon aiming systems. Another significant development was the reorganization of the PAF's structure into three regional commands--northern, central and southern.[13] Overall, the inventories of combat aircraft in both India and Pakistan increased, although in India the increase was far greater in quality of combat aircraft.

Navies

The increases in land and air forces have overshadowed the changes in the Indian and Pakistani navies. Yet the clearest shift in balance of military power has taken place with the navies. India has begun the transition from a coastal to a blue-water navy. There has been an across-the-board improvement in India's relative position in submarines, frigates, and destroyers (appendix 6). India also improved its position in mine and antisubmarine warfare forces. Pakistan maintained its position in light forces. Naval inventories increased in both countries.[14]

Pakistan organized a Maritime Security Agency (MSA), equivalent in function to India's Coast Guard. The new force consisted of the destroyer *Badr* and four patrol boats, all transferred from the Pakistani Navy. The tasks of the MSA will be to protect fishermen and the 200 mile exclusive economic zone, as well as to conduct oceanographic research, rescue operations, and pollution control. The MSA will therefore give the Pakistani Navy more flexibility and allow it to concentrate on its military mission.

Defense Production

As in previous periods, India maintained its superiority in defense production. And as before, the scientific and technological progress had more of a potential rather than actual significance for India's military balance of power with Pakistan. For example, defense production work began on the licensed production of the T-72 tank, the MiG-23 fighter, and the Type 209 West German submarine. The LCA project still depends on foreign technical aid. In 1987 the Indian and American governments reached an agreement for the supply of

US jet engines for the Indian LCA program.[15] India made progress though in indigenously developing missiles, radar systems, electronic countermeasures equipment, aircraft test equipment, and remotely piloted aircraft.

Related to defense production is India's space program, which, as several observers have pointed out, has implications for military reconnaissance, command and control, weather forecasting in military planning, and the production of ballistic missiles.[16] India became the world's seventh space power on 18 July 1980 when it launched an Indian-made satellite, the *Rohini-I,* from an indigenous launch vehicle, the SLV-3. The Indian Space Research Organization (ISRO) successfully launched two more *Rohini* satellites in 1981 and 1983.

ISRO is still at an early stage in its space program, and it is using foreign technological help to develop a self-reliant space industry. The United States, USSR, and Western Europe have all helped to launch Indian-made satellites or satellites made for India. So in this respect India's space program is genuinely nonaligned.

At present India's space establishments are working on a new generation of larger launch vehicles (Polar Satellite Launch Vehicle (PSLV)) and Geosynchronous Satellite Launch Vehicle (GSLV), on an indigenous remote-sensing satellite, the Stretch Rohini Satellite (SROSS), and an indigenous successor to INSAT. The SROSS program was setback in March 1987 by the failure of a test launch of the satellite vehicle. The space establishment expects to resume testing of this in 1988. The aim of India's ambitious space program is to make the country self-sufficient in space by the mid-1990s. So far India's space programs have been for civilian purposes (communications, remote sensing, meteorological), but the progress to date has given India the capability of at least producing intermediate range ballistic missiles.

Pakistan's defense production capabilites are still limited. In the 1980s Pakistan began using its Chinese-built and financed tank and aircraft rebuilding facilities, and it continued production of light aircraft at Kamra. Pakistan's government gave more attention to its space program. In 1981 it upgraded the status of the Space and Upper Atmosphere Research Committee (SUPARCO) to the status of a commission, and gave it the task of launching national communication satellites in the future.[17]

Military relations between India and Pakistan in the 1980s have been tense. The causes of this tension were Pakistan's arms purchases from abroad, military conflict in the remote Saichen glacier of disputed Kashmir, rumors and fears of attacks on each others' nuclear facilities, and a mobilization scare in 1987 when the armed might of both countries was arrayed along their borders in a state of war readiness. In the 1980s, military relations between the two took on more of a nuclear tone. Nevertheless, both countries tried to continue their No-War Pact talks, resolve the Saichen glacier dispute, and formalize a verbal agreement between Zia and Rajiv of December 1985 not to attack each other's nuclear facilities.

The strengthening of military assets in South Asia generated fears of an arms race in the subcontinent among the governments of India and Pakistan. While India sought to reassure Pakistan that it would not take advantage of the Afghan situation to weaken Pakistan, India also found an increase in Pakistan military might to be unacceptable.

The Indian government argued that, given Pakistan's past record of hostilities, it would likely use its new foreign military aid against India at some point. In particular, Indian defense planners feared that Pakistan had greatly enhanced its capabilities of attacking Indian strategic targets, such as air bases, communications, and nuclear installations. India would also be less able to respond to a possible Pakistan military attack in Kashmir by launching an attack across the international boundary in the Punjab and Rajasthan.[18] Furthermore, the Indian government doubted Pakistan's intentions as well as its capabilities, noting that the bulk of Pakistan's armed forces were deployed against India rather than Afghanistan.[19]

Islamabad defended its military buildup with several arguments. The new arms were meant to replace Pakistan's obsolete military inventories and to increase Pakistan's deterrent rather than offensive capabilities.[20] India retained such an overwhelming military advantage that any Pakistani attack on India would be suicidal. Even with Pakistan's new weapons, India would keep its military edge in the future when its new Soviet, British, and French arms purchases arrived.

As for the record of past conflict, Islamabad argued that Pakistan had been the victim of Indian power. Such a record accounted for its troop deployments against India. Pakistan now found itself confronted by three major security threats: Afghanistan and the USSR on the western front; India on the eastern front; and domestic front of potential secession in Baluchistan, the NWFP, or Sind. Pakistan's defense planning had to meet a combination of military attacks from all three fronts (for example, a combined Soviet-Indian attack, or a Soviet or Indian-backed insurgency in the periphery) rather than just an attack on one front. The Pakistan military still remembered the 1971 as an instance of a joint Soviet-Indian attack on Pakistan.[21]

Further, Islamabad argued that its new arms met its defense needs against Afghanistan and the USSR. The multirole F-16 aircraft would allow Pakistan to defend, among other things, its air bases against Soviet attack. Some of those bases, such as Sargodha, are closer to Afghanistan than they are to India.[22] The F-16s would also be the backbone of the PAF's combat aircraft in the 1980s and 1990s, besides being a symbol of America's long-term commitment to Pakistan's security.

To outward appearances, the Indian and Pakistani positions on the build-up of military assets were irreconcilable. But while these positions were at odds and increased tensions between the two countries, the Soviet intervention in Afghanistan also made Indian and Pakistani authorities aware of the opportunity costs of their continued conflict. The opportunity costs included the failure to reach a common diplomatic, political, and even, military response to the Afghanistan crisis. The Indian government hesitated at first to publicly condemn the Soviet invasion; it preferred to privately voice its objections to Soviet leaders. As the occupation continued, the Indian government became increasingly aware of the security threats to South Asia. As a regional power, India's security perspectives were wider than Pakistan's. The presence of Soviet troops on the edge of the subcontinent threatened not only to increase Soviet intervention in South Asia (direct military or subversive intervention) but also to increase a counter American presence in the Indian Ocean, the Middle East and South Asia.

Nor was that all. India had a direct interest in a stable Pakistan now that Pakistan stood as a buffer between India and the USSR and India and Iran. A Pakistan fragmented into several unstable states on India's northwest border would increase the chances of foreign intervention. The possible formation of transregional states such as greater Baluchistan or Pakhtoonistan would also break up the regional unity of the subcontinent.

Save for Kashmir, Indian and Pakistani interests do coincide on the question of Pakistan's territorial integrity. This is a point that Indian External Affairs Minister, Narasimha Rao, stressed to the Pakistan government and public opinion. It was also a point that Zia emphasized to the Indian government. In a news interview shortly after the Soviet invasion, Zia said, "We are a buffer state between the Soviet Union and India and a strong, stable buffer state is also in India's interests."[23] A logical upshot is that India has an interest in maintaining Pakistan's defense capabilities. After Rao's talks with his counterpart, Agha Shahi, in Islamabad in June 1981, both sides issued a joint statement in which they "agreed that each country had the sovereign right to acquire arms for self-defense."[24] The all-important problem is that, so far, India and Pakistan have failed to agree on what constitutes arms for self-defense.

A new phase in Indo-Pakistan relations opened in November 1981 when Zia unexpectedly offered India a No-War Pact. This followed Pakistan's acceptance of the United States economic and military aid package that was concluded with the Reagan administration in fall 1981. Although the Pakistani offer was consistent with India's long-held policy since independence of signing such a pact, the Indian government was clearly surprised. Pakistan had boldly seized the initiative in normalizing relations. In contrast, India's response was faltering and guarded. It argued that Pakistan's offer was indirect and vague to boot. It also suspected the offer as a trap; Pakistan might lull India into talks until Pakistan started receiving its American arms. After all, Pakistan had also made a similar offer to India when it accepted American arms aid in 1954.[25]

To regain the initiative, the Indian government proposed that the two countries sign a much more comprehensive Treaty of Peace, Friendship and Cooperation. Not only was the Indian proposal designed to be more positive than a simple No-War Pact, it was also designed to test Pakistan's good faith in creating a security-community by seeing how far Zia was prepared to go in promoting economic, scientific, cultural, and military cooperation with India. The Foreign Ministers of both countries held initial discussions in New Delhi in late January 1982. These discussions were partly successful. The Pakistani side clarified its No-War Pact proposals. The Foreign Minister, Agha Shahi, also welcomed an Indian proposal to set up a joint commission in the functional areas of trade, cultural relations, and scientific and technological cooperation.[26] Further talks were set for the first week of March 1982 when both sides would begin substantive negotiations on a No-War Pact. Unfortunately, India postponed these talks on 24 February 1982 because Pakistani representatives raised the issue of Kashmir in a meeting of the UN Human Rights Commission in Geneva. For India, this violated the principle of bilateralism.

New Delhi and Islamabad eventually resumed the No-War Pact talks in November 1982. Both sides, though, still differed on the form and content of an agreement. It is unlikely that Pakistan sought a terse No-War Pact statement since that would not concretely serve Pakistan's security interests. It would say nothing, for example, about Indian troop deployments against Pakistan. A terse No-War Pact was also probably not in India's interests. The Indian government felt that the Simla Agreement of 1972 already served as the functional equivalent of a No-War Pact. Besides, India had several issues it wanted to discuss with Pakistan, including Kashmir and the Karakoram Highway, foreign bases, troop reductions, and troop deployments.

What progress has been made during the negotiations? One visible progress has been the establishment of a five-year Joint Commission, which both countries signed at the Nonaligned Movement Conference in New Delhi in March 1983. By May 1984 both countries had made progress on combining the drafts. These efforts ground to halt as India accused Pakistan of aiding Sikh terrorism.

By 1988 negotiations were still underway on a normalization agreement. Under Rajiv, the treaty negotiations appeared to be making progress. Both countries began to consider merging the drafts of their proposals. Major stumbling blocks were foreign bases and raising Kashmir as an issue in international forums. Pakistan's representatives saw no need for a provision about foreign bases, because both India and Pakistan are already members of the nonaligned movement. Pakistan also wanted the flexibility and room for maneuver to raise the issue of Kashmir in the United Nations. At the end of bilateral talks in Islamabad in December 1986, Indian Foreign Secretary A. P. Venkateswaran seemed to imply that the Kashmir issue would be solved after all other issues had been settled.[27]

Nuclear Security

Besides the hoary problem of arms supplies from abroad, Indo-Pakistani security relations in the 1980s acquired a new dimension: India charged that Pakistan was developing nuclear weapons. Rajiv conducted an active diplomatic campaign to prevent Pakistan from acquiring this capability. India's position was that it will be forced to reassess its policy on nuclear weapons if Pakistan acquired the bomb. It is likely though that the Indian government has already conducted a review of its policy and taken contingency measures in the event of Pakistan acquiring the bomb.

Pakistan's declared position was that its nuclear program was for peaceful purposes and that it had neither the capacity nor the will to develop nuclear weapons. It sought arms control with India on the basis of sovereignty and reciprocity.

Zia's government made several proposals to manage the nuclear issue between the two countries. Zia proposed that India and Pakistan should simultaneously accede to the Nuclear Non-Proliferation Treaty and accept the full-scope safeguards of the IAEA. He also proposed mutual inspection of each other's nuclear facilities, a joint declaration renouncing the acquisition and development of nuclear weapons, and establishment of a nuclear-weapons-free zone in South Asia.[28]

The problem with this Pakistani diplomatic approach was that it was becoming stale. The Pakistan government knew that India was unwilling to take up these offers, and yet it persisted in making them. India objected that the Non-Proliferation Treaty discriminated against nuclear haves and have-nots. It was unwilling therefore to adhere just to please Pakistan. Nor would a nuclear free zone in South Asia safeguard Indian security; it would not take into account Chinese nuclear capabilities. Disarmament would have to be global. Finally, the Indian government objected to mutual inspection because it feared that it could be easily evaded, particularly for the plutonium already produced by Pakistan.

The only progress made was at a meeting of Rajiv and Zia in December 1985 at New Delhi. They agreed that their countries would not attack each other's nuclear facilities. This was a verbal agreement, and both leaders left it to their staffs to turn it into a formal agreement.

In Islamabad in December 1986 the Foreign Secretaries of India and Pakistan reported progress on the negotiations for a peace treaty and of a formal agreement not to attack each other's nuclear facilities. Indian Foreign Secretary Venkateswaran claimed that very good progress had been made on the proposed treaty against attacking nuclear installations, although "a few technical aspects" remained to be discussed.[29]

IDENTITIVE CAPABILITIES, POWER AND INFLUENCE

Relations between India and Pakistan have been affected by both unfavorable and favorable national values. The unfavorable ones include, first, Pakistan's continuing belief in the two-nation theory and India's belief in secularism, and secondly, Pakistan's desire to rejoin the Commonwealth and India's opposition to this reentry. Favorable national values include a desire to remain nonaligned and devote their national resources to economic and social development. Each of these favorable and unfavorable values will be discussed below.

The Indian government remained committed to secularism as a principle of its political system. What seemed uncertain though was the implementation of that principle and adherence to secularism among India's population. In 1986 Rajiv Gandhi's government introduced a bill in Parliament to give a greater role for Muslim law in divorce cases of Muslim couples. Rajiv's actions resulted from the Shah Bano case, in which a divorced Muslim woman obtained an alimony judgment against her former husband. The husband and several Muslim groups argued that Muslim personal law should prevail in this case. Rajiv's attempts to give priority to Muslim law were denounced by Muslim modernist women and Indians who felt that the government was backtracking from the secular model in order to win electoral support from the Muslim bloc of voters.

Intercommunal conflict also strained Indian secularism. Muslims were upset over the dispute over the holy places of Babri Masjid and Ram Janmaboombhi in Uttar Pradesh. Hindu fundamentalism remained strong. Communal violence broke out in Ahmedabad, and Bangalore during this period. Sikh terrorism continued to be a problem in Punjab and other parts of India. Certain Sikh terrorist attacks (for instance, singling out Hindu victims) were designed to inflame relations between the Sikhs and Hindu communities.

Zia's government continued to reaffirm Pakistan's Islamic identity. In the political system, he preferred a partyless system with separate electorates for Muslims and non-Muslims. In the legal system, he promoted the primacy of the *Sharia* (Islamic Law) and attempted to implement the Sharia by introducing an Islamic system of punishment and a system of Shariat court benches.[30] In the social system, the government established rules for the use of Urdu instead of English, a dress code for women and government servants, and rules for regulating relations between the sexes. In the economic system, the government attempted in 1986 to amend the Constitution and introduce Islamic economic principles.

Even in the interpretation of Islam itself, India and Pakistan seemed to move further apart. The Pakistan government interpreted the Sufi tradition more in terms of its consistency with the *Sharia* than in its secular aspects.[31]

In contrast to Pakistan, the Indian political elite still upheld mainly western concepts of government and law, such as representative democracy based on the free organization of parties and nondiscrimination between religious communities and the sexes.

How have the changes in identitive assets between the two countries affected their regional cooperation?

Religion as always has been an irritant in relations. The Pakistani government voiced concern over the Hindu-Muslim rioting in Gujarat in 1985.[32] This brought an angry Indian response of Pakistani meddling in Indian domestic affairs. While Pakistani officials saw Indian secularism as a sham, there was also mistrust within India about Zia's Islamization. Government officials saw that policy as being carried out by Zia for instrumental and expedient reasons--to maintain himself in power.

Pakistan's Islamization had little impact on Indo-Pakistan relations. This is partly because there have been inherent domestic limits to Islamization. Sections of Pakistani society have resisted either the concept or application of Islamization. These include modernists, middle class women, leftists, and religious minorities such as Barelvi Sunnis and Shias who were suspicious of Zia's Islamization because they saw it as a form of Sunni domination. Moreover, Islamization failed to integrate ethnic minorities like the Baluchs and Sindhis into Pakistani society. For these minorities, Punjabi domination is as important a factor as Islamization in determining whether Pakistan stays united or not.

Furthermore, India continued to have several advantages in limiting the drift of national values between the two countries. It has a larger number of Muslims than Pakistan. Despite the communal conflicts, it has attempted to demonstrate that these Muslims are doing as well, if not better than, their fellow Muslims in cultural, political, and economic development under Indian secularism. The Indian government has demanded that it be represented in international Muslim forums since it has the world's fourth largest Muslim population.

Pakistani rulers still saw Indian values as a threat to their ideological system. While India has been keen to increase ties and communication between the two countries, Pakistan has footdragged. At the Indo-Pakistan Joint Commission meeting in July 1985 both sides agreed to increase cultural, educational, journalistic, travel, and tourism contacts. Group tourism was to be promoted and the number of pilgrims from both countries was to be increased. There was also to be an exchange of visits by various groups and organizations like women's organizations, lawyers' associations and old boys associations including Jamia Milia and Aligarh Muslim University. Pakistan accepted an exhibitions of Indian Urdu books.[33] The details of these agreements were left to be settled in a formal document.

Little scholarly attention has been paid to Pakistan's recent attempts to rejoin the Commonwealth. Yet this issue has important consequences for Indo-Pakistan identitive relations. Pakistan hoped to increase its security by rejoining the Commonwealth. By being part of a multilateral organization, Pakistan would safeguard its international identity. After the Soviet intervention in Afghanistan, the British, Canadian, and Australian governments all strongly favored Pakistan returning to the fold.[34] Pakistan's official policy, though, was that it would only return if the Commonwealth members unanimously asked it do so. In this way, Pakistan could save face, but it also meant that India had a virtual veto on Pakistan's reentry. Its refusal to let Pakistan back in is coercive rather than punitive. India has implicitly set conditions to Pakistan's reentry--a return to democracy in Pakistan and a promise by Pakistani governments that they would not raise bilateral issues in Commonwealth forums as they have done in the past.[35] The first of these condition seems to have been met in 1988. The question now is whether Benazir Bhutto will accept the second conditions. Pakistan's reentry might improve identitive relations by allowing both countries to reaffirm their common historical heritage, but even so Pakistan's Islamization policy is likely to reduce the impact of that historical heritage. In any case, the Commonwealth issue has been a small irritant in Indo-Pakistan relations.

Differences in national values over the role of religion in nation-building, the form of political system, and membership in the Commonwealth have been offset by a growing Indo-Pakistan identity of values on the demands for a new international economic order. Both countries have criticized each other's less-than-impeccable nonalignment credentials (India, for Pakistan's new security relationship with the United States, and Pakistan, for India's close relationship with the USSR). But both countries have taken similar positions on issues such as debt relief, foreign aid, and trade liberalization in developed countries. These similar positions have been expressed in bilateral meetings and multilateral forums such as the Nonaligned Movement and the newly created South Asian Association for Regional Cooperation (SAARC). For instance, Foreign Minister Yaqub Khan praised India's "able leadership" in the Nonaligned Coordinating Bureau on Namibia, and lauded the role played by India, particularly of its late Prime Minister Indira Gandhi, in upholding the cause of the nonaligned movement.[36]

In summary, Indian and Pakistani values on religion and its role in the political system remained as far apart as ever in this period. Indeed, Zia's policy of applying Islamic principles to Pakistani society moved both countries further apart in national values but did not impede Indo-Pakistan relations. The return of a civilian government to Pakistan and Pakistan's participation in the Nonaligned Movement appeared to narrow the gap in values between India and Pakistan. The narrowing, however, masked important differences that still remained in religion.

CONCLUSION

Indo-Pakistan relations in the 1980s have been mixed. Relations have improved in some areas. Both countries have recognized the economic benefits of increasing their bilateral trade and have been willing to separate trade from political and military disputes. In November 1981, Pakistan proposed a No-War Pact to India, and negotiations began on an agreement to create a security-community. Relations have also improved in the identitive field. The Pakistan government was more willing to permit cultural exchanges with India.

Cooperation has inched forward. Pakistan demanded safeguards for its economic, political and cultural sovereignty. Both countries have been unable to increase their trade, despite their complementary economies. Kashmir has been a continuing obstacle to improved relations. India reacted strongly when the Pakistan government raised the dispute in international forums. Both countries have also suspected each other of encouraging separatism in their territories. In security matters, both countries have been concerned by the Soviet occupation of Afghanistan and the Iran-Iraq War, but this concern has not been translated into common diplomatic and political positions. One reason is that India and Pakistan have been divided over the issues of American arms sales to Pakistan and Pakistan's incipient nuclear weapons program. Finally, in identitive matters, Pakistan's Islamization has not been a major obstacle to improved relations. Still, Pakistan's government has made it clear that it will maintain Pakistan's separate religious and cultural identity in South Asia.

Notes

1. The Reagan administration's view of the strategic importance of Pakistan is contained in the testimony of James Buckley, Under Secretary of State for Security Assistance, Science and Technology, Department of State, in U. S., Congress, House, Committee on Foreign Affairs, *Security and Economic Assistance to Pakistan, Hearings and Markup before subcommittees of the House Committee on Foreign Affairs*, 97th Cong., 1st sess., 1981, pp. 19-24 and 294-98.
2. Zia estimated this arms deal to be worth at market rates some US $6-7 billion. Interview with Rodney Tasker, *Far Eastern Economic Review* 16 October 1981, p. 44.
3. US Arms Control and Disarmament Agency, *World Military Expenditures and Arms Transfers 1986*, p. 78 and 88.
4. World Bank, *Pakistan: Review of the Sixth Five-Year Plan. A World Bank Country Study*, (Washington, D. C.: World Bank, 1984), p. ix.
5. Indian Planning Commission, *The Seventh Five Year Plan 1985-90, vol. 2* (New Delhi: Planning Commission, 1985), p. 129.
6. Ibid., p. 144.
7. "Pak-India Trade: Expansion Potential," *Pakistan Economist*, 6 February 1982, pp. 18-19.
8. *Tribune* 27 April 1985.
9. Leonard S. Spector, *Nuclear Proliferation Today: The Spread of Nuclear Weapons, 1984*. (New York: Vintage Books, 1984), pp. 96-97.
10. *Tribune* 23 April 1985. The Tehrik-i-Istiklal withdew from the MRD in October 1986.
11. *Dawn* 27 September 1983.
12. *Tribune* 17 April 1986
13. *Asian Recorder* 25, 44 (28 October-3 November 1980), p. 15721; and 28, 32 (6-12 August 1982), p. 16734.
14. For an analysis of the Indo-Pakistan naval balance, see Ashley J. Tellis, "The Naval Balance in the Indian Subcontinent: Demanding Missions for the Indian Navy," *Asian Survey* 25 (December 1985): 1186-1213.
15. *Tribune* January 8, 1987.

16. Jerrold F. Elkin and Brian Fredericks, "India's Space Program: Accomplishments, Goals, Politico-Military Implications," *Journal of South Asian and Middle Eastern Studies* 7 (Spring 1984), p. 50.

17. K. M. Amer, "Paksat: A Place in Space," *Pakistan and Gulf Economist*, 5-11 November 1983, p. 12.

18. *Statesman Weekly*, 11 July 1981.

19. See, for example, the statement of India's Foreign Secretary, R.D. Sathe, in the *Times of India*, 9 March 1980.

20. Zia's interview with Rodney Tasker, *Far Eastern Economic Review*, 16 October 1981, p. 43.

21. Stephen P. Cohen, "Pakistan," in *Security Policies of Developing Countries*, ed. Edward A. Kolodziej and Robert E. Harkavy (Lexington, Mass.: D.C. Heath, 1982), p. 102.

22. Ibid., p. 104.

23. *Statesman Weekly*, 8 March 1980.

24. Text in *Pakistan Horizon* 34 (Third Quarter 1981), pp. 194-95.

25. Sarvepalli Gopal, *Jawaharlal Nehru: A Biography*, vol. 2: *1947-1956* (London: Jonathan Cape, 1979), p. 186. For a comparison with the US MDAP period of the 1950s, see Sarbjit Johal, "India's Arming of Pakistan: Indian Views in the 1950s and 1980s," *Strategic Studies* (Islamabad) 9,2 (Winter 1986): 68-80.

26. *Statesman Weekly*, 6 February 1982.

27. *India West* 2 January 1987.

28. *Pakistan Horizon* 38 (Fourth Quarter 1985), pp. 127-29.

29. *India West* 2 February 1987.

30. William L. Richter, "Pakistan," in *The Politics of Islamic Reassertion*, ed. Mohammed Ayoob (London: Croom Helm, 1981), pp. 144-46.

31. Katherine Ewing, "The Politics of Sufism: Redefining the Saints of Pakistan," *The Journal of Asian Studies* 42 (February 1983): 251-68.

32. Pakistan's Minister of State for Foreign Affairs, Zain Noorani, told the National Assembly that Pakistanis could not remain indifferent to the plight of Indian Moslems with whom they had "ties of family and bonds of religion and history." *India West* 21 June 1985.

33. *Tribune* 5 July, 1985.

34. Zubeida Mustafa, "Pakistan's Foreign Policy--A Quarterly Survey," *Pakistan Horizon* 34 (Fourth Quarter 1981), p. 17.

35. "P.M. Opposes Pak Reentry into Commonwealth," *Statesman Weekly* 26 September 1981.

36. *Tribune* 27 April, 1985.

CHAPTER NINE

CONCLUSION

Indian and Pakistani governments have made faltering attempts to normalize their relations since the Soviet invasion of Afghanistan. Both are currently working on a draft of a peace treaty. The outcome of these negotiations will be determined by several factors, including Indian and Pakistani relations with the major powers--the United States, USSR and China. Also important will be how Indian and Pakistani policymakers calculate the international and domestic costs and benefits of regional cooperation. Finally, India's capabilities and responsiveness as a core area will affect normalization between the two countries.

To conclude this study, this chapter assesses the relative capabilities of India as a core area and of Pakistan as either a countercore or as potential partner in regional integration. The final part of the chapter will then review Indo-Pakistan relations between 1947 and 1986 in light of the hypotheses of this study.

MATERIAL CAPABILITIES, POWER, AND INFLUENCE

Economic

Since independence, India has successfully established one of the most diversified industrial economies among developing countries. Its GNP ranks twelfth in the world; Pakistan's ranks forty-seventh.[1] The structure of their economies has also changed (table 9.1).

These aggregate figures mask several Indian economic weaknesses. The differences in per capita income between India and

Pakistan are small; indeed, Pakistan's GNP per person of $338 is higher than India's $ 258).[2]

Table 9.1

India, Pakistan, and the United States: Distribution of Gross Domestic Product (Percent)

	Agriculture		Industry		Services	
	1965	1985	1965	1985	1965	1985
India	47	31	22	27	31	41
Pakistan	40	25	20	28	40	47
U.S.	3	2	38	31	59	67

Source: World Bank, *World Development Report 1987* (New York: Oxford University Press, 1987), pp. 206-207.

The poverty in both countries has several implications for their regional capabilities. First, the Indian economy is still structurally weak, with agriculture accounting for a large proportion of GDP. Secondly, both countries have the potential for raising productivity and for mobilizing more domestic resources for economic development. According to several estimates, India and Pakistan are using only a fraction of their potential in agriculture and industry.[3] Both governments could mobilize more resources by increasing taxes in the agricultural sector and by managing their economies more efficiently. An indication of this has been the increase in investment in India's stock exchanges following Rajiv's economic liberalization in March 1985.

A final implication is that although Pakistani governments have noted India's larger absolute capabilities, they have been able to compare Pakistan favorably with India in per capita income. This has reduced their perceptions of India as a core area in South Asia.[4]

Yet India is clearly not another Pakistani economy writ large. The relative per capita GNP figures may suggest this, but there are noticeable differences in kind between the two economies. First, India's natural resources (coal, iron ore, other minerals, and oil) and its industrial base are qualitatively superior to Pakistan's. This makes comparisons of the GNP figures misleading, as we have seen for each of the six periods of Indo-Pakistani relations examined in this study. Secondly, in absolute terms, Indian governments can mobilize more resources than Pakistan for purposes as varied as industrial investment, military expenditures, or foreign economic and technical aid programs. Thirdly, India's larger population and economy allows its governments to spread the economic burdens of defense, which are much less per capita than Pakistan's.[5]

Future Indo-Pakistan economic relations will depend upon how each government perceives the economic strengths and weaknesses of the other. To be able to impress Pakistan and its neighbors in South Asia, the Indian government must be able to demonstrate superior economic growth. To enhance its position as a regional economic leader or core area, it must show that it is a "crore area"--that it can consistently generate tens of millions of rupees for internal development and external aid. (In South Asia the term "crore" refers to 10 million units of measurement.)

Here India has uneven capabilities as an economic leader in South Asia. On the positive side, the Indian market is much larger now than it was at independence, and could accommodate increased Pakistani exports of engineering goods, metal products, and food and raw materials.[6] The economies of both countries could become more complementary, making it possible for them to increase their bilateral trade without harming their programs of national economic self-reliance.

Besides trade, the Indian government has several other assets, such as an educated labor force, entrepreneurial skills, and experience in joint ventures, which it can use to increase economic cooperation with Pakistan. Some of the economic aid currently provided under the Indian Technical and Economic Cooperation Program (ITEC) could also be provided to Pakistan. This includes (a) provision of training facilities in India to Pakistanis, (b) dispatch of Indian experts to Pakistan, (c) gifts of capital goods, equipment, drugs, medicines, etc., (d) financial assistance for conducting feasibility surveys, and (e) undertaking specific projects in joint ventures.[7] It would not be difficult for the Indian government to increase such aid to Pakistan, just as India has done for its regional neighbors and other developing countries.

On the negative side, the Indian economy is limited in its ability to provide other resources to Pakistan, particularly capital and other raw materials and industrial goods. Pakistan's capital needs are larger than those of India's smaller neigbors, and India is unable to compete with current Western and Middle Eastern sources of capital to Pakistan. India also has a limited ability to provide large quantities of coal, steel, and energy to Pakistan; to provide these would mean sacrifices by India. For example, the Indian government has given a high priority to domestic oil exploration and production, but increased oil production in the Seventh Five Year Plan (1986-91) is unlikely to meet India's growing domestic needs.[8]

Under these circumstances, Pakistan's relative economic bargaining position with India is good. Since 1980 it has become self-sufficient in food and could export its surpluses to India. This, plus the beginnings of heavy industrialization in Pakistan, makes the two economies complementary. Exploiting and developing these complementarities will depend on the willingness of Indian and Pakistani governments to increase potentially beneficial economic cooperation.

Nuclear Energy

Nuclear energy has acquired both an economic and a symbolic significance for the two countries. Since the 1950s, both governments have emphasized the potential contribution of nuclear science to their domestic development. The Indian government began to develop domestic resources and to acquire foreign assistance in order to become self-sufficient in civilian nuclear energy. A consistent official policy of both governments has been to develop nuclear energy for peaceful purposes--energy, scientific and technological spin-offs, and applied uses in medicine, agriculture, industry, and so forth.

How have India and Pakistan fared in these programs? There are five major criteria for comparing their performances: (a) from the initial starting point at independence, (b) the extent of present self-sufficiency, (c) comparisons with other countries, particularly developed ones, (d) contribution to domestic energy needs, and (e) capabilities of producing nuclear weapons.

Both countries have undoubtedly made impressive progress compared to their initial starting points at independence. Their nuclear energy capabilities have been built literally from scratch. It is true that India had greater initial advantages than Pakistan and has done much better in training skilled workers and establishing physical plant and research facilities. But comparing Pakistan with India tends to overshadow the achievements that Pakistan has made in its own right. In relative terms, Pakistan now has the most sophisticated nuclear program of Islamic countries.

India and Pakistan still depend upon foreign technology and supplies for their nuclear energy programs. India is still far from achieving self-sufficiency. The Bhabha Plan envisaged, first, natural uranium heavy water reactors to produce plutonium; secondly, the use of this plutonium and India's abundant thorium reserves in fast breeder reactors to produce uranium 233; and, finally, developing breeder reactors using uranium 233. There are weaknesses in the first stage in producing enough plutonium, and the fast breeder reactors of the second stage are only at an experimental stage of development. Presently India is self-reliant in research, instrumentation, nuclear fuel fabrication, and in designing and constructing power reactors. It depends on imports of heavy water and special metals. Pakistan is even more dependent upon foreign assistance and will need more foreign technical and financial assistance to increase the number of its power reactors.

The Indian and Pakistani nuclear power programs are small compared to the developed countries. The growth of nuclear energy in the United States has dwarfed that of India and Pakistan (appendix 8). Clearly, the Indian program has a long way to go before it can be considered in the league of the United States, USSR, France, and Britain. In relative (and regional) terms, however, it is only important for India to establish its superiority in nuclear energy development over China and Pakistan. Here it is succesful; among developing countries, including China, India has the most advanced and self-sufficient nuclear power program.

Nuclear energy forms only a small proportion of the installed power capacity of India and Pakistan. In 1983 it accounted for 2.0 percent of India's and 2.9 percent of Pakistan's net installed electric power capacity. In contrast, it accounted for 9.9 percent of the United States' capacity.[9] These proportions are unlikely to increase much for India and Pakistan, given the technical and financial constraints on their programs.

The contribution of Indian and Pakistani nuclear power programs to their ability to produce nuclear weapons is controversial. Still, several conclusions can be made. First, the civilian power programs give only a rough indication of their nuclear weapons capabilities. Some observers suggest that civilian programs are misleading since a nation determined to produce nuclear weapons could bypass a civilian program altogether and produce weapons-grade material in facilities especially dedicated for this purpose.[10] Secondly, both countries can produce a small number of weapons. India demonstrated its capabilities in the May 1974 "peaceful nuclear explosion." Pakistan has yet to demonstrate a similar capability, although President Zia claimed that Pakistan had this capability.[11]

Finally, technical and economic constraints prevent both countries from producing a large number of weapons. The current size of plutonium stocks in both countries is small, and India, in particular, needs these stocks to advance to the second stage of its civilian program. A nuclear weapons program in both countries would be expensive in terms of "dedicated facilities," and delivery and command and control systems.[12] Given India's and Pakistan's present level of mobilization of economic resources and nuclear development, civilian and military nuclear programs would compete for scarce resources.

Although India and Pakistan can produce a small number of nuclear weapons for punitive and coercive uses, their civilian programs also give them the ability to influence each other towards greater nuclear cooperation. Such cooperation has been overshadowed by the attention paid to the potential nuclear conflict between the two (for example, reports of preemptive strikes, possible nuclear blackmail, and nuclear weapons collusion between Pakistan and China and between Pakistan and Islamic countries). Nevertheless, there is a political and scientific basis for cooperation between the two countries.

Both have declared a commitment to the peaceful uses of nuclear energy, and both have experienced cut-offs and delays of nuclear technology and supplies by developed countries. Peaceful nuclear cooperation would be consistent with their foreign policies of South-South cooperation and of reducing their dependence on the developed states.

Scientifically, both could share knowledge of the operations of their power reactors and other facilities in the nuclear fuel cycle, as well as knowledge of the peaceful applications of nuclear energy. India could offer Pakistan training places in its research and educational institutions. It could also supply power reactors and isotopes.[13] A basis also exists for cooperating in regional nuclear fuel cycle centers; and, if Pakistan's peaceful intent is assumed, the controversial Pakistani uranium enrichment plant could also serve India's needs.

The above are only mentioned to show the potential cooperation between the two countries. Actual cooperation will depend on several factors, the most important being political. Indian leaders such as the late Mrs. Gandhi, have repeatedly offered nuclear cooperation to Pakistan.[14] But cooperation would depend on the Pakistan government's willingess to become interdependent with India in this nationally important field. It would also depend on the Indian government's willingness to share knowledge and supply items that might be used to increase Pakistan's own nuclear weapons capabilities. Given these obstacles to cooperation, two conclusions are indicated. First, nuclear cooperation will likely follow political normalization and probably after trust has been established over several years. Secondly, the most feasible cooperation between the two countries may be in coordinating their international negotiating positions toward the developed countries on such issues as the interruption of fuel supplies, preventing collusion among suppliers of nuclear materials and technology, and ensuring the supply of enrichment services.[15] This cooperation in multilateral forums like the IAEA and the Nonaligned Movement would itself be a confidence-building measure for more specific nuclear cooperation between the two countries.

Political

By political capabilities is meant the skills each country's political elite has in legitimizing the political system, in politically integrating the country, and in extracting resources for domestic development. A regional power could use these political assets to prevent smaller regional states from developing a particular type of political system. Or, alternatively, a regional power could bolster the smaller states by giving them economic, diplomatic, and military support.

The political assets of the two countries have varied remarkably since 1947. India took an early lead over Pakistan in political development, particularly in political leadership. The Indian political elite successfully established a constitutional system, expanded political participation, developed a federal system with strong state loyalties, maintained civilian control of the military, and conducted economic planning. All these successes kept the political system integrated despite multiple challenges (ethnic, linguistic, regional, and religious) to the system.

Conclusions about the current strength of India's political integration depend on the particular institutions one examines.[16] At the state level the picture seems to be one of fragmentation. Regional discontent has flared up in the northeast, Punjab, and Kashmir. In some states, regional groups have demanded that they be given preference in education and employment over people who do not speak the predominant state language. Such demands have obstructed the free flow of labor in India and have created ethnic and linguistic conflict at the state level.[17]

Despite regional instability and complex social division, there is contrary evidence that India is more nationally integrated today than it was in 1947. This is the result of the intervening growth of several national institutions; for example, public sector companies, the armed forces and defense production establishments, and scientific and technical institutions.[18]

Pakistan's political development since 1947 shows a decline and collapse of constitutional government, followed by military rule, the secession of East Pakistan, a period of civilian rule under Bhutto (1971-77), and then military rule again (1977-88) followed by a return to civilian rule in 1988. This record has been labelled "persistent praetorianism," although a more accurate label may be "cyclical praetorianism."[19]

As in India, it is difficult to estimate Pakistan's political integration. The positive factors promoting integration are: a common Islamic culture; greater acceptance of Urdu as a national language; perceived external threats from Afghanistan, the USSR, and India; and the existence of national institutions, such as the armed forces, and educational and scientific institutions. The negative factors include internal differences over the definition of an Islamic society. There are also ethnic conflicts between *mohajirs*, Biharis, Sindhis, and Pathans. In Baluchistan, the NWFP, and the Sind there is resentment of Punjabi domination of national life. Although it is difficult to say whether the positive or negative factors predominate, it is likely that Pakistan's political integration has more resiliency than outside observers give it credit for. (As in India, domestic opposition to the central government should not necessarily be equated with secession.)

Given the regional unrest in India, it could be argued that Rajiv Gandhi's government is too absorbed in domestic politics to pay attention to its relations with Pakistan. Or it could be argued that he will try to compensate for these domestic failures by being more aggressive towards Pakistan. Like his mother before him, he has often talked of "foreign powers" having a hand in India's problems in the Punjab. On balance though, both Indian and Pakistani governments are able to control their internal political behavior. This allows them to be responsive to each other. Each can use its political capabilities for power and influence.

For power purposes, each can support autonomy or secessionist movements in the other country. The Indian government could support such movements in Pakistan's Baluchistan and NWFP. Similarly, the Pakistan government could support movements in Kashmir and the Punjab. But such support has its costs and benefits. The costs include weakening the other country, creating an opportunity for intervention by external powers, and setting a precedent for one's own political integration. The benefits, however, include using threats of support to deter interference by the other country in one's own political system.

Besides power, there are several ways in which New Delhi can use its political assets to influence Islamabad. It could stop supporting autonomy or secessionist movements by denying moral, financial, and other support to opponents of the Pakistan government. It could stop making public statements about supporting particular political groups withing Pakistan. More positively, New Delhi could offer its diplomatic services for mediating internal conflict in Pakistan and it could also openly declare its support for the new democratic government against any domestic opposition or return to military rule. The problem here, though, is that this positive support may be interpreted by Islamabad as an interference in Pakistan's internal affairs. Scrupulous noninterference is more feasible for New Delhi than positive support, which may be resented.

The Indian government faces definite choices in using its political assets. Should it show that it is committed to the Pakistani state regardless of the regime or should it show a clear preference for democratic regimes? In the latter choice, the Indian government would uphold the national values that it sees as most important, particularly constitutional government. Whatever course is chosen, the use of its political assets is likely to test New Delhi's diplomatic skills and responsiveness to the utmost.

MILITARY CAPABILITIES, POWER AND INFLUENCE

As the dominant military power in South Asia, the Indian government has several capabilities of punishing, coercing, or influencing Pakistan. These capabilities have steadily increased since independence, and even though the Pakistani military has revitalized since 1979, India's present capabilities are much greater than Pakistan's. India's armed forces number 1.2 million men, a significant total, globally as well as regionally.

As in the past, India's military assets are intended to deter Pakistan from settling the Kashmir issue by force. India's military assets--diversified defense production industries; large, well-equipped armed forces; and the ability to produce and deliver nuclear weapons--are all part of these deterrent capabilities. For instance, although India has demonstrated only what it calls a "peaceful nuclear explosion," the implications for a nuclear weapons capability are clear to Pakistani governments. They have to anticipate the possible Indian reaction to Pakistan's demonstrating its own nuclear capability. Current Indian policy is to forego the production of nuclear weapons but to reasess that policy if Pakistan goes nuclear.[20]

New Delhi has several capabilities for influencing Pakistan to form a regional security-community. The most important of these are geopolitical advantages and the ability to provide military aid. India's geographical advantages derive from Pakistan's lack of defensive depth and vulnerability to land attacks from the east and west. By contrast, India's larger territory allows it to defend in depth against conventional attacks. If Pakistan were invaded from the west, India could assist Pakistan's defense. Although India's capabilities have been built for national purposes to defend its long borders and coastline, the marginal costs of using these capabilities for regional defense would be small. As Rose and Kumar note, "One fact little noted outside the region is that all the South Asian states except Pakistan have already been brought within the matrix of an Indian security system which is regional rather than national in scope."[21]

One key element in this regional security system is India's expanding arms industry. The Indian government can export more weapons; specifically, small arms, ammunition, artillery pieces, small and medium-sized warships, naval dockyards, training aircraft, helicopters, and aircraft testing rigs. This export capacity is likely to increase as the Indian government steps up production to reap the economies of scale, as domestic needs are met, and as domestic production of new items releases older weapons systems for export.

Like economic, nuclear, and political assets, India's military advantages over Pakistan are not one-sided. Pakistan has certain military advantages that it can use to influence India. In geopolitical position, for instance, Pakistani governments realize that India needs a strong, stable Pakistan just as much as Pakistan needs defensive depth. Moreover, India's borders with Pakistan are difficult to defend. Indian governments can hardly wait for an invader to reach the plains of Punjab before defending India against a conventional military attack. Although Pakistan is sandwiched between India and Soviet-occupied Afghanistan, it is supported on its flanks by China and the Middle East. Hence Pakistan has geographical access to these areas for military assistance.

India's government will be under certain disadvantages in providing military aid. First, Pakistan has little need of Indian manpower, particularly pilots and technicians, for it has these in abundance and even provides them to Middle Eastern countries.[22] Secondly, Indian cannot yet export sophisticated weapons like high-performance aircraft. India still depends on Soviet, French, British, and West German assistance to develop its defense industries. Nor would the quality-conscious Pakistan government want India's cast-off weapons. For all these reasons, India's military aid is likely to be limited to small arms and ammunition, artillery pieces, small and medium-sized naval craft, radar, expertise in setting up defense production establishments, and carrying out defense research and development.

The actual provision of Indian military aid will depend on several factors, such as extraregional strategic developments (for example, military threats from Afghanistan). Another factor will be Islamabad's willingness to accept Indian military aid, which in turn will depend on Islamabad's cost-benefit calculations of military cooperation. Large-scale military aid is unlikely until the present differences over Kashmir, Chinese assistance, foreign bases, and troop deployments are settled. So the extent of military cooperation will depend, first of all, on whether a peace treaty is concluded, and, secondly, on the type of treaty--does it allow for consultation in case of an attack by a third country or is it merely a No-War declaration?

IDENTITIVE CAPABILITIES

India's identitive assets could be used by the Indian government to increase regional cooperation with Pakistan, even though these assets have more often been a source of conflict between the two countries. As with material and military assets, there are two distinctive uses of identitive assets: for power (punitive and coercive) and for influence.

An example of the punitive use is retaliation against religious minorities by members of a religious majority. In other words, religion would be used as a "communal irritant" or weapon.[23] Pakistani governments accused Indians of carrying out such a policy during the partition period in order to punish the Muslims for demanding Pakistan. Although Indians today are in a better position than Pakistanis to conduct this policy (the Muslim minority in India is larger than the small Hindu minority in Pakistan), it would be repugnant to and foreign to the Indian elite. This punitive use of assets has never been part of official Indian policy, because it would betray some of the ideals of the Indian elite--respect for the individual and his or her rights, democracy, and secularism.

Indian governments, however, have used identitive assets for coercion, if by coercion is meant country A preventing country B from following a course of action that A disproves of. India's coercion has taken the form of denying Pakistan's two-nation theory by pointing out that Hindus and Muslims form part of the same civilizational area and share the same history, languages, customs, and so forth. The Muslim League and postindependence Pakistan governments denied this: Hindus and Muslims were incapable of living side by side because the numerically larger Hindus would dominate the Muslims and threaten their way of life. They saw the major threat to Pakistan's national values to be India's secularism and composite Hindu-Muslim culture, which seemed to offer South Asian Muslims a competing model of national development. Pakistani governments have tried to use religion for nation-building,[24] but India's identitive assets have centripetally drawn Pakistanis back to the subcontinent.

Zia's government attempted to apply Islamic principles to all walks of Pakistani society. If successful, this would have reduced the identitive ties between India and Pakistan. India's assets were too significant to be ignored, and there were domestic constraints in Pakistan in implementing Islamization. Islamization did not preclude improved relations between the two countries; this may be because, as Richter points out, Islamization has solved Pakistan's identity crisis and made it more confident in interacting with India. It may also be because Islamization has defined what types of cultural contact are permissible.[25] Moreover, the policy of Islamization is unlikely to be followed by Benazir Bhutto. Her policy of legitimization will be to devote resources for domestic economic development, a policy which will bring Pakistan closer to the Indian model of economic and social development.

Today India and Pakistan have several identitive assets that they could use for influence. They could emphasize "religion as a great ideal,"[26] invoking the values of religion irrespective of its communal and national utility. Such a use would be a positive- rather than negative-sum activity. They could promote Urdu literature and further those national values that emphasize international equality between the developed and developing countries.

The Indian and Pakistani governments have already moved closer together in some of these areas. The Indo-Pakistan Joint Commission, established in March 1983, is a mechanism for increasing economic and cultural contact between the two countries, such as in trade, pilgrimages, and scholarly contact. The SAARC has also moved to increase identitive ties in South Asia. India will hold archeological and historical conferences. Proposals have also been made in SAARC to consult and adopt common policies on preserving antiquities. India and Pakistan have begun coordinating their policies on the New International Economic Order (NIEO). Both have taken similar positions on issues such as debt relief, foreign aid, and trade protectionism in developed countries. If this coordination serves to promote world order concerns and does not degenerate into mere anti-Western rhetoric, then both countries could benefit, regionally as well as globally.

Even assuming that the basic differences between India's secularism and Pakistan's two-nation theory remain, identitive relations between the two countries will likely improve. But a high order of mutual responsiveness is needed from both governments. Indian governments will have to avoid denying the two-nation theory. With Pakistan already an established fact, such statements serve no real purpose and instead only inflame relations. For their part, Pakistani governments will have to abandon the myth that Indian goverments are hostile to Pakistan.

In summary, this review of India's capabilities as a regional power and of Pakistan's as a regional challenger or partner has shown that integration between the two is likely to be limited, but that it is nonetheless possible. Although no attempt was made to argue that this integration is inevitable, several areas were identified for possible cooperation in trade, nuclear energy, political integration, military aid and identitive cooperation.

Because of the past record of conflict and present suspicions, integration, if it were to occur, will likely take the form of confidence-building measures (for example, the Indo-Pakistan Joint Commission) and of coordination on international issues like the NIEO. Successful cooperation on the international front could itself further regional integration. Finally, it was suggested that integration will come about only as a result of a high, but achievable, level of mutual responsiveness.

INDO-PAKISTAN RELATIONS AND PLURALIST INTEGRATION THEORY

The theoretical framework of this study is the pluralist pretheory of integration. This is the most comprehensive one for conceptualizing integration in developed and developing countries. A key task for developing countries is to create security-comunities, which Deutsch defined as a group of people which have attained, within a territory, "a 'sense of community' and of institutions and practices strong enough and widespread enough to assure for a 'long' time, dependable expectations of "peaceful change among its population."[27]

Indian and Pakistani governments have been grappling with this basic problem ever since independence: How to reach a political accommodation within the region acceptable to both countries. The many attempts to create a security-community include Nehru's offer of a No-War Pact in 1949, Ayub's offer of a joint defense of the subcontinent in 1959, the Indus Waters Treaty of 1960, the Tashkent and Simla Agreements, Pakistan's proposals for a Nuclear Weapons Free Zone in South Asia, Pakistan's recent offer of a No-War Pact and India's counteroffer of a Treaty of Peace, Friendship and Cooperation, the various proposals for a mutual reduction of military force levels and expenditures, the Indo-Pakistan Joint Commission, the pledge not to attack each other's nuclear facilities, and the recent multilateral consultations in the South Asian Association for Regional Cooperation (SAARC).

Of course, it could be argued that these attempts at forming a security-community show the absence of community. Behind these attempts is unremitting Indo-Pakistan hostility. One variant of this view is that Indo-Pakistan relations are inherently conflictive because of Pakistan's two-nation theory and Indian secularism. Another view takes the antagonism even further and traces it to the basic conflict between Islam and Hinduism. The various wars fought between India in 1948-49, 1965, and 1971 are all adduced to prove this atavistic antagonism. One author aptly calls this the *communal conflict with armor model* of Indo-Pakistan relations.[28]

The key assumptions of this model are the inevitability of conflict and the predominace of emotion over rationality. This model was responsible for our framing the null-hypothesis of this study:

1. Where emotional factors predominate, national policy-makers do not weigh the costs and benefits of integrating with other countries.

There was little evidence of irrationality in Indo-Pakistan relations to support this hypothesis. True, Indian and Pakistani leaders and publics have often been emotional and have seriously misjudged the relative capabilities of the other country. But there is more evidence that both countries have been calculating in their relations.

First, during the Pakistan movement, Pakistani leaders like Jinnah and Liaquat Ali Khan were aware of the opportunity costs of their adherence to the two-nation theory. Yet they believed that Pakistan would provide more opportunities for Muslims than a united India, which would be dominated by Hindus. It could be argued that they were still being irrational because a "mutilated, truncated, and moth-eaten" Pakistan would not be worth having economically. This argument assumes though that Muslim League leaders weighed two alternative strategies for Muslims: the political benefits of Pakistan and the economic benefits of staying in India. Clearly they did not, for they saw these benefits as incommensurable. As Liaquat told Mountbatten in 1947, "If your excellency was prepared to let the Muslim League have only the Sind desert, I would still prefer that and have a separate Muslim conditions in those conditions than to continue in bondage to the Congress with apparently more generous concessions."[29]

A second example of rationality can be found in Ayub Khan's memoirs. He claimed that his assessment of Pakistan's relative military weakness during the "war scare" of 1951 was crucial in dissuading Liaquat from declaring an all-out war against India.[30]

Finally, even that most emotional of Pakistani leaders, Zulfikar Ali Bhutto, was careful in his policy towards India after he assumed power in December 1971. A politician, who had declared a thousand years of struggle against India and who had vowed that his people would eat grass if necessary to produce the nuclear bomb, prepared his people for their reduced status in the subcontinent after the 1971 Bangladesh War.

Nor does the communal conflict with armor model stand up to empirical scrutiny when we examine the actual wars between the two countries. Those wars have been fought by two professional armies with similar British traditions, so much so that these traditions have mitigated these conflicts. The first Kashmir War, 1948-49, and the September 1965 War could even be called "Sandhurst Wars." And the 1971 War was not fought between Hindus and Muslims but between predominantly Hindu India and Bengali Muslims against West Pakistani Muslims.

Other explanations are needed to account for why India and Pakistan have failed to form a security-community. One is the attention hypothesis:

2. Regional powers in developing areas may be too preoccupied with their domestic development to devote attention to regional integration.

There was no evidence to support the hypothesis that leaders of regional units become so absorbed in nation-building that they cannot pay enough attention to other units. Indian and Pakistani governments paid much attention to each other after independence, and necessarily so, for partition left many unresolved disputes between the two countries. One only has to read the extensive correspondence between Indian and Pakistani Prime Ministers on Kashmir, refugee movements, the war scares, and the Indus waters dispute, to see the painstaking attention that they paid to each other. Moreover, this was at a time when their domestic problems were immense.

The attention hypothesis makes two assumptions: that there is a necessary contradiction between a country's development and regional cooperation and that domestic concerns take priority over regional and international concerns. Postindependence Indian governments, though, have defined India's security in regional terms because India's security perimeter corresponds to the natural defensible borders of the subcontinent rather than to India's international border. Thus Nehru in 1950 defined India's security perimeter in the Himalayas to include the Nepal-Tibet border. There is no evidence that Indian governments neglected regional security. On the contrary, they saw India as the core area in South Asia--witness their attempts to bring the Himalayan states into a regional security system, their attempts to insulate the subcontinent from the external powers, and their concern with the domestic poltitical stability of the South Asian periphery.[31]

Where the attention hypothesis seems to be more valid is in international rather than domestic politics. As the larger regional unit, Indian governments have focused their attention on the central balance--the triangular relations between the United States, the USSR, and China--while Pakistan, the smaller unit, is preoccupied with its balance with India. For example, when Indian governments mobilized military resources after the 1962 Sino-Indian War, this also changed the Indo-Pakistani military balance. In short, Pakistan, whether it likes it or not, is affected by the competition between the larger powers.

Even with this asymmetry of international attention, Indian governments have not been ignoring Pakistan. Indian policymakers have realized that their relations with the larger powers have had an impact on their relations with Pakistan. The post-1962 military build-up and India's "peaceful nuclear explosion" of May 1974 were conscious policies to show Pakistan that this asymmetry of international attention is inherent in the asymmetry of power between the two countries.

This suggests that responsiveness depends not on absorption in domestic and international tasks but on the opportunity costs--domestic and international--of paying attention to the messages of the periphery. The third hypothesis of this study states:

3. A regional power will concentrate on its internal development when it perceives the costs of internal development to be smaller than the costs of regional integration.

This assumes that the policymakers of the regional power are rational, that they weigh the domestic and international costs and benefits of devoting resources in money, manpower, time, and so forth, to domestic and regional tasks. To test this hypothesis, we need to specify what the perceived costs are to policymakers. One important opportunity cost is between safeguarding national sovereignty and devoting more resources to domestic economic and social development. This has been a common complaint of Indian and Pakistani policymakers since independence: they have lamented that their conflicts have taken away resources that otherwise could have been more profitably devoted to domestic development. The discussion of the null hypothesis showed that these opportunity costs are more apparent than real; national security has been incommensurable with economic development. The national values of secularism or Islamic way of life have taken precedence over welfare.

Both countries have often been unresponsive when regional integration on the other's terms involved unacceptable costs. Pakistan's unwillingness to participate in an Indian regional security system and Nehru's rejection of Ayub's joint defense of the subcontinent in 1959 both show that unilateral responsiveness is insufficient. For successful cooperation, mutual responsiveness is required.

What are the specific conditions under which both the regional power and periphery become mutually responsive? From this study, two major conditions stand out: domestic political stability and agreement on solving the Kashmir dispute. Because the last condition has been absent, Indian policy has been to increase its assets to keep the status quo. Pakistan's policy has been to mobilize external support. The fourth hypothesis was:

4. Regional integration is more likely to be successful where the regional power can convince the periphery that it can match or surpass any material, military, or identitive support to the periphery from extraregional powers.

This hypothesis assumes that the periphery will sooner or later decide that it has no alternative but to accommodate the regional power. It also assumes that external support encourages the periphery to be less responsive to integration with the regional power.

India's policy since independence has been to wear down Pakistani diplomatic and political resistance. The aim has been to show Pakistan that external support will not be enough to make Pakistan a countercore and that external support will always be matched or surpassed by Indian power. Since the dramatic tilting of national power after the 1971 Bangladesh War, Pakistani governments have recognized that some accommodation is necessary with the stronger India. They have been unwilling though to accept what they call Indian "hegemony." Pakistan has still been able to receive assistance from the United States, China, and the Middle East, even though India has been able to counter the effect of this external assistance.

India's policy remains that of neutralizing Pakistan's countercore role. This is the only policy available to the Indian government, as long as it is unwilling to settle bilateral disputes militarily and as long as Pakistan makes Kashmir a precondition for improving relations between the two countries. The Indian government's policy has been to deter Pakistan militarily and to offer regional integration in the hope that Pakistanis will realize the need for integration and accept what Indian policymakers inelegantly call the "regional facts of life"--that is, Indian dominance.

Thus, an overall conclusion to this study is that India has several capabilities as a core area but that regional integration has been hindered by an absence of mutual responsiveness between India and Pakistan. The basic conflict between core and countercore remains. The task for the leaders of both countries is to remove this basic conflict and to create a security-community in the subcontinent. The past attempts at peace show some of the mechanisms that are still needed to create dependable expectations of peaceful change--changes in troop deployments and concentrations, a treaty of normalization, formal guarantees of nuclear renunciation, and regular meetings of the Indo-Pakistan Joint commission.

Notes

1. U. S., Arms Control and Disarmament Agency, *World Military Expenditures and Arms Transfers 1986* (Washington, D. C.: US Government Printing Office, 1987), p. 16.

2. Ibid, pp. 78, 88.

3. In 1982 Mr. Swaminathan, a member of the Indian Planning Commission, noted that India could produce more food, since it was only using about 25-30 percent of its production potential at current levels of technology. *Statesman Weekly*, 23 January 1982.

4. This was particularly true of Ayub Khan's and Bhutto's governments. See Bhutto's views on India's economic capabilities in *Foreign Policy of Pakistan: A Compendium of Speeches Made in the National Assembly of Pakistan 1962-64* (Karachi: Pakistan Institute of International Affairs, 1964), pp. 93, 103.

5. India's defense expenditure per capita in 1984 was $9; Pakistan's $21. As a percentage of GNP, India's defense expenditure was 3.9 percent; Pakistan's 7.1

percent. International Institute for Strategic Studies, *The Military Balance 1986-87* (London: IISS, 1986), p. 214.

6. S. M. Javed Akhtar, "Pakistan's Trade with India," *Indian and Foreign Review* vol. 20, no. 16 (New Delhi, 1-14 June 1983), p. 8.

7. T. N. Kaul, "India's Economic Cooperation with Developing Countries," *Foreign Trade Review* 7 (January-March 1973), p. 336. The list of possible joint ventures includes manufacturing automobile spares, components and accessories, glass bottles, vials, machine tools, bicycle parts, compressors, high precision tools, chemicals, aluminum and electronic goods. Akhtar, "Pakistan's Trade," p. 8.

8. Mr. Satish Chandran, Secretary of the Indian Energy Ministry, noted that India would still depend on imported oil in the future as the gap between domestic demand and output widened in the 1990s and beyond. "Land-based bio-mass fuels must be developed." *Statesman Weekly*, 2 January 1982.

9. United Nations, *Statistical Yearbook 1983/84* (New York: UN Statistical Office, 1984), p. 826, 829, and 830.

10. M. Zuberi, "Nuclear Safeguards: The Servitudes of Civilian Nuclear Technology," in K. Subrahmanyam, ed. *Nuclear Myths and Realities* (New Delhi: ABC Publishing House, 1981), p. 12. A "dedicated facility is defined as "a facility built indigenously (possibly clandestinely) in order to produce fissile material for nuclear weapons. It might be a plutonium production reactor, a uranium enrichment plant or a reprocessing plant." U. S. Congress, Office of Technology Assessment, *Nuclear Proliferation and Safeguards* (Washington, D. C.: Government Printing Office, 1977), pp. 15-16.

11. Zia's interview *Time* 30 March 1987.

12. Pro-bomb Indians differ over the cost of a nuclear weapons program. Low-cost estimates are to be found in Subramaniam Swamy, "A Weapons Strategy for a Nuclear India," *India Quarterly*, 30 (October-December 1974): 271-75. Higher-cost estimates are found in K. Subrahmanyam, "Costing of Nuclear Weapons Program." *Institute for Defense Studies and Analyses Journal* (New Delhi) 3(July 1970):82-88; and "Indian Defense Force in the Eighties?" *IDSA Journal* 5 (April 1973): 457-71.

13. In the past, India has provided Pakistan with isotopes, H. J. Bhabha, "Development of Atomic Energy in India," *Indian and Foreign Review*, 2 (15 October 1964), p. 10.

14. Letter of the Indian Prime Minister to the Prime Minister of Pakistan, 22 May 1974, reprinted in *Pakistan Horizon*, 27 (Third Quarter 1974), pp. 197-198. Immediately after Rajiv's meeting with Zia in New York in October 1985, Pakistan's government claimed that both countries had agreed to begin a technical dialogue. A group of technical experts would meet shortly. Rajiv Gandhi denied that the Indian government had discussed initial technical discussions but admitted that "we are only trying to see how we can initiate it." "Gandhi-Zia Talk Fails to Allay Suspicions on Nuclear Program." *India West* 1 November 1985.

15. These international cooperative issues are analyzed thoroughly in Joseph A. Yager, *International Cooperation in Nuclear Energy* (Washington, D. C.: Brookings, 1981).

16. Paul R. Brass, "Pluralism, Regionalism and Decentralizing Tendencies in Contemporary Indian Politics," in A. Jeyaratnam Wilson and Dennis Dalton, eds.,

The States of South Asia: Problems of National Integration (London: C. Hurst & Co., 1982), p. 224.

17. Weiner concludes that these demands have prevented the formation of an internal common market in India. *Sons of the Soil: Migration and Ethnic Conflict in India* (Princeton, N. J.: Princeton University Press, 1978).

18. This is the argument of Robert L. Hardgrave, "The Northeast, the Punjab, and the Regionalization of Indian Politics," *Asian Survey*, 23, 11 (November 1983), pp. 1172-73.

19. William L. Richter, "Persistent Praetorianism: Pakistan's Third Military Regime," *Pacific Affairs* 51 (Fall 1978): 406-26.

20. "Pak may force N-policy review: Foreign Secy," *Tribune* (Chandigarh) 1 January 1987.

21. Leo Rose and Satish Kumar, "South Asia," in *Comparative Regional Systems: West and East Europe, North America, the Middle East and the Developing Countries*, ed. Werner J. Feld and Gavin Boyd (New York: Pergamon Policy Studies on International Politics, 1980), p. 264.

22. See, for example, Shirin Tahir-Kheli and William O. Staudenmaier, "The Saudi-Pakistani Military Relationship: Implications for U.S. Policy," *Orbis* 26 (Spring 1982): 155-71.

23. P. C. Mathur, Virendra Narain, and M. V. Lakhi, "Intraregional Relations: A Study in Infrastructural Determinants," in *Foreign Policies in South Asia*, ed. S. P. Varma and K. P. Misra (New Delhi: Orient Longmans, 1969), pp. 94-97.

24. Ibid.

25. William L. Richter, "Domestic Factors in Pakistan's India Policy." Paper presented at the 35th Annual Meeting of the Association for Asian Studies, San Francisco, California, 25 March 1983, p. 7.

26. Ibid.

27. Karl W. Deutsch et al., *Political Community in the North Atlantic Area* (Princeton, N.J.: Princeton University Press, 1957), p. 5.

28. Stephen P. Cohen, "The Strategic Imagery of Elites," in *Defense Policy Formation: Towards Comparative Analysis*, ed. James M. Roherty (Durham, N. C.: Carolina Academic Press, 1980), p. 171.

29. H. V. Hodson, *The Great Divide: Britain--India--Pakistan* (London: Hutchinson & Co, 1969), p. 224.

30. Ayub Khan, *Friends Not Masters* (London: Oxford University Press, 1967), p. 40.

31. For a fuller treatment of the Indian government's interests in the domestic stability of its regional neighbors, see Cohen, "Strategic Imagery;" and Leo E. Rose, "India and its Neighbors: Regional Foreign and Security Politics," in *The Subcontinent in World Politics: India, Its Neighbors, and the Great Powers*, ed. Lawrence Ziring, rev. ed. (New York: Praeger, 1982), pp. 35-66.

Appendix 1

India and Pakistan: Imports & Exports by Area 1948-85 (percent)

	1948	1954	1962	1965	1971	1979	1985
I. INDIA							
Pakistan							
X[a]	17.0	1.8	1.4	0.9	0.0	0.1	0.1
I[b]	20.0	2.9	1.6	0.9	0.0	0.5	0.2
UK							
X	21.8	31.6	23.7	18.5	10.6	7.6	5.1
I	28.6	24.1	16.6	11.3	11.5	10.9	7.2
USA							
X	15.9	15.5	16.9	18.4	17.2	13.8	22.9
I	20.3	12.2	29.2	33.5	23.2	16.5	10.2
USSR							
X	1.2	0.4	5.4	10.9	14.1	7.5	15.7
I	0.6	0.2	5.5	5.8	4.9	7.5	7.4
Middle East							
X	6.1	7.5	9.1	9.3	12.1	14.9	8.8
I	12.2	11.9	8.7	5.1	11.9	22.6	18.9
II. PAKISTAN							
India							
X	48.7	9.1	9.8	5.4	0.0	1.8	1.3
I	45.4	4.9	3.0	1.9	0.3	0.6	0.2
UK							
X	7.0	19.4	17.4	13.6	9.7	6.3	5.4
I	20.1	28.5	17.8	14.8	11.2	7.0	6.1
USA							
X	6.3	6.6	8.9	9.2	10.1	5.8	10.0
I	5.9	6.4	38.0	35.0	24.8	12.7	13.9
PRC							
X	1.3	7.3	0.6	8.2	4.5	1.2	2.1
I	5.1	0.5	0.6	1.8	3.7	3.0	2.4
Middle East							
X	0.2	0.8	7.7	7.1	11.3	23.1	18.1
I	1.1	6.2	5.3	3.0	7.1	20.8	25.1

Sources: International Monetary Fund, *Direction of Trade Annuals*, 1938-54, 1962-66, 1970-76, 1985.

a. X = exports b. I = imports

Appendix 2

India and Pakistan: Military Manpower, 1947-87
(in thousands)

Year	Total	Army	Air Force	Navy
1947				
India	300.2	280.0	9.2	11.0
Pakistan	155.9	150.0	2.3	3.6
1953				
India	351.0	325.0	15.1	1.0
Pakistan	260.4	250.0	5.5	4.9
1962				
India	596.0	550.0	30.0	16.0
Pakistan	247.7	225.5	15.0	7.7
1965				
India	844.0	800.0	28.0	16.0
Pakistan	258.3	230.0	20.0	8.3
1971				
India	980.0	860.0	80.0	40.0
Pakistan	367.0	340.0	17.0	10.0
1979				
India	1,096.0	950.0	100.0	46.0
Pakistan	429.0	400.0	17.0	12.0
1987				
India	1,262.0	1,100.0	115.0	47.0
Pakistan	480.6	450.0	17.6	13.0

Sources: Lorne J. Kavic, *India's Quest for Security* (Berkeley and Los Angeles: University of California Press, 1967), pp. 85, 235-56; William J. Barnds, *India, Pakistan and the Great Powers* (New York: Praeger, 1972), p. 100; and the International Institute for Strategic Studies, *The Military Balance*, 1965-66, 1971-72, 1979-80, and 1987-88.

Appendix 3

India and Pakistan: Army Divisions, 1953-87

	Infantry	Mountain	Armored	Independent[a] Armored
1953				
India	6	-	1	-
Pakistan	5	-	-	1
1962				
India	8	-	1	1
Pakistan	6	-	1	1
1965				
India	9	11	1	1
Pakistan	6	-	1	1
1971				
India	13	10	1	2
Pakistan	12	-	2	1
1979				
India	16	11	2	5
Pakistan	16	-	2	3
1987				
India	20	9	2	7
Pakistan	17	-	2	4

Sources: Lorne J. Kavic, *India's Quest for Security* (Berkeley and Los Angeles: University of California Press, 1967), pp. 85, 97-98; and the International Institute for Strategic Studies, *The Military Balance*, 1965-66, 1971-72, 1979-80, and 1987-88.

[a]Brigades

Appendix 4

India and Pakistan: Tank Inventories, 1953-87

	India (1)	Pakistan (2)	Ratio (1) to (2)
1953	600	n.a	n.a.
1962	1,000	800	1.25
1965	1,450	1,100	1.31
1971	1,450	870	1.67
1979	1,900	1,065	1.78
1987	2,750	1,600	1.71

Sources: Lorne J. Kavic, *India's Quest for Security* (Berkeley and Los Angeles: University of California Press, 1967), p. 97; and the International Institute for Strategic Studies, *The Military Balance*, 1965-66, 1971-72, 1979-80, and 1987-88.

Appendix 5

India and Pakistan: Combat Aircraft, 1947-87

	India	Pakistan	Ratio (1) to (2)
1947	100	35	2.86
1953	288	128	2.25
1962	670	160	4.19
1965	590	130	4.54
1971	625	285	2.19
1979	630	256	2.46
1987	701	381	1.84

Sources: Lorne J. Kavic, *India's Quest for Security* (Berkeley and Los Angeles: University of California Press, 1967), p. 97; and the International Institute for Strategic Studies, *The Military Balance*, 1965-66, 1971-72, 1979-80, and 1987-88.

Appendix 6

India and Pakistan: Naval Inventories, 1947-87

	Aircraft carriers	Cruisers	Destroyers	Frigates	Submarines
1947					
India	-	-	-	2	-
Pakistan	-	-	-	2	-
1954					
India	-	1	3	7	-
Pakistan	-	-	3	2	-
1962					
India	1	2	3	13	-
Pakistan	-	1	6	2	-
1965					
India	1	2	3	10	-
Pakistan	-	1	5	2	1
1971					
India	1	2	3	18	4
Pakistan	-	1	2	5	4
1979					
India	1	1	1	20	8
Pakistan	-	1	6	1	6
1987					
India	2	-	4	21	11
Pakistan	-	-	7	-	8

Sources: Lorne J. Kavic, *India's Quest for Security* (Berkeley and Los Angeles: University of California Press, 1967), appendices 9,10, p. 124; and the International Institute for Strategic Studies, *The Military Balance*, 1965-66, 1971-72, 1979-80, and 1987-88.

Appendix 7

Aircraft Design and Development in India and Pakistan

INDIA

I. INDIGENOUS PRODUCTION

System	Type	Work began	Prototype flight	Output
HT-2	Primary trainer	1948	1951	160
Pushpak	Light monoplane	1958	1958	64
Krishak	Light monoplane	1958	1959	68
Kanpur I	General purpose	1960	1961	n.a.
Kanpur II	General purpose	1961	1961	n.a.
HF-24	Supersonic fighter	1956	1961	125
HJT-16	Basic jet trainer	1959	1964	190
HF-24 M IT	Tandem trainer	1967	1970	18
HAC-33	Light STOL transport	1974		n.a.
HPT-32	Basic trainer	1974	1981	20
HJT-16MkII	COIN/ground	1974	1976	20
HTT-34	Trainer	1984		0

INDIA

II. LICENSED PRODUCTION

System	Type	Licensor	Date of License	Output
Vampire	Fighter bomber	UK	1953	230
Vampire T.55	Conversion trainer	UK	1953	50
Folland Gnat	Lightweight fighter	UK	1956	215
HS-748 Avro	Transport	UK	1959	80
Alouette III	General purpose helicopter	Fr.	1962	297
MiG-21FL	Trainer version	USSR	1967	180
MiG-21M	Trainer version	USSR	1972	150
MiG-21bis	Fighter	USSR	1976	220
SA-315B Lama	General purpose helicopter	Fr.	1971	140
HS-748M	Transport	UK	1972	20
Gnat-2 Ajeet	Fighter	UK	1973	79
Gnat-2 T-2	Tandem trainer	UK	1978	0
An-32 Cline	Transport	USSR	1980	0
Jaguar	Fighter	UK	1979	20
MiG-27	Fighter	USSR	1983	12
Do-228	Transport	FRG	1982	23

PAKISTAN

LICENSED PRODUCTION

System	Type	Licensor	Date of License	Output
Saab	Light aircraft	Sweden	1974	125

Sources: Stockholm International Peace Research Institute, *The Arms Trade with the Third World* (New York: Humanities Press, 1971), pp. 744-53; and *Yearbook 1984* (London: Taylor & Francis, 1984; Michael Brzoska and Thomas Ohlson, eds., *Arms Production in the the Third World* (London and Philadelphia: Taylor and Francis, 1986); and *Jane's All the World's Aircraft*, various issues.

Appendix 8

India, Pakistan, and the United States: Nuclear Power Generating Capacity, 1962-86

	Installed Capacity		Under Construction	
	Number of Reactors	Net MWe	Number of Reactors	Net MWe
1962				
India	--	--	--	--
Pakistan	--	--	--	--
United States	3	452	2	133
1965				
India	--	--	3	596
Pakistan	--	--	--	--
United States	4	515	5	2,275
1971				
India	2	396	3	640
Pakistan	1	125	--	--
United States	17	7,949	55	47,911
1979				
India	3	602	5	1,087
Pakistan	1	125	--	--
United States	70	50,901	88	96,408
1986				
India	6	1,154	4	880
Pakistan	1	125	--	--
United States	99	84,592	21	23,301

Sources: International Atomic Energy Agency, *Nuclear Power Reactors in the World 1987* (Vienna: IAEA, 1987).

INDEX

The Centers for South and Southeast Asia Studies of the University of California at Berkeley coordinate research, teaching programs, and outreach and special projects relating to South and Southeast Asia. The Centers publish a Monograph Series, an Occasional Paper Series, a Language Teaching Materials Series, the Berkeley Buddhist Studies Series, and the Berkeley Working Papers on South and Southeast Asia. Abstracts of manuscripts for consideration should be sent to the Publications Committee.